Collected Po

TOM RA W ORTH was born London
worked in the United States and Mexi
Poet at King's College, Cambridge, ir   ᴊince 1966
he has published more than forty books   ᴊ of poetry, prose and
translations. His graphic work has been shown in France, Italy, and the
United States, and he has collaborated and performed with musicians,
painters and other poets. In 1991 he was invited to teach at the University
of Cape Town, the first European writer thus distinguished for thirty years.

TOM RAWORTH

Collected Poems

CARCANET

First published in 2003
by Carcanet Press Limited
Alliance House, Cross Street
Manchester M2 7AQ

A CIP catalogue record for this book
is available from the British Library

ISBN 1 85754 624 5

The publisher acknowledges financial assistance
from the Arts Council of England

Set in Monotype Ehrhardt by XL Publishing Services, Tiverton
Printed and bound in England by SRP Ltd, Exeter

Contents

Acknowledgments

The poems in this collection are in rough chronological order, and are taken from the following books, some of which collected work published in earlier, smaller editions:

The Relation Ship (Goliard Press, London, UK, 1966); *Haiku* (Trigram Press, London, UK, 1968); *The Big Green Day* (Trigram Press, London, UK, 1968); *Lion Lion* (Trigram Press, London, UK, 1970); *Moving* (Cape Goliard, London, UK/Grossman Inc., NY, 1971); *Act* (Trigram Press, London, UK, 1973); *Back to Nature* (Joe DiMaggio, London, UK, 1972); *From the Hungarian* (privately printed, Bowling Green, OH, USA, 1973); *Ace* (Goliard Press, London, UK, 1974); *Bolivia: Another End of Ace* (Secret Books, London, UK, 1975); *Cloister* (Blue Pig Press, Paris, France/Northampton, USA, 1975); *Common Sense* (Zephyrus Image, San Francisco, USA, 1976); *The Mask* (Poltroon Press, Berkeley, USA, 1976); *Logbook* (Poltroon Press, Berkeley, USA, 1976); *Four Door Guide* (Street Editions, Cambridge, UK, 1979); *Sky Tails* (Lobby Press, Cambridge, UK, 1978); *Nicht Wahr, Rosie?* (Poltroon Press, Berkeley, USA, 1979); *Writing* (The Figures, Berkeley, USA, 1982); *Lèvre de Poche* (Bull City Press, Durham, NC, USA, 1983); *Heavy Light* (Actual Size Press, London, UK, 1984); *Tottering State: Selected and New Poems 1963–1984* (The Figures, Berkeley, USA, 1984); *Lazy Left Hand* (Actual Size Press, London, UK, 1986); *Visible Shivers* (O Books, Oakland, USA, 1987); *The Vein* (The Figures, Gt Barrington, MA, USA, 1991); *All Fours* (Microbrigade, London, UK, 1991); *Blue Screen* (Equipage, Cambridge, UK, 1992); *Eternal Sections* (Sun & Moon Press, Los Angeles, USA, 1993); *Catacoustics* (Street Editions, Cambridge, UK, 1996); *Survival* (Equipage, Cambridge, UK, 1994); *Emptily* (The Figures, Gt Barrington, MA, USA, 1994); *The Mosquito and the Moon* (Ankle Press, Cambridge, UK, 1994); *Silent Rows* (The Figures, Gt Barrington, MA, USA, 1995); *Muted Hawks* (Poltroon Press, Berkeley, USA 1995); *Clean & Well Lit* (Roof Books, New York, USA, 1996); *Etruscan Reader V* (Etruscan Books, Devon, UK, 1996); *Meadow* (Post-Apollo Press, Sausalito, CA, USA, 1999); *Landscaping the Future* (Porto dei Santi, Loiano, Bologna, Italy, 2000).

Poems from *Four Door Guide* are rather scattered. They came from different periods, and in this *Collected* have been put in more or less chronological sequence. *Clean & Well Lit* was a selection over some years; many of the longer poems had been previously published as separate books. Thus I have included them here under their original publication and date. Nothing from the chapbook *Pleasant Butter* (USA, 1972) is included, as no copy was available.

I thank everyone involved in these, and other, publications; and especially Judith Willson, Grant Shipcott, Sarah Rigby, Neil Powell and Liffy Grant for their skills and patience during an unusually complicated job. Any errors in the text are probably mine, and spelling inconsistencies that remain are intentional. The poem 'Dark Senses' is *in memoriam* Barry Hall (1933–1995) and the poem 'Out of a Sudden' is *in memoriam* Franco Beltrametti (1937–1995).

Tom Raworth, Cambridge, November 2002

This book is for my family and friends, living and dead: small return for what they have put up with for forty years.

Waiting

she made it a
noise
      entering the room
as he sat holding
a cigarette   grey
smoke &
      blue
he was too   sound
of children moving so
much outside he wrote
small she
spoke he
cut a pack of tarot cards page
of (shall we go she said) pentacles re
versed meaning prodigality
dissipation liberality un
favourable news

Not Under Holly or Green Boughs

(for David & Nicole)

the voices move.   they are walking.   it is time
it is time.   they are moving, walking
talking
      some thing faintly sweet
      the lemon drops
           dialogue

a pause they
speak in   place

      this is hans in front of
them and in the background they are held and
also in the movies

this is the banner.   music.   the whiskey
in the sunlight enters the water like gelatin   the gravel
white.   flags are frayed.   as she smiles the skin
tightens along her nose

                        a record we save for certain days

in spain the garotte   twenty years
the woman said drawing the number large with her finger
a tightening screw, the lines got less   he
would keep them in a drawer in this new room
with the old stool
                              years ago
a forecast of a present war.   this
is our job

                  gipsy on the packet moves through the smoke

the place was empty the stairs
had marks of old carpet the
aircraft's trail dispersed into cloud
he entered the car at the lights and gave me an apple

we passed the arch at seven
already in the sunlight the flame was invisible   a place
you can get a drink at any time.   here
the garden is thick with weeds.   dandelions
buttercups.   yellow.   we tilt back out heads
they have stopped.   they are looking

Sing

a certain
drum beat   it is that
of skin

the button found
still
      vibrating

produce
the body   this
small thing?

i hold, here
only the fat remaining   sound
of a fingertip lighter
without ring   it

is the pressure of air i
don't remember

Bitter Moon Dances

1 *to start*

waking and misreading my watch – nostalgia? – suddenly i felt at home
        again, gunfire in the night
the dream lasted an hour in the dream an hour passed – i woke again
        wondering what graham mackintosh looked like
hold my hand – i feel lonely now – cries cries they lie on the floor the cat
        disturbs them
kitten i tried to drown holding it under the water – it moved in the palm
        of my hand sound rising with the bubbles – a power i didn't want
sometimes it comes ready in pieces – sometimes i have to try and trap it
        like this, spraying out words to keep the thread from breaking
camouflage was the other thing i suddenly felt at home with
bitter moon dances a phrase we overheard
it was her cheek i kissed and the inside of her arm warm – this hand

2 *the voyage – translate these sentences*

it was the 21st october when we arrived at the capital
the guide was showing the tourists the most important monuments in
        the city
first we went to a rather big factory and later to a smaller one
i arrived at 4.30 in the train from malaga and stayed 3 hours
it was just striking 6 when we went to look at the city

3 *the indian problem*

16,000,000 catlin said and the estimate is now some hundred thousands
the later map shows how they were pushed west

Anniversary

the train runs, trying to reach the end of the darkness

for the time that is left, if you will permit
i will recant and withdraw from my insecurity
see, i give you this bullet with my name on it
how neatly it fits your mouth.   certainly
the words that trigger it are unknown to both of us
as yet.   i have worn channels in the air of this room
that are mine, a way of progressing
from desk to door to table.   just now not
thinking, i touched the tip of my cigarette
to the head of a moth walking by my paper knife
& realised only when it spun and spun and fluttered
what i had done.   a comet.   the patterns in the sky

the six of us move in the night
each carrying a different coloured torch

The Blood Thinks, and Pauses

then crossed the menai strait to
anglesey   the water dark
below the bridge   a still day
the white flashes only
                                gulls
you talked and your head
                        was touching mine

& i was thinking (we were
                              the only people there
in that compartment   no
corridor   the water below
still, and the train stopped)

                              about my first peach
that day, after the war   i
was seven it was two
and six
            a hot day   we walked the back way home
beside the railway   to the left
the embankment   grass & weeds i
could smell them and the hot pavement
the tar melting in the road   gravel
moved gently as we crossed &
                  i sucked the peach stone dry

i had been talking to you and
            thinking this and other
things
            he wants, he had said
a poetry of violence   gulls
dropped
            looking for peach stones

You Were Wearing Blue

the explosions are nearer this evening
the last train leaves for the south
at six   tomorrow
the announcements will be in a different language

i chew the end of a match
the tips of my finger and thumb are sticky

i will wait at the station and you
will send a note, i
will read it
            it will be raining

our shadows in the electric light

when i was eight they taught me *real*
writing
        to join up the letters

listen you said i
preferred to look
            at the sea   everything stops there at strange angles

only the boats spoil it
making you focus further

Wedding Day

noise of a ring sliding onto a finger

supposing he *did* say that?
we came by the front
sea fog twisting light above the pebbles
towards the cliffs towards the sea

i made this pact, intelligence
shall not replace intuition, sitting here
my hand cold on the typewriter
flicking the corner of the paper.   he

came from the toilet wearing
a suit, people
didn't recognise him, down the length of
corridor.   the room
was wooden, sunlight   we stood in a half circle

noise of two cine-cameras

i wonder what's wrong with her
face, she said, because
there's nothing wrong with it really   i
inhabit a place just to the left of that phrase.   from

a bath the father took champagne later
whiskey.   through the window we watched the frigate's
orange raft drifting to shore

i mean if you're taking *that*
attitude
              we rode in a train watching the dog move

noise of a bicycle freewheeling downhill

The Others

(for Anselm & Josephine)

she said nothing
leaned on the stone bridge   the wind
howled in my ear, pause
between the dropping
of the record & the music

dust   the wind   the streets
already in shadow

we walked   someone
playing the piano in a tiled room

oh
said her mother a
mister dante called you
                              beatrice

September Morning

as the window opens the sun slides along the wall
the bird simply steps from the ledge, out
drops,   being dead
is not to be able to brush the dirt from your fur to
have slugs
            on your eyes

now, the early morning, the children
stand, looking, in
slippers on the wet grass

nearly covered i am afraid to drop earth on your head
the sea, the sea fills the whole horizon

My Face is My Own, I Thought

morning   he had gone
down to the village   a figure
she still recognised from his walk

nothing
        he had explained
is won by arguing   things are changed
only by power
                and cunning   she still sat
meaning to ask what
did you say   ?   echo in her ears

he might just have finished speaking   so
waiting and
            taking the scissors
began to trim off the baby's fingers

Morning

she came in laughing his
shit's blue and red today those
wax crayons he ate last night   you know
he said eating the cake the
first thing nurses learn
is how to get rid of an erection say
you get one whilst they're shaving
you, they give it a knock like
this, he flicked his hand and
waved it down she
screamed, the baby stood in the doorway
carrying the cat
in the cat's mouth a bird fluttered

But I Don' *Love*

but i don' *love*
you she said   there were
drops of sweat
                on the receiver
warm sun the sky
on the horizon turquoise   a faint
haze
        red trains crossed the bridge

they played war forecast music   as they
walked down the hill the brown
girls passed
                driving their own cars

the tree had not been climbed
they disturbed the dirt   it grew
like a ladder
from below the sound of water on the leaves

but she said you stroked her
hair she said she is like a
cow you are so
obvious

the gardens of the houses go down
to the stream   there are a few
allotments the path
was overgrown   they walked single file
under the north circular road   the tunnel
chalk inscriptions latest dated 1958
                                        no sound
from the cars overhead
                              the lake
dark red flowers   green
scum no
current a red
ball
        stationary in the middle

Notebook

follow the same pattern
the door closes you
look at it, walk
to the other wall
try to reach the window
sit on the bed then
get up, look in your
pockets for
something with which to scratch your
name

        morrell came out of it o.k. (see
        jack london or 'chronicles of san quentin')
        went on to be in charge of the prison keys, why am i
        here, my hands tied?

again years,
not a constant, a
fraction of *age*.   eight
at eighty like one at ten?

>   morrell said 'i've been throwin' people down &
>   cuttin' their throats all my life.
>   i don't know what honor is.   but
>   if you wanna give me a chance to cut *your*
>   throat, why, all right.'

escape: i know what i'm saying
each day get six library books, never read them
instead the children's comics, old books again

figure the angles and still say sitting, perhaps
finally make it with a laugh, i quote:
the simplest of all
was the successful escape of a cripple
who hobbled away in full sight of the guards
all of whom were confident that he surely could not be serious.

>   summer of '52 i was in ireland
>   my aunt's cottage, chickens
>   outside, corduff, lusk, county
>   dublin. beside it the stone schoolhouse where ashe taught
>   my cousin pat and i argued, english
>   bastard he said, what
>   could i do but call him
>   irish pig and fight?

none of them really sees it they
like poetry, take
nourishment at one remove ignore
the life that feeds it   they
are intense, like
folk music, the worst sort, are
not as i
was, 27 this year
i cannot move with them
the ends they want i must assume
we have, to work.   arguing
the same things year

after year the boundaries
never move

     thursday seventeenth of june i
     am writing this at sea, frost
     covers the portholes
     i'm on my way to the goldfields
     dawson city – won't dig,
     i'll take marked cards   still

thursday, sun,
showing the dust on the windows
seeds fly outside, a tree?
here? this is a note
on where i am now
for someone who won't see,
my brother who died
when? a rumour, things
said whilst i sat quiet
in the corner of the room, the curtains
moving along the bamboo on their brass rings

She Said Bread, Fred

(for Race & Elizabeth)

in black & white
the cigarette end is silver

organ music, the women
in black
     (goza church EHV
                  ree sunday
comerainorshine   she said a

fine day
we are passing the coast of africa
smell from the land of animals & hot wet leaves

i am dancing
yes, free
of this, they are
asking questions
eyes like a fly

       (you are two thousand miles away in malaya singing
       blue moon & i walk through the door & you smile &
       keep right on singing.   i

open the cupboard
in it lies the head i wore long ago when i was a soldier my
god, the rain on the night sea

The Third Retainer

they would not say the thing

       name the monster
       name the monster

fascination of perspective   trees
seen from the train
fog on the hills
         iron staircases
against red brick with shadows

they left holes
in their
     arguing   to drop in
communication a
printed circuit he saw it as, a

handkerchief caught in a branch
waiting for a stronger wind

News

the letter came in the morning with the rain mist
cold, i put it in my pocket
knew how you had written it
standing in the doorway said
the child is dead

later, the envelope crumpled, thinking
of a line, found it in a book

'that picture's awful dusty' jesse said.   the

irregular star-shaped patterns of the blood

Three

smell of shit when i lift him he knocks the book from my hand
i hold him up she pulls at my leg the other comes in with a book
he gives me his book picks up my book she pulls at his arm the other
is pulling my hair i put him down he pulls at my leg she
has taken my book from him and gives it to me i give him his book
give her an apple touch the other's hair and open the door

they go down the hall all carrying something

I Mean

all those americans here writing about america it's time to give
        something back, after all
our heroes were always the gangster the outlaw why
surprised you act like it
now, a place
the simplest man was always the most complex you gave me

the usual things, comics,
music, royal blue drape suits &
what they ever give me but unreadable books?

i don't know where i am now my face seems exposed
touching it   touching it

as i walk this evening no
tenderness   mad laughter from the rooms   what
do i know of my friends, they are always
showing small kind parts of themselves

no pacifist i am capable of murder
                    the decision is not
this, but not
to sic on the official   the paid
extension of self   to react at the moment

oh, this ain't no town for a girl like dallas

jean peters to widmark 'how'd
you get to be this way?
how'd i get this way?   things
happen, that's all'   but

we ain't never gonna say goodbye

follow me into the garden at night
i have my own orchestra

November 1964

in those countries people move through the stone arches carrying
     cases   lines of poplars
lead to the water   it is difficult
     to place the smells   from the air
the streets could be also
water

                    moving in boats they miss each other
touch with sticks leaving
           marks   noise
           of our plane frightens them
we have messages

first the books were removed at night   the children's clothes
ornaments   pictures were taken down   letters piled into boxes   we
moved quickly and the rain held off

they dip those sticks in the
           water and as the boats
           rise and fall they touch
each other softly, watching;
           damp trails are left on their
bodies which quickly become inflamed

making jokes i secretly terrorized my children   i lay on the bed
watching the sky change   peach to salmon   the clouds a dark blue
smoke blew across   a plane passed, reflecting the sun

we land in the field   children
           run towards us as
we remove our harnesses   they
touch their fingers gently to the silk
as it still moves

There Are Lime-Trees in Leaf on the Promenade

(for Ed & Helene)

the blossom blows
                         across the step
no moon.   night, the curtain moves

we had come back from seeing one friend in the week
they celebrated the twentieth anniversary of victory.   fireworks
parades.   and all across the town the signs the french
people are not your allies mr. johnson   who were

then, the old photographs.   garlanded the tanks with
flowers now
choke-cherry
            a poison   we came
separately home

the children were there
covered with pink blossoms like burned men   taking
the things they laughed
                  at the strange coins, tickets.   ran
around the house pointing up at the plane then
the only noise

there can be no dedication   all things in their way
are   the actual scars   tension.   the feeling
of isolation.   love
for me in one way is waiting for it to end

what to do? the woman, they said
lived on a boat   swans
built their nests behind the lockgates   the eggs
when the gates were opened
smashed.   each time in pairs the swans
would hunt out ducklings, and whilst one
held off the mother, would drown them
beating them under the water with their wings

we heard the phone ringing in the empty house then went to bed
later than morning we spoke for the first time

the sun just through the trees but still dark in the room
she with the hem of her dressing gown torn sitting at my desk
i looked at the things and touched them
                  waiting to hear the voices

we had come back from seeing one friend in the week
they celebrated the twentieth anniversary of victory.   now
speaking to them for the first time i thought of him
from that same country living in a different place.   his tongue
he said, felt heavy now whenever he spoke english

there would not   perhaps   be time

saturday may 15th.   the sun higher   covered
with a faint sweat i read sun tzu
the art of war   'anger
may in time change to gladness.   vexation
may be succeeded by content,
                                    but a kingdom
that once has been destroyed
can never come again into being; nor can the dead
ever be brought back to life.   hence the enlightened ruler
is heedful, and the good general full of caution'   i read
the wind blowing the blossoms in that week
two thousand four hundred and sixty five years after

I Die of Thirst beside the Fountain

they pass & i turn
but you know this
                        the act
revolves around itself
                              my time
goes marked by letters, some
enthusiasms vanish.   in arguing
with you i've used up many books but
the work is too much   i have no
energy
           to mould them   sky darkens now
the snow is grey   sounds of cooking a
movement of plates

this room is cold
and i'm in trouble

Recognition

i didn't think you'd
look like that he
said & went into the dark

i examine myself in the mirror
behind me and again
behind me the
window she looks through i
didn't think you'd
look like that i say she
smiles and
walking towards me
touches the back of my neck from behind
i peer round the corner looking for alice

       sound of a knock upon the door

Down There on a Visit

the street pattern of black and white
my friends love me like a *dog* i am forgiven my small lapses
paper sticks on my lip finger slides towards the heat
i went around expecting them to give me
something wanting to touch and hold it all
i went into their rooms they were careful
i watched them taking care not to watch me they
were afraid of nothing only through
people i thought i could touch something

city boy there in that walled
place thirteen churches a
cathedral full of saints' bones
hair blood bits of moses' staff only
one thorn from the crown?

in the sun the raindrops cast no shadows
a hand moves away the flames ash fills the fingerprints

The Dublin Zurich Express

so many things
i might almost go to them i
lean over the table
eating now
not thinking
crushing cigarette packets
end here? in this room
endless like
xavier?

i wonder what's happening outside
look out the window but then for
example i'd have to fetch
a chair, climb on the table
no. stop here.
demand some kind of treatment this
crying is a bit worrying

understand my predicament
now i have got here there are two paths
no decisions, stop now.
i see my lines
not
growing poems but a notebook for prose

Sliding Two Mirrors

sliding two mirrors together to
make a puzzle of his face

oh she said moving across the room

19 years after the liberation i arrive there   soldier
carrying a guitar   a

                    ring
        you gave me   twisted
        where it caught and broke your
                    finger   smell

of must from the drawer with the japanese soldier's hat
            a yellow star it also
travelled   diamonds
on the backs of german prisoners singing at christmas

and jeremiah clarke
who wrote the trumpet voluntary and later
shot himself through the head
in the precincts of st paul's cathedral   for love

in some way cheated
like monica vitti with black hair

For Paul Dorn

you said i
will not be here then

(the difficulties of packing   how
to move that enormous box

i noticed the shelves
were warping   on the knots
the sap was sticky

you still talked &
following your gestures from memory
i argued

(in the ashtray an apple core a
spoon with milk skin

the window didn't shut tight &
it rained
        you moved the cups

from the wall a bull watched us

Six Days

monday

i was alone then looking at the picture of a child with the same birthday
a key turned in another lock there was a noise through the window
the cigarette made noises like a cheap firework
in the ruins of so much love in this room i must leave something
the morning was sunny it is easier to die on such a day a blister under
      your foot and easier still to mention it
a need to explain this and a french dictionary i worried how to carry the
      bottle in my case with only a cork
sweat dripped from my nose in the picture a man wrote in a room
      behind a peacock there were two clocks in the room and two
      watches twenty nine bottles four of them my own
i wanted to share everything and keep myself it would not work
on the door a drawing of a lion in this room on the mirror in soap it said
      write
the plane was always level and the moon dipped

i had cleaned the room all my taste had gone the whiskey tasted like milk
      chocolate
i had bought all the books for my friends my shoulder still ached from
      the case i would be carrying more back
a leaf i had found and given to her all green with four brown eyes
five years ago i had stood on those steps the next month she was
      wearing a white dress the car was late i combed my hair in a
      window in the tube it was still summer i
was and still am addicted to self-pity

a handkerchief to my face and the blood dried i would have left it
the shelter smelled of earth there was a shovel inside to dig yourself out
      nine paving stones in the path

a tall brown girl in jeans who came up the steps of the bridge something
    about rhythm the line and breathing
motions

tuesday

the whiskey began to taste like whiskey the cigarettes still made noises
i had not noticed that beside the peacock was a quieter bird in front of it
    a dish and through the window a countryside
day of daniel there had been noise and i fitted a lock to my door
a long while ago i read silone 'i came home' he said, when he was able to
    continue
'and told my parents the doctor had advised me to return to my native
    climate.'

so wrote to you this letter
my jacket was wet from the window it was all grey except for one green
    tree by the pantheon
there was a sound of water in the streets the americans wore white
    trousers and red shirts
i counted my money it was tuesday i ate salt because i was still sweating
then the rain stopped and it was all white the tree vanished there were
    red tiles

he was five and he said to me why are you not nice look i gave you that
    calendar
i bought him a toy french car every year he looked after them and never
    lost the tyres
i was aware of having a family the policemen all had moustaches
bought oranges and chocolate, bread, wine and coca-cola
soda à base d'extraits végétaux
i could not write anything without repeatedly using i someday i would
    get over it
my teeth ached from politeness it felt like october '62

they take up the cobbles and re-lay them in the same pattern
they wear blue jackets and blue trousers and blue caps
the stones are grey underneath is sand
they do this every year and wash the public buildings

let me tell you about the needles i said
isn't it the truth? you find them everywhere.   even in bay city.

wednesday

today it is warm and the americans wear blue nylon raincoats
it is with a 'c' she said shall i wait outside a skin formed on the soup
there were brown leaves already it was only july
and between the grey stones drifted green buds dead fish in the river

i have no love and therefore i have liberty it said on the wall and
          underneath with my key i scratched 'lincoln'
pas lincoln she said bien sûr i answered an elastic band floated by
there are statues of all the queens of france she said there was cream on
          her nose
my throat is sorry do not go down those alleys at night there are thieves
          and murderers
this cinema is the biggest in europe maurice thorez est mort
enregistrez un disque a way to send letters

when we left ravensbruck she said we could not stop laughing and joking
          for half an hour

thursday

in the musée national d'art moderne there are three modigliani
          paintings two sculptures a copy of matisse's book 'jazz' five statues
          by germaine richier a plaster construction to walk inside statues by
          arp a restaurant and a reconstruction of brancusi's studio
it was half past three the girl in the american express looked sad and
          shook her head
everyone was kissing it was like a commercial for paris
on a newsstand i read in the guardian about the strike they said at the
          british council library mr ball has left?
in les lettres nouvelles june 1960 i read requiem spontané pour l'indien
          d'amérique with a footnote saying little richard – jazzman célèbre

from a corner of his studio the stairs went up to nowhere
there was a blowlamp and an axe a pile of wood
i looked at myself in brancusi's mirror and it was round

friday

they were painting the outside of david's house white
30 rue madame i would not have recognised it
posters say tous à la mutualité avec pierre poujade
pigeon shit runs into apollinaire's left eye

the light through her sunglasses makes her eye look bruised
other pigeons coo a sound of water splashing men shovel the leaves as
      the yacht is thrown it moves
a blue balloon the carts stand there are cigarette ends in the gravel
wearing a black dress with green spots gold sandals an indian girl walks
      through the gardens reading a music manuscript

on the steps at night five spaniards singing *la bamba*
long r's and a noise like a cricket
she moves another chair to rest her feet

one spot of nail polish on her stocking little song you have been pushing
      behind my eyes all day

saturday

a letter came i felt very strange at gloucester road she said after you went
      and i had kisses from four people
i wanted to be there people move into church a door slams the car
      moves

i could not say i tried
i said i
could not   people have hair on the backs of their hands
what did we eat we ate sausage a stew
of onions tomatoes and courgettes below in the square they played
      boules
six men and a fair brown woman in a black dress

emptiness a taste of brass the holes in my head filled with warm sand
a scar beneath her left eye yellow bruises inside her elbows
in the *marais* we bought sweet cakes in the heat without shirts there were
      still tattooed numbers
birds walk inside the dry pool the flowers are dark and even
on the wooden floor the cup broke quickly calvados a faint smell of
      apples

looking at the etruscan statues in the louvre there is a green patina on
        my hands my expression has taken its final shape
everything becomes modern inside these cases there is nothing without
        touching

children crawl under the glass   things are reflected several times

The Wall

and in the morning said
                        let's go
(trying it for sound) a
crust forming on my eye rims
my stomach moving, moving
here, four a.m.   tick of a clock
seats creaking.   she said
tanzen-wir?   a girl
24   she said   went on
i forget the german   .   the canal is too cold
and played the radio we
did not dance
                through black
bakelite and wire we were connected
     music coming into my left ear these
noises around me   now
i shut my eyes to recapture it   what
?   i felt   the
        music coming into my left ear (*high noon*)
        i could not hear all she said   TRAVEL
now   what was that, the rhythm i meant at the beginning?

but we did not dance and she made me a cup of coffee?
and in the early morning (later than this, now
the connection is broken – i touch the bare brass of the plug –
but she is still there) with me (listening to the music)
she went out into the street

                    it is cold
i hold her hand in my pocket
dew forms on my moustache   o
it is familiar to her now, my face, a single car
is parked in the square, now
i can understand all she's saying

A Pressed Flower

and now there is a movement another
child   i am unable to help you
at all times – irritated when you clutch my hand now
still spellbound when you talk

there is no decomposition
                          at the same moment
evening
          only the ground is dark, the sky still palest blue, and
your grandfather whom i also love is perhaps dying
these first weeks of the new year   because
you are me i tear at you *how*
can i channel it?   the children
develop my faintly irritated voice   they wave their hands

at the other end of the line i say
there is no answer   but the room there
is filled with people looking at the phone

Who is Hannibal's Descendant, Leading his Elephants against the Tanks?

at last i've done it!
put the white horse inside the carnation
staggering in the heavy air
it vanishes among the petals

all the women i meant blend into one
i give her this book of reality
she curtseys in her delicate velvet
as the race continues in the heart of the flower

The Blown Agent

her blue gown is taking the smoke
the dust on the hem of her blue gown
blue gown – that's nice

in the low corridors of the old school   that smell
and her blue gown, poor dog
all those years the cake had lasted
we collected the dust in a matchbook

immobile   the petals   the horizon   the the
lonely in the room and no room to click my fingers
over my head   moon   moon

on a bicycle, after the cars had left, her blue gown, going

Ah the Poetry of Miss Parrot's Feet Demonstrating the Tango

we were leaving on a journey by slow aeroplane
that was the weapon you had picked for our duel
flying above a gigantic playing-card (the five of spades)
from one corner to the other – our goal the gilt edge

this is a pretense (i quote your note), a cut, take the short way
because justice is what the victim of law knows is right
your stockings rasped in the silence, the engine stopped
and i wished it had been a ten of clubs with more landing space

it was a game in the air, flock wallpaper in the cockpit
outside feathers grew from metal, flapped, and we began to climb
from the mechanical smoothness to the motion of a howdah
i picked up the card, removed my goggles, and began to dance

Hot Day at the Races

in the bramble bush shelley slowly eats a lark's heart
we've had quite a bit of rain since you were here last
raw silk goes on soft ground (result of looking in the form book)
two foggy dell seven to two three ran
crouched, the blood drips on his knees
and horses pass

shelley knows where the rails end
did i tell you about the *blinkered* runners?

shelley is waiting with a crossbow for his rival, the jockey
all day he's watched the races from his bush
now, with eight and a half furlongs to go
raw silk at least four lengths back disputing third place
he takes aim

and horses pass

his rival, the jockey, soars in the air
and falls.   the lark's beak neatly pierces his eye

North Africa Breakdown

it was my desert army.   no fuss.   no incidents.
you just have to be patient with it.   take your time.
a child leaving a dirty black car (with running boards)
wearing a thick too large overcoat : grainy picture.
each night round the orange dial of the wireless.

or innocence.   oh renaissance.
a dutch island where horses pull to launch the lifeboat.
we are specifically ordered that there shall be no fast cars.
where can we go when we retire?

it was their deduction we were afraid of
so shall we try just once more?
nothing is too drastic when it comes to your son, eleanor.

and nothing works in this damn country.
no it's not a bit like home.

You've Ruined My Evening / You've Ruined My Life

i would be eight people and then the difficulties vanish
only as one i contain the complications
in a warm house roofed with the rib-cage of an elephant
i pass my grey mornings re-running the reels
and the images are the same but the emphasis shifts
the actors bow gently to me and i envy them
their repeated parts, their constant presence in that world

i would be eight people each inhabiting the others' dreams
walking through corridors of glass framed pages
telling each other the final lines of letters
picking fruit in one dream and storing it in another
only as one i contain the complications
and the images are the same, their constant presence in that world
the actors bow gently to me and envy my grey mornings

i would be eight people with the rib-cage of an elephant
picking fruit in a warm house above actors bowing
re-running the reels of my presence in this world
the difficulties vanish and the images are the same
eight people, glass corridors, page lines repeated
inhabiting grey mornings roofed with my complications
only as one walking gently storing my dream

Southland

so i aim into the sad world of the deaf and dumb
the quiet cars, the impossibility of calling someone back

which light?   my but the prison was clean.
weightlifting and art classes.   goodness, who had a letter?
red fur and dying carnations.   the land reclaimed from the sea
by cunning and the use of slaves.   the speed of clouds.
speak into the microphone!   who by doing our work
questioned our power and we beat them
blows falling in their heads never breaking the surface.

so protected by glasses i was a sole traveller
leaving town, spitting in the road, no lifts
and an unsolved murder in the next county

last thing i heard the happy sound of people being entertained

Now the Pink Stripes

now the pink stripes, the books, the clothes you wear
in the eaves of houses i ask whose land it is

an orange the size of a melon rolling slowly across the field
where i sit at the centre in an upright coffin of five panes of glass

there is no air   the sun shines
and under me you've planted a quick growing cactus

Don't Follow My Toes

well, helmut, uncle friedrich will show you where he was
try on this belt, this old aircrew jacket
the 'cosmetic way' to remove unwanted hair surely, quickly
yes, the italians were always underfoot

an inflated tonsil i am looking at.   your right, or mine?
it is noon, it is summer, and birds fly through the shadows of the
    empty station

Wham! – The Race Begins

my *first tur*kish de*light* – and in an *opium* den!
whitey should think whitey on seeing whitey
45 starters today – one of them a giant rat

she, running (to catch up) with her breasts
the rosetta stone finnegans wake in *their* language:

'come, come, i'll stay and won't go washing'

Collapsible

behind the calm famous faces knowledge of what crimes?
rain on one window showing the wind's direction

a jackdaw collecting phrases 'it's a chicken!'
nothing lonelier than hearing your own pop in another country

                whose face with bandages was singing
her breath always only half an inch from the corner of my eye

Got Me

did you ever fall asleep making love in a rocking chair?
i did, and i remember every minute.   that's really
when i began to drink, then i drank again, and finally some more
then i started to hang little heavy baskets of drink on my thoughts to
        keep them down
which was about the same time i wrote my famous corrected poem, you
        may remember it

XXX XX

xxxxxxxxxx fall asleepxxxxxxxxxxxxxx rocking xxxx
xxx and xx remember every minute. xxxxxxxxx
xxxxxxxxxxxxxxxxxxxxxxxxxxxxxxxxxxxxxxxxxxxxxxxxxxxxxxx

Shoes

shoes come from leather leather
comes from cows come from milk no
no milk comes from cows come
from shoes baby shoes
                come
from there to here hear
the shoes of blind children shoes
shuffling tripping a blind child falls into a cement mixer
a deaf child is crushed by the ambulance racing to the blind child who is
        the child of some dumb man who makes shoes

that evening he cries over a piece of leather stained with milk
the tear marks make a pattern he tries to read to read
he wants to cut the leather into the shape of a gingerbread man

he wants very much to have his child back
to ride on the cows back

The Lonely Life of the Lighthouse Keeper

snow falling on the lemon trees
the cowboy shivering in his saddle
what patience required to make *models*!
goodbye, pablo, it's all in the cause of the revolution

he used to turn on just to gloat at the *pauses*

now for the slow movement

Inner Space

in an octagonal tower, five miles from the sea
he lives quietly with his books and doves
all walls are white, some days he wears
green spectacles, not reading

riffling the pages – low sounds of birds and their flying

holding to the use of familiar objects
in the light that is not quite

Love Poem

there have been so many other men in my pause life
don't be frightened pause it's just my pause way
(he's going to force his *way* into her *life* – well folks
that's why we came out here to the free west

section 2

i've never said you were unattractive.   that's another
distortion.   i've just said unattractive to *me* at this *time*
certainly men would be attracted to you but let them have six
years of *this* sort of thing then see what they'd be like

3.

'he speaks for all of us'

4. continuing

how there are some nauseating actresses who *must* at some stage of their
    careers have played cripples (once i tried to let a smile be my umbrella.
    i got awful wet)

on to 5

like the balinese say 'we have no art, we just do everything as well as
    possible'

6. (and approaching the bend)

where is the thing i want to hold? the heroin i take is you and *that* is
    sentimental.   which is not sex but something more subversive

7.

too far.   look back.   you've missed the point

8. the end

yes the sun i love i *came* through the window
and the last rays were *in* the park

Sky

(for Ron Padgett)

of the burned building but the frame stays
my room was there, stopping the clouds from entering
and i was inside.   i opened the window – sky!
a skylight – blue again!   a trapdoor in the floor
saw the roof of an airplane passing under me

i somersaulted slowly in that room not touching anything
blind almonds falling

Continuation

the caps are blue
not teeth, but like the whites of brown eyes

corruption of instruction   don't want to hear it
shit even then he had mis-remembered it &
if he recalled the name i wouldn't know
the red petal turning yellow &
i'm turning grey over
a moving coloured lantern slide of another possibility

now 14 years after, staring from the train at st cloud 8.15 a.m. somehow
      expecting her to be there and recognisable
behind a fixed smile ripping with my teeth loose flesh round the ulcers
the only sound feet as the wind blows dust in the sunlight
song of the regular bell and the still bodies burning under the statue of
      verlaine

but what i really care is that she came walking, walking disguised as
      anyone
a motorcycle passing early morning in the rain

These Are Not Catastrophes I Went out of my Way to Look for

corners of my mouth sore
i keep licking them, drying them with the back of my hand
bitten nails but three i am growing
skin frayed round the others white flecks on them all

no post today, newspapers and the childrens'
comic, i sit
in the lavatory reading heros the spartan
and the iron man

flick ash in the bath trying to hit the plughole
listen to the broom outside examine
new pencil marks on the wall, a figure four

the shadows, medicines, a wicker
laundry basket lid pink with toothpaste

between my legs i read

        levi stra
         origina
      quality clo

              leaning too far forward
into the patch of sunlight

What Is the Question

the pen tip moves along the edge of purple shadow marking a white line
    down the road
a car is approaching my left eye sees it reflected filling half a lens
and all out*side* the rim is black
though with *some* shapes moving, faint patches, more the lingering
    images from some unseen light
down there, *under* where i am standing, in the area i can't see, and if i
    bend down the lens that car will pass over my head and the dazzling
    light will draw me and make me finally tumble down

only a distant noise as the darkness meets again after my heels

Going Away Poem for Lee Harwood

the woodsmoke hangs in the air between the trees
click – it is winter, the smoke vanishes
and now the orange flames provide a movement
across the water – it is the children
pay for it   their faulty articulation
not really jerks but a slowness of legs and larynx

seen in the flashes of blue light from the train wheels
as we are travelling, separated from the crude metal
by point 008 of an inch of candlewax
left by the spraying machines that only run at night

                                        fever

asleep in a beached boat, covered with foreign newspapers
in a city on a bay where even the light is different
as the deprived are always the state of the nation

Gitanes

where do all the cigarette ends go? the world should be littered with them
i reach for one like an oxygen mask when the trip gets bumpy
sometimes i smoke 5,000 a day, alternating between white and yellow
(i also drink cider and breed lettuce
here on my small farm printing fake photographs of my parents)

the ivy has grown over my inscription
lines spread from the nose, greasy, across the forehead
she's breaking up! i try to block them with cigarettes
filling the wrinkles with ash, smoothing it over, applying make-up

no, that was in '38.   i'm heading that way fast
matches all gone i vainly rub the end on my bristles
friction should do it, no, that was douglas fairbanks jnr. on t.v.

did you see him?   i almost smoked my ear
here, stepping off the pavement, damn fool, i bet he'd been smoking
all those books under their arms.   a rhythm of footsteps.   sheets
      blowing
with cigarette burns.   and they don't flush down the toilet first time

well girls, *shave* those books from under your armpits
she did, and there was a small hole from which she pulled
a never ending cigarette, yellow, white, yellow, white   ·

so we went into the labyrinth and killed the minotaur, holding on
but coming back, half-way, we found it burning
and a gnome had eaten the ash.   puff puff, puff puff

Georgia on my Mind

he sees the quickest pizza in the world
he sees light flashing in the photo machine
he sees returned bus tickets

he smells two elastic bands around two daisies
he smells the same shirt all week

he hears a million men marching on wheaties

Tom Tom

awakening this morning by the baobab tree
the bright colours of my clothes fading
catarrh a slow trickle in the back of my throat

the animals whose names i know only in dialect
in this place as the day grows and the air vibrates

eyes nose and mouth the dark green of our statues
face of an ape the symbol of justice and death gone

gone chaka the welder of a thousand tribes

Introduction

now weather spans the arches and the tree is drawn
a weight of blossom dissolving in the mud
filling the footprints
he returned to the scene
to see policemen sniffing at the shape of her shoe
and dancing
smiling in the frost as the cast hardened

Oratorio

who came first?
as joseph asked that question the ball went into the pocket
everything was a gamble and music began softly in the background
both with amnesia
again the violins
it was possible then
that they were really there
only a few feet from the main line
hold back the credits
joseph took a leaf and kissed it
he looked this way and that
around the circle
but the diamonds in her hair were soft bird droppings

Variations

do you remember a hill, miranda?
and the times we'd sit on the cool veranda
talking of films was it bande a
part from you there is no-one miranda
and just about here i had planned to
change the rhyme
just one more time
a reverse. last line

miranda. a hill. i remember. do you?

Adagio

you are dead old woman and dead your husband
a wet leaf in your mouth pulled cutting the tongue
what a loving glance he gave you
tall men carrying you walking like horses

Saraband

behind the trees
where i can not hear the voices
inside the tent
its tasselled curtains and deep carpets
balance the candle against the grey image
ah
i tell you
a banjo
here miles below the city
among the roots of trees
smaller than an ant
the bridge is swinging

Nocturne

or is life cold?
in the early hours as the fire is dying
dance
take another bottle
bunch up the pillow
to sit staring with only a blanket
it's time the flying saucer left
my thoughts like grease around you
as you swim across

El Barco del Abismo

where there are magpies across the road i camp alongside the circular
    stone tomb of a gipsy

my image i do not recognise in the mirror stepping out of them and into
    it

el sabotaje
sabotear
el saboteador
camuflar

all the boats go out to sea
all the men go home to tea

AND THE SUNN IS AT LAST very stong so I dont wanr to open py
    e eyes

Title from Sr. Martinez Ruiz' Latin American History lecture on Thursday, May 9th.
1968 at noon. I was so impressed I stopped listening.
First line written on Saturday, May 11th, 10.30 a.m. while drunk on a coach taking
us to Almuñecar to visit an avocado pear plantation. In fact I can't read my hand-
writing. Part of it could be 'i caw too long with'.
Next line Saturday, May 11th, about midnight. That was a strange day.
Four lines from a Spanish Vocabulary, Sunday, May 12th, about 4.p.m. Something
else Roy pointed out in the same book: in a list of words to do with crime, police, the
law, etc. was the Spanish for 'tapered trousers'.
Two lines written by Ben Raworth (4) and sent to me in a letter which I read at 10.29
a.m. on Monday, May 13th.
And then it was May 14th, when I found the last line in a letter from David Ball at 6
a.m.

The Sure Grip of a Cats Paw

we are eating hops
beside the distant market
you and i
and the plane lands
look at its wheels

cubierto de polvo
rice hops off the plate
and takes to the air
you and i
beside ourselves in the distance

eating each other
you and i
spinning like rotors
voice cleaves the ruby
the roar of engines ring marks left by glasses

The Explosive Harpoon

régis couldn't break the pistol
corridors of panes against which the grass buckles
frozen glass sprays from his fingertips
as the blood on the leaf runs (dissolves)

cybernetic pain give me grace
the pigeon sees nothing still
caps in your mind that explode for years

wind blows in her cheeks, apparently
now is a word i like and morning, morning now
you think with my voice and all
your factories are circled by yellow machinery

your arrow's point the other
as are areas only can understand

fires in the hole behind the heather
stream overgrown with grass the daisies at an angle
the immigrant arrives   his face contained the mix to now

our town has been taken by whales, and children ride on them
and the bird on the horse through the black flames

Gibil – Burn the Wizard and the Witch!

maritime thoughts of an interview
and questions   the crowds
smile 'nigger'   carved stone
says the streets are enough thanks

the 'c' note from the bank
is flat in the half
cast dream of brown
gunfire, in the gunfire, in the rocks

on them the dream
floats as a scum of beer
death of all bubbles the extent
of their coloured world

Kew: The Museum or Library of Plants

the world is growing out of them
eight trumpets running from block to block
pressure of hymns forms the roofs of churches
so flutes would be cold here, and a drum
still organ pipes spear the body still
continuing how inert they lie

for possession of the corpse
a mirror shows the signal
of apples and the giant moored
her hat held down by pins
the plate passes   there must be a spoken way of getting there

the dead were found by their servants
we could like in dreams – why not?

Joseph Saves his Brothers for Ever

1.

they said they had both had dreams and did not know their meaning

recently ruined in the sixteenth century
i did not think of them for a long while

her finger squeaked on the pane

2.

in three languages
the blue packet
for months without company
i had to
the next one
no contact
the right hand side

i am he you thought as lost

3.

it's really a dry period
dials show through bodies
salt goes brown
the pilot realises the earth is up

train the bird
who wouldn't

The University of Essex

(for John Barrell)

1. *gone to lunch back in five minutes*

night closed in on my letter of resignation
out in the square one of my threads had broken loose
the language i used was no and no
while the yellow still came through, the hammer and the drills

occasionally the metabolism alters
and lines no longer come express
waiting for you what muscles work me
which hold me down below my head?

it is a long coat and a van on the horizon
a bird that vanishes   the arabic
i learn from observation is how to break the line

(genius creates surprises : the metropolitan
police band singing 'bless this house'

as the filmed extractor fans inflate the house with steam

2. *walking my back home*

the wind
is the wind
is a no-vo-cain band

and the footstep
                          echoes

i
have conjured *pe*ople

3. *ah, it all falls into place*

when it was time what he had left became a tile
bodies held shaped by the pressure of air
were clipped to his attention by their gestures

my but we do have powerful muscles
each of us equal to gravity

or sunlight that forces our shadows
into the pieces of a fully interlocking puzzle

4. *good morning he whispered*

the horrors of the horses are the crows
the bird flies past the outside the library
many heels have trapped the same way
he tolls, he lapsed with the light from so many trees

check the pattern swerves with the back
the tree that holds the metal spiral staircase swings
aloft the hand removes a book and checked it
for death by glasses or the angle food descends

5. *the broadcast*

she turns me on she turns on me
that the view from the window is a lake
and silent cars are given the noise of flies dying in the heat
of the library   the grass outside goes brown
in my head behind my glasses behind the glass in the precinct
thus, too, they whisper in museums and banks

Extract from the Mexican Government Book of Home Cooking

(for José Emilio and Cristina Pacheco)

TLATELOLCO

TLEIQUE?

        TOTOLIN
        TETL
        TLAXCALLI

AXCAN?

        DISPARADOR
        CABEZA DEL PERCUTOR
        BALA

VOILA!

TOTOLTETLAXCALLI

Tlatelolco: the Square of the Three Cultures; Tleique?: what things?; Totolin: chicken; Tetl: stone; Tlaxcalli: bread; Axcan?: then?; Totoltetlaxcalli: omelette.

The Silken Cord   December 4

barbara besider tower
i remembered how to walk
vinegar

was dawn
was inky, turquoise, was purple was white

how about to walk

leaves fall through the night
now he is sleeping by the window
tío protect us from rockfalls and numb my tongue

The Needle

that the mind moves, still
in the learned dance of words
seems the interest the dead
flowers pattern on the thin curtain
before the memory of the dream of the man
who sleeps in his reported dream

quartz   and it was broken   8 : 15

lead plate roofs the impulse
implosion yet another core
preventing forms the solid he carves

an eye watering   two hooters   distortion

The Worst Poem

electricity flooding the taking place reduction
how hearing letters after not talking
heavy pace flies on screen
food reaction eccentricity

nothing i can do spins it off
though the ugliness almost completes the circle

Going to the Zoo

shapes that come in the night
three tulips through my window
hair brushed in the next room

the black panther extends his leg
here is the site of the battle of maldon
mum ee mum ee mum ee

the order is all things happening now
no way down through you float in the density
so sensitively turned on the animals

The Phone Keeps Ringing

my hand hurts (sloopy) 'the dream'
'his hand hurts (sloopy) "the dream"'
tree   fly buzzing   forcing in

look at the diamond! (yes : the laser)
retina weld retina weld retina weld
my eye a glass hand the diamond scars

Reverse in through Driving

seneca mixtures eye light phone keeps ringing
sloopy (his hand) green hand cars on the gravel ringing
branch spring pulls the leaves back out the draught
kept on walking (pputttt : quiet door) flaTTTTT
light goes through us all. they : embarked
punctuation blows it (mixtures) misdialled the number
light fills and weighs heavy getting number

see FIVE NATIONS. adj. of this tribe.

The Window Display

lemon break (write it out) anything he wanted
boring boring slough the skin
keep everything open mix metaphors contact board
another slice? off nearly with the cake lift
lack precision (explain it to them) how they watch
look with one hand find your feet

There are Forty-seven Pictures of her Walking out of Central High

anemone gloam and i'm walking (time) survival
kit survives 'droves of them leaping every night to the coast'
head aches (the delicate poem to express my grief escapes me)
being them to know and nobody RED EAGLE comes to break
the formal CRIES THE clarity of time
the women i love DREAM still three monkeys lean
back and towards one white one black one brown
down the stair trip (them) pulsing with the day
a fraction second lag is how you know you built the bridge

How Can You Throw It All Away on this Ragtime?

(for Jim and Nancy Dine)

the sound track cut flickered to the past connection
inspiration came on to her like at coffee

the twelfth period begins with one lizard
cold blades of itzcoliuhqui

he can not move in clothes that are not his
trigger to many connections

of course the key slips through the grating
trust marginal thoughts

some like shoes will fit
the will to make out

Lion Lion

the happy hunters are coming back
eager to be captured, to have someone unravel the knot
but nobody can understand the writing
in the book they found in the lions' lair

Lemures

1.
lovat on the cancered hand
lemniscus — or was it franz lehar?
i can't consult it any more

2.
it's all coming back to me, thanks
that skill again now
and in nahuatl

Travelling

1.
cold feet   the rain drips into itself on its round trip
round heels

2.
you liked the lions and you heard them roar
the word that is forgotten always shows
a medical kit – how can i thank you boys enough!
i couldn't live with myself if i didn't

3.
anthea's eyes on the dark corde du roi
in my fantasy the car continues slowing down

4.
my pig, painted with flowers, receives the money
ooo   ooo   ooo   (oo   oo   oo?)

First Man? On Mars

of celandine and bright water, not on this planet
zeppelin, zeppelin, it makes me cry
how i dressed you in my mind in edwardian clothes and met you for the
        first time
in the manner a little archaic   i ate it
the pans all we had left CUT an alien 'hand' CUT puzzled how to
        unscrew? the knob
velvet to your ankles white lace to your throat and around it a band (the
    arrangements are so predictable

is it my metier to be a policeman? i wonder
the CUT right or left? CUT cut? *how many?*

the shadow i make outside is the first shadow this shape here
as i am in my mind the total knowledge of earth. what was it?
bright this way and that.   did it move?

i am william tell's most accurate shot, listening to your rustle
oh my!

archaic in your manners you curtsey. yes
it is opening. i race to remove your bright clothes
the arrangements are so alien. it makes me eat it CUT
it ate me   i ate it   i am it looks like home

Jungle Book

stranger. a curious hand touches the snow raising pigeons

they want us to compete so they need only read 'the best'
next line
this curiously carved hand is for scratching the ice to attract the seal's
    attention

come, take my place in the long hibernation dream of the hamster

The Plaza and the Flaming Orange Trees

lions sit at the door of their hut staring over the snow
by the radiator she suddenly sat down – 'daddy!'
what have i to do with this music?
the spinning and reversing tapes dispose of *that* (she knows
he didn't get the job – 'daddy?'

boy the poor are funny
and when a white man dies it tightens up
'you must sing for us!' what – right now?

day the first indian reached the ocean and dust blew over the water
i unburdened myself to the compassionate face of a lion

Dear Sir, Flying Saucers! Flying Saucers! Flying Saucers!

(for Asa & Pip)

he is taking a glass but the hand of his shadow touches the door
the day has warmed the pebbles   now why is this?

his passport   his papers   the letter of credit
says people are born in high places that empty

there is no imagery to explain this new feeling
outside the range of sound and sight   he worries about
the other three   packing, packing, his head
turning over the surface still dreams of the water

Strike, General

incendiaries burst over the field
the oranges dent moss and shake
bright gas is caught by the evergreens

fan spins
cup to lip — all those boats to do it
what did you want to know about america? you can fly or go by sea

Unease

what quintessence as she walked to the door
it is a privilege we allow to the meanest and most despicable of our
        prisoners
the terminal buildings will be out of sight

the hand has calluses as you shake it
RISK OF SCATTERED LIGHT SHOWERS
no doubt she did it with my blessing

Provence I

in the morning there is opera, faïencerie
dance dance to break off the filter

singing songs he could not play on his teeth

edge edge dance dance
in the morning to opera along the cliff road

his teeth were the filter and filled
with gold

that would not take an edge the bark
whittled whittled into a tooth pick in mourning

Provence II

so i rode to my lady's castle
horse stepping gently through screaming vines
the noise of our train filled the valley

my lady was sowing
sweep sweep of her arm
white seed slashed like water

oh my lady is brown, red
and crumbling on the green velour
smear of my seed   horse   stop

Provence III

the tape of my mother does not have that high pitch
the ape swung from the high tree

crash of the door took my mother under the ape's arm
she spun over my daughter in the brown dust

Provence IV

stone or heart, the ashes surround my plate
the horse i ride on is dappled with leaves
that would break the skin. i wait for the sound of a car
in the noise of the valley bringing a spoiled gift

The Lemon Tree

(for Roy Wallis)

a.
across the bare plain dogs pass in the sun
pepsi-colon say the signs and breakW-ater
the hard lacquer of the only cypress that stands
in the glare of old bones, the houses made from them

b.
there is no way to stop crying into my cigarette
tears the taste of medlar fruit
of rinsed saucers no way the tiles
are coming true

c.
across the street smooth girls behind their glasses have it made
but in the end what gift do they give
guarded so carefully soaked every day in sweat
powdered, perfumed, exchange, cambio, wechsel

d.
who had the pylon and the rest
of all that over the caves on the hill
without speaking german or clicking or
hearing the children leave school dancing
hearing the cloth cameras the silent
roar of the famous lions i obviously
came all this way to see

e.
i am learning spanish
but in granada we buy before we try
tiene gracia he said: gracia (f) grace,
attraction; favour; kindness; jest,
witticism; pardon, mercy; pleasant
manner; obligingness, willingness.
(pl.) thanks, thank you

f.
it was only glass, albert, and the cyclist was an illusion
hello albert, in my glass, in my room, i sleep in your tree

King of the Snow

the hunchback child gets finally to me
in sewage washing oranges towards the cave
she drifts, eating a yellow jelly cake

in a dry ravine the bones make orange dust
that wind drifts into words   the lemon tree
edges towards the child towards its children

a lemon bursts   the orange pus congeals
two elements that form a crooked hand
of bones   that gives the child a message

Metaphysics of Magicians

grey lights of the train
waiting for lines
purcell and the branches dancing
twisted into the room

finger brushing opaque glass mosaic
perhaps the steel core is lost
night and the train crossing
another room and smaller again

heth is the chariot
crab lotus and amber
wed to a chair
guarded by mirrored facets

tree after tree of orange

the lines between them

South America

he is trying to write down a book he wrote years ago in his head
an empty candlestick on the windowsill   each day
of his life he wakes in paris to the sound of vivaldi in summer
and finds the space programme fascinating since he still doesn't know
how radio works   as in the progress of art the aim is finally
to make rules the next generation can break more cleverly   this
        morning
he has a letter from his father saying 'i have set my face
as a flint against a washbasin in the lavatory. it seems to me
almost too absurd and sybaritic' how they still don't know
where power lies or how to effect change
he clings to a child's book called 'all my things' which says:
ball (a picture of a ball) drum (a picture of a drum) book (a picture of a
        book)

all one evening he draws on his left arm with felt-tipped pens
an intricate pattern   feels how the pain does give protection
and in the morning finds faint repetitions on the sheets, the inside
of his thigh, his forehead   reaching this point
he sees that he has written pain for paint   and it works better

The 'Speed' Novel

but you should take those layers off
so it can not be just imagination — the 'speed' novel
discussion of rapid detail

separating the rings prepared the bases
'if you think we're on the run'

Floral Luncheons and Service Dinners

(for piero heliczer)

the name was that anticipated
some would call it but we
know the changed vision of the capital

cold mornings on the bridge
nothing to chance
the machinery and ritual of bleeding

and for his every shout
she had secretly written her sad reply
the loveliness of long distance

Come Back, Come Back, O Glittering and White!

life is against the laws of nature, this we know
from nothing bangs again the heart each time
shadow and light push back across the lawn
the grass that feels them both of equal weight

and memory keeps going, clutching the straws
of similarity in taste or scent
flickering in laminates or spiralling through tracks
the perfume of you was and keeps on going

Claudette Colbert by Billy Wilder

run, do not walk, to the nearest exit
spain, or is democracy doomed
we regret that due to circumstances beyond our control
we are unable to bring you the cambridge crew trials

if you're counting my eyebrows
i can tell you there are two
i took your letter out and read it to the rabbits

describe the sinking ship
describe the sea at night
he lived happily ever after in the café magenta

how to preserve peaches
they're counting on you for intimate
personal stuff about hitler and his gang
it's a chance i wouldn't miss for anything in the
wait in holland for
instance watching the windmills
that's more than flash gordon ever did

all those bugles blowing
in the ears of a confused liberal
so long
pretty woman
wake me up at the part where he claims milwaukee

You Can Stroke People with Words

unanimously they omitted
this practice for the night
what i decide is right
as the filter of these ambiguities

the arm in the photograph
appears to rest on a real stone
in the briefing huts on the previous afternoon
it was my practice never to leave my seat

small muscles flexing
sable
sable
throwing the strategic bomber at the man in the street

On the Third Floor and a Half

grains on a spoon
the barrage balloons
echo in the bay

a polite gesture with the tray
to let her pass
away with gentle movements

stirring into the foam
a train where they have changed
the destination plates

Chancer

others turn off and now he rides the right straight way
the shadows uniform in their direction

in the town of D., among strangers
he asked to be going home, silently

one inch from the dark shore
bound to the ship as by a spell

this is a model of you i made
it contains thumbnail he thought went into the flames

Venceremos

(for Mike Gonzalez & Chris Allen)

death came as the lion spoke but nothing changed
the audience stayed sitting   he moved miles
entering their pores he seized each one of them
as they began to cough, to move again, to lap the snow
his mane two feathers floating in the thermal dust
he went five ways and left five different tracks

My Son the Haiku Writer

now the melody
in the pattern of shadows
one shadow behind

slow cello music
pushing the velvet armchair
as the rain comes down

thin layers of glass
spinning up in the thermal
what can stop them now?

time under pressure
dawn. and the green butterflies
crossing the ice-cap

bells of red thunder
the cross of an ape in dreams
my house where i sleep

tracked down by process
inside the dentist's peephole
, but i fixed him good

voice under voices
i would recognise her walk
twenty strings vibrate

spinnets of silver
one hair caught between my teeth
whose? i've been away

anonymity
the black cloud came down firmly
in music and love

wax filtered sounds through
earth where imagination
spreads a boned circle

the method signs off
measuring the depth of cause
in the case of grass

a mould of eyelids
under the singing emblem
cough. and he dropped them

astride the rider
eyes are light like the star light
soft mellow vowels

coughing of amber
strictures between the pillars
in my chair in my

the problems of form
within this limitation
he drops a sylla...

The Moon Upoon the Waters

(for Gordon Brotherston)

the green of days : the chimneys
alone : the green of days and the women
the whistle : the green of days and the women
the whistle of me entering the poem through the chimneys
plural : i flow from the (each) fireplaces
the green of days : i barely reach the sill
the women's flecked nails : the definite article
i remove i and a colon from two lines above
the green of days barely reach the sill
i remove es from ices keep another i put the c here
the green of days barely reaches the sill
the beachball : dreaming 'the' dream
the dreamball we dance on the beach

gentlemen i am not doing my best
cold fingers pass over my eye (salt)
i flow under the beachball as green waves
which if it were vaves would contain
the picture (v) and the name (aves)
of knots : the beachball : the green sea
through the fireplaces spurting through the chimneys
the waves : the whales : the beachball on a seal
still : the green of days : the exit

Reverse Map

out of the dream in which she has gone
in a man's jacket and hat : through the streets
that were at once granada, the lawcourts
searching for a file or a book left with her
compelled to travel the same route
to complete the ritual each time. she was not
in the room where the party was, now darkened
night after night   'hello fink'
but in the other house : again travelling the route

the journey is always anti-clockwise
and the loneliness is there before awakening
it is a dream known to be dream
and can not bring a moment's satisfaction

Who Would True Valour See

everything is done to the ticking of a clock
how is she to be known in the dream?
water's the way past the membrane projected
around us : we recognise the jamming
the same piece of film : we
are pointing the wrong way
how is she to be everything out of the dream?
now the hand does not move
is anything still true the membrane shakes
this morning i remember nothing

He Called it Greenland to Encourage Settlement

there they go, wound up, the jelly people : no feelings
street lover : hot shots to take *all* the points
his son, whom i caused to be educated

the crushed bright paper bird lay in the crate bottom
i would say she was a very lonely person
can you pinpoint when this murder was committed

knights in white armour have passage through walls
and ring as the old throw the old on the bonfire

Live from Athens, He Explains

speak to me in dreams, i am no child of now
yug   rum   swe   den
when it is night it is everywhere night

i speak of a time i remember (do you hear the echo
?) when there will be no flattening of explanation

The Corpse in my Head

(for Juan Agustin Palazuelos)

thoughts, memories, dreams, continue in the clamped skull
day after day : she re-enters as reported speech
and the hero of the dream has his own subconscious
his subjective memory of those encounters : breakfast
at the savoy : the intruder : the view
from a high flat roof of river and dead iowa trees

the seasons waver with the slides
he makes one move : a two-page flicker book

Helpston £9,850 Stone Built Residence

the view is again unapproachable
my hand and jacob's ladder : the dogs dream
there are again crossed knives on the plate : flower
rose : as you grow i weaken
how can i tell you the accent in which i say
o mercy : o room pressures with music

no, you are a rabbit, you change constantly
a dog : a clown : you juggle
the surface mysticism of the rich
which has eaten our country boys : boys
touch wood : swing the swing : the journey seen
through scraper-board windows NO clapboard houses

The Stroboscopic Forest Light Plays

(for Marco Antonio and Ana Luisa Montes de Oca)

gently : the walk to the door
and candles blow wild

the ghost has remained in the language

Purely Personal

dawg put'n fleas 'n m'bed : well, evenin' draws in
red lamp : orange lamp : green lamp : cold (fill it in later)
'for the sun always shines in the country of the elephants'

all information is false
as light blows out the room after the slide performance
'n we're closer than we thought

tired and lonely here on the perimeter
tonight i couldn't give a fuck for anyone
all i see is black : you can recapture nothing

Notes of the Song / Ain't Gonna Stay in *This* Town Long

the face in the dream is a name in the paper
bicycle shop smells ('sometimes my brain sings')
ice crystals bleed : these songs are songs of love

the levels write : they say
please let me in : the lights go out
(sometimes my nails sing)

Entry

major turnpike connections in eastern united states
audubon, witchcraft, akbar
all for san francisco

ordinary people
i have killed poetry
yes   and i had to tell you
books are dead
refer others to your own
experience perhaps
identical thoughts flicker
through each head at the same time
intelligence was the invader from space
and won   defend your planet

now that sounds intelligent

Train de Nuit

the light goes out and includes the train in the night
dreams of children : they sleep in their dreams

sight of train in the night
as the lights return

gare d'amiens

Railway Express

water tower thumb tacks hold the country down
as white ice rivers jolt perspective
we move by
rocks and wrecks of cars

green bridge
        yellow house
blue sea   red buoy

sun light explodes on the water's surface

Blue Pig

hearing the paper hearing the sound of the pen
like a seance : i will dictate these words
who dat?   she had a woollen
hat : he was so *frien*dly then

Four Late Night Poems

1. *translation*

crystal falls
i looked after her

2. *fire works the beauty of war*

band across the water
early today police frog men searched a milk filled lido

3. *magaden to never*

susumen
yakutsk
buyaga
aldan

4. *hooked*

clover
 lover
clever
 lever
closer
 loser

Shooting Sticks

it should be obvious
what i am doing
to anyone aware of the day
taking sighs
out of sights
moving off to the heart

The Title : Hear It

you are now
inside my head
better you were
inside your own
love
tom

Good Morning

(for Mike Horovitz)

the glowing bird that pecks inside my head
is going out   it proves to be
more plastic than insane
or so it makes me think
or seems to me

a wonder that i see it by its light
glowing inside my head   a tree
a leaf vein as i fall
and is my shadow soft?
and am i free?

Your Number is Up

colour t.v.
works in a drawer
colour t.v.

The White Lady

on the phone   meeting the white lady
smoke hangs solid in the cab   i speak to the driver
in spanish   the arrangements have been made

Lie Still Lie Still

o lady speak
for if there is a dream
then let it be
paranoia

is seeing how language works
what it means   the face of a wolf
glares back through the glass

blossom   honey
my favourite poem
is
still
is

You Can't Get Out

this is no way
to find me
you plot your own course

in the still dark room
the blue man's skin
shows white tattoos

and you read on
and but
and so slowly

Stag Skull Mounted

9.00 pm. May 1st. 1970

(for Ed Dorn)

mounting a stag's skull remains
the province of a tiny man
who standing on a bolt peers
across eye socket rim at antlers
(the magnetic north) that are not his
heads   east again
upon a giant brown and white
saint bernard   which leads me
to today   obsessed by thoughts
of drowning in hot water in the dark
the hound's bark drifts
through trees in the night spring air
venus is out

8.00 pm. May 5th. 1970

each evening the girl with a twisted spine
passes my window   as the weather warms
her dresses thin and shorten and useless pity
for the deformed and lonely leaves me
only this   i can not love her and her life
may be filled with warmth   i project my past
sadness on to all   the weight
of my thought of her misery may add
the grain that makes her sad   i should be dead
which is why today the roman wall
is not the wall the romans saw

11.08 am. May 7th. 1970

matthew coolly looks out from his comfortable seat in the suitcase. it is in
the case that he travels with father unwin on the missions that require
matthew to be minimised.

'found poem'

9.30 pm. May 13th. 1970

the dog is at my feet
thin paper blocks my nose, round wax bumps over me
all magical instruments must be duplicated

the way is not a direction
but a smoothing of decay

i am a ping pong ball from face to face
idea to idea   and what i do
is a disservice
                to crystalise
the doorway   the landscape beyond
to withhold knowledge   to fashion
this from the jerks of thought and vision

12.15 pm. May 19th. 1970

(for Kenneth Koch)

the government has explained the situation to us
pigeon in the beech tree

first a shoe shine then the whole wide world
Frank O'Hana

(the plane dropped in an effort

the government has explained the situation to us

pigeon in the beech tree
first a shoe shine then the whole wide world
Frank O'Hana

(the plane dropped in an effort

the government has explained the situation to us

pigeon in the beech tree first
a shoe shine then the whole wide world
Frank O'Hana

(the plane dropped in an effort

pigeon in the beech tree

the government has explained the situation to us
first a shoe shine then the whole wide world
Frank O'Hana

(the plane dropped in an effort

this vehicle is fitted with a hope anti jack knife device 1)2)3)4)

9.30 pm. May 24th. 1970

'and'   nobody
minds and covers blown
blossoms and leaves with love
zap zap zap zap 'and'?
the british rail insignia

'petrol burns'   'tomorrow's another day'

10.30 am. May 26th. 1970

wild animals wouldn't drag me
in the rain gentle
men wear hats to the zoo today
i wake to read contracts
and smile that ron in his title
fused jerry lee lewis and john ashbery
with gracious goodness well
every packet bears the maker's signature
as it says on the box
of farrah's original harrogate toffee

(10.00 PM. EST. JUNE 1st. 1970
just for the record,
'great balls of fire!' was
something my mother and grand-

mother used to say (before
j. l. lewis, bless him).
                              love,
                              ron)

Noon May 29th. 1970

i can not find my way
back to my self i go
on trying

the sparkling games
flickering at the end of my youth

12.10 am. June 1st. 1970

the time is now

12.256 am. June 1st. 1970

looking at my watch

11.42 am. June 2nd. 1970

opposites are timeless

it is the moment all time
is our selection

he had cultivated europe by the throat

9.37 am. June 3rd. 1970

this is my handwriting

1.31 pm. June 5th. 1970

(for Ted Berrigan)

my up
is mind made

absolutely empty

now here comes thought thought
is laughing at language language
doesn't see the joke the joke
wonders why it takes so long

but it's friday
and it's a long way down

10.26 pm. June 5th. 1970

word

10.59 pm. June 5th. 1970

10.45 am. June 6th. 1970

word: a
a: the
the: the

in
    adequate language
            i love you

8.06 pm. June 10th. 1970

poem

9.25 pm. June 10th. 1970

poem
poem

7.19 pm. June 29th. 1970

organic

7.21 pm. June 29th. 1970

education

7.22 pm. June 29th. 1970

laugh

7.40 pm. June 29th. 1970

this trick doesn't work

The Corner

what speaks of change
should not be heard

where water brings
that idiot's sound

what sound of change (ha!)
should water bring

that idiot's what
should not be sound

Greetings from Your Little Comrade

at the ballet he reads 'history of the ballet'
a strange convoy of desperate men and the woman they forced to go
      with them
it's true what his uncle patrick said

at the ballet her   history of the ball'
range of separate men   woman forced
it's a 'this' – cleopatra's aid

he missed the meeting
shooting along (alone)
squeezed her as

wide of the mark
at some speed
simultaneously

Moonshine

the plastic back
of chairs – the

of chairs – the
look at that

my moment
what it should have

storm of static
with one line clear

List

(for Bob)

he gives up
the hand up raised

she stands up
up he is describing nothing

some trip up
too he calls up down

Writers / Riders / Rioters

the present is surrounded
with the ringing of ings

which words have moss on
the north side was a linear trick

this is the moment
my shadow is thrown on air

Reference

this is the poem from which i quote
'this is the poem from which i quote'

And His Share of the Loot, if I Know Shorty Fleming

a b c d e f g h i j k l m n o p q r s t u v w x y z

© ?

Logbook page 106

would have explained it. But asymptosy seems destined to leave it to Vespucci. The two styles fight even for my handwriting. Their chemicals, even, produce nothing more than wax in the ears and an amazing thirst. That seems to 'even' things, for those who regard it as a *balance*, or think the wind blows *one way*. The third day of our voyage was perilous. Multitudinous seas incarnadine. But the small craft that came out to meet us contained us and went sailing into the sunset, carrying only ten pages of my logbook (106, 291, 298, 301, 345, 356, 372, 399, 444 and 453), slightly charred by the slow still silent instant. And it was in that same instant (as everything is) that we recognised that in addition to our normal crew we had a stowaway – the author of *The Incredible Max* who, alone and unaided had, on a long string, hauled the dinghy *Automatic Writing* (out from Deus ex Machinette) – or how else could he be explained? The eloquence of his moustache (you will understand) bulged neatly over and under his belt. He spoke of himself as ceaselessly sweeping up the leaves that fall from the trees. We tried to tell him about the other seasons – 'Fall DOWN : Spring UP!' we made him repeat. 'Fall DOWN : Sweep UP!'

Logbook page 291

beepbada beep beep. Or the pages. Or the faces in the trees' silhouettes at night. Around us was the countryside of Whimsy where, huddled around leaping orange fires, the natives let their cigarettes dangle unlit in their mouths, thinking only petrol or butane could light them. Stripping bark from each native to reveal our track we followed one string of dulcimer notes after another. Nothing is lost, or confused, in this country – not the PENGUIN ENGLISH DICTIONARY, nor the RED PEN, nor the YELLOW PEN WITH GREEN INK (Patent Applied For). At night in the forest we slept, listening to the creak of our future oars. 'Let us', said one of the natives whose language we could speak, but imperfectly, 'build from these trees a thing which we call a "ship" – from the wood remaining I will show you how to make "paper" – on this "paper" (once we set sail) I shall show you how to "write" (with a charred twig from the same tree) – and if your grandmother is with you, here's how we suck eggs.' From the shore we watched the 'ship' approach us. We set sail in small craft to meet the strangers, pausing only to write pages 106, 291, 298, 301, 345, 356, 372, 399, 444 and 453 of the logbook, charring

Logbook page 298

a fair day. Afraid I think only in words: that is to say I am able to say 'that is one of the things we have no word for'. And when our journey takes us into the dark (en una Noche osCUra... roll up... roll up!) I am quite able, by touch, to say to myself 'this is another of the things we have no word for that I've never felt before'. And so, pausing nly to drop an 'o', flick cigarette ash into the waste paper basket – ash which lands in the exact top right hand corner of the only piece of paper in the basket, which I now have beside me, reading on the reverse (hidden in the basket but the grey pattern of type through paper attracted my eyes) 'THE CHANGING CRICKET BAT: a clever sleight of hand trick which will mystify your audience' – and look through the window at a man in a white suit turning the corner, I reach the end of my sentence. At the same moment the record changes. I type in time to the snare drum 'every branch blows a different way'. Ash fills my fingerprints making a soft cushing sound as I type on, pausing only this time to watch my fingers move, have a pain in the stomach, pay close attention to three words in the lyric. Now it is almost time for

Logbook page 301

or, indeed, as an out-of-space static. I am writing, perhaps, the story of
Atlantis: and if you can only see the peaks, and think a detailed descrip-
tion of *them* is sufficient, then grown gills, swim down, and get over that
molecular distinction of 'the surface' and think a detailed description of an
out-of-space static; or indeed, *as* an out-of-space static. I am, and think a
detailed description of them is sufficient. The pen scratches on the paper,
the rain raps on the window. The ship has sailed, and from inside the
beer bottle we read the label in reverse through the brown glass:
'ƧИAMUЯT' And the twig from the tree outside is stationary and dry,
stuck into the neck of the same bottle. And the bottle stands on the table
(the wood of which came from Finland) next to the empty cigar box
('Elaborados a mano' in Cuba) near the Olympia typewriter (from West
Germany). Until finally writing becomes the only thing that is not a
petroleum by-product, or a neat capsule available without prescription.
And think a detailed description of them is sufficient. I am writing,
perhaps, the story of Atlantis, and if you can only see, then grow gills,
swim down and get over that molecular distinction of 'the surface'. Until

Logbook page 345

the ticket on which we saw, turning it over, the words **MAFIA MONEY**
in Cooper Black type. Which meant that at that moment (the ship comes
in, the craft go out – and beneath them all is Atlantis, the form of our
voyage) we were thinking about Germany and how to get there. Two
scouts had been dispatched to the new *Casa della Pizza* on the corner
of Head Street to bring back provisions, and I was again left with the
logbook. Today's happenings bear no relation to the beauty of, for
instance, a brass chronometer or a sextant. But a burst of happiness comes
(at the same instant as the t.v. blurts 'Cliff Richard in Scandinavia') on
turning over in my papers a letter which arrived this morning from our
point scout Joe. 'You're goina FIND me / out in the CUNtry' sings Cliff.
The audience laughs. Do you remember the author of *The Incredible
Max*? He is here too, on the telephone. But residual beams flicker
'TEEN TITANS' and the beautiful codex: 'So you girls want to do
your thing in my shop? Well, let's play it by ear and see what kind of
"vibes" occur.' Against which can only be set the thought of the New

Band of Gypsys: Jimi Hendrix, Janis Joplin, Colonel Nasser, Erich Maria Remarque and John Dos Passos. Or how do YOU think? A play with unlimited cast, each saying one line only. Or the poem that

Logbook page 356

frequent deaths do not affect the bedding. Swimming around in the glass with the scent of juniper entering our lungs we screamed out. But our cries were drowned by voice-carrying laser beams which, activated by the CO_2 in our breath, boomed THE RIVER MEDWAY HAS OVERFLOWN ITS BANKS NEAR TONBRIDGE... THIS WOULD IMPLY THAT THE INFINITIVE WAS *OVERFLY*. TO *OVER-FLOW* HAS THE PAST PARTICIPLE *OVERFLOWED*, NOT *OVERFLOWN*. The information was just in time – although in the bulb-shaped glass the pressure of the voice had forced us under the surface – for the giant finger that dipped in, stirred us around, and re-ascended to stroke the rim of the glass, created, as it gathered speed, a perfect C sharp, which shattered our prison and caused the clear sea to overfly. How neatly all the solutions are labelled 'Paradox'! And how much we owe to Adam who never bit the apple, but rolled it along the ground, thought 'wheel', and so bought us death, clothes, and 200 different kinds of washing powder. These last few nights I wake, unable to change the film running through the two projectors behind my eyes. Of course the stars were nearer before we could fly – why else should the universe expand? And what goes on behind my head, these nights when blood spatters and snails down the shiny celluloid? Mirrors lie. This voyage can only

Logbook page 372

caps. I have been from one to another of my friends and I feel uneasy. I understand now that I have been dead ever since I can remember, and that in my wife I met another corpse. This is the way salt is made. We, the salt, get put on and in things. But we are our different taste: I am in Maine. Did your salt taste different today? What did you expect this to be? I am sodium – I realise now my fear and love of water. Chlorine.

We have combined to save you from our separate dangers and become the sea. Sodium rode in the bus taking care not to sweat. In front of him the strange tracery ASHTRAY. To his left SAFETY EXIT – LIFT BAR – PULL RED CORD BELOW – PUSH WINDOW OPEN. He copied this tracery as the bus sped along the dotted line. Across a pale green metal bridge. To the left grassy hillocks, then pines. In the distance a black horse cropping. He counted four blue cars, one after another. The green tinted windows of the bus announced a storm. TS 536, another blue car, overtook the bus. The is MAINE, he told himself. And the selectors threw up 'an island off the rocky coast of Maine'. An exit road curved down. A truck called HEMINGWAY passed. What strange mutations will come from that grassy strip between the lanes – never walked on, fed by fumes, cans, paper, tobacco and

Logbook page 399

subtlety is only what you see looking around inside your head with a torch: beating your radar pulse there to yourself and back and describing the journey. No, that was something else. Red. Until the day I ( )ed that intelligence and intuition were the same, and passed through *that* fence. The word I choose so precisely becomes next day the key word in an advertising campaign to sell a brand of stockings, because the word means *what comes to mind first*. And as a 'writer' and 'artist' I should have sensed the direction of that word. As the renaissance painter should have sensed his picture on the packet around those same stockings with SIZE NINE printed across the detail which took him three days to paint. Because the stockings are always been there, and we are all USEFUL... and the packet was one of the things for which he painted the picture. Like the con of ecology which has been fed and fattened to keep your mind *off*. Buy CLEAN MACHINES. So long as we are all satisfied that matter cannot be destroyed it is a closed world. 'Art' says only 'This is how I do this' – and a form can be used once only. 'He planted that word twenty years ago so that its weight is now exactly right' – that's the message of 'culture', the real, cold, science. The last message to come through on the old transmitter was ELECTRICITY WILL STOP... and we have no way of knowing if the last word was message or punctuation. So before

Logbook page 444

can work the transmitter we've forgotten the message. The card retrieved from the bottle floating by said only

o

how you grow

and as we stared a foresight appeared above the o, and it became the muzzle of the rifle whose butt, as the picture tilted, was cracking Rosa Luxemburg's skull. And the circle of paper from within the o fitted first neatly into the hole of an old early morning return bus ticket, took off, was lost for an instant in a swirl of confetti, and finally settled in George Kimball's empty eye socket as he searched in the sawdust under the table for his glass eye. And the sawdust, the table leg, the confetti, the bus ticket, the rifle butt, came from the SAME TREE, whose final total of seasonal rings, said aloud, is the name of god. On the coast of Maine the stones are a foot in diameter. On the northern coast of France they are an inch. Their travels tilt the earth's axis towards another Ice Age WHICH WILL KILL THE VEGETA-BLES. For this is the battle: between the vegetables and the rocks. And we are the disputed territory – we, and the water we come from and are. And fire is the flint destroying the tree (though it be coal – the vegetable in disguise). And mushroom and hemp are the settlers moving west.

Logbook page 453

I'm not going to make it to the lift in time, nor change my name, and the dialogue echoes off the walls of the set. It's the front room, and the queen's picture flickers into a limp book called Jimi Hendrix because all books are dead and we live where the edges overlap. The material is transparent, but the seam is already ripping down from Orion. And I am busily sweeping up the last few words in a country without an ear, whose artists are busy filling in the colours they've been allocated in the giant painting-by-numbers picture of themselves, because they think an interview with the man (now a physicist in Moscow) who was the boy on the Odessa Steps *makes a connection*. Full moon. High tide. Because it's all gesture, and nobody ever talked in words.

N~~I~~NE POEMS

mine

for Rory McEwen

HE IS VERY BADLY BURNED

those gestures, the italian menus
Colour

OUSTED

thinking of italy brings mabel normand to mind
i   speak   your   *weight*

LEON : A POEM (after Kenneth Koch)

Naples : sleeping with women

Naples : sleeping with women

FOUR

red candles
black fist
black glasses
snow

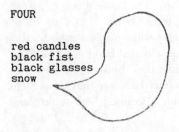

IN THE DART ROOM

running scared,
big egg   S   beating the pavement

VISUAL PETRARCHAN SONNET WITH INTRUDER

black

red

rouge

noir

schwartz

Красный
rojo

negro

blue

brown

bleu

brun

blau

braun

LINE RON HAD UNDERLINED IN 'JEFFERSON AND/OR MUSSOLINI'

all genius worries the dud, i think, by reason of the overplus

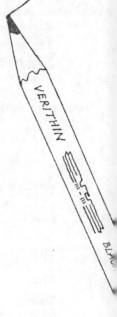

MOVING

pictures

erato
ERRATA

Energy Gap

(for Nicolas and Irmgard Born)

music of the dance fades   she shuts the door
from the window they watched a train
'i guess that is a different train' he said
film cuts music off

A Fall in French Furniture

outside the prison stars are born
grape fruit of the vine
ohio, not an allegory

isn't that breath taking
mexico rattles rhythmically

my life
inside a mirrored sphere
my skin mirrored

(it says here you're a great clarinet player)

Toxophily

small squirt of
describable sadness
tenor's the one with the bend

tenor's the ace that
shattered a steady beat
sil   hou   ette

studios have 'kleig' lights
it's a small town
we could go back, too

at night, with eyes closed
facing myself
air marks on a bowstring

Surgical Names: John

every home has a sharp knife
where's the sharp knife? you had it in the garden

One Two Three

One

wasp hovers

smell of caramel
people teach

Two

theses (for david)
puppets : throats with knuckles
i believe in programming

moi je je je moi moi

Three

here
in the city
slaughterhouse

CO_2 activates the voice beam

Surgical Names: Joe

his head in silhouette is a dove
landed on his shoulders   the space
between hand, hip, his foot on her shoulder
in the shape of an hour glass   he will slip

this is a cracked caruso record
its effect on the world is yet to be discovered
◄——— Eastern Airlines Route Map
(now that was a re-cap)

humidity affects all thoughts below cloud base
rain washes down fragments of ideas
to the waiting rats   who know
bts f th potry o kats, bake, an yats

yes, the sculpture is of a rat
rat-time   rat time

to get back to the buffalo flight
zoo poem : (zoëtrope – look that up)
'the pen is mightier than the sward'
(an optical toy that shows
figures as if alive and in action)

We Must Get to the

window frames
tree
behind it lies
bottom of this

Star Rats

1.
moon
rust
train

2.
home
train
towel

3.
train
dust
mirror

Surgical Names: Frank

heads
tails

Can You Hear Me, Mother?

re-cap
train carries day
house memories
a sentence for the hidden movements

sniper
from day train aim
at day window
put out the night full stop

Flat One

pleasure of the mind
is one's own picture

you get what you put
no, that's too active, rather flat water
river reflection, presence of the reaction

Flat Two

chords of flat speech
river laps at the bottom / underground river
true landscapes of all arts
mingle around senses

Surgical Names: Ted

i

wonder

Taxonomy

the albatross drawer
this is the drawer where we keep the albatrosses

T.V.

toads of lake titicaca
200 to the acre
one billion toads in lake titicaca

Sailor Song

take a fix
hit or miss
exaggerated contract
strychnine pull

sea
see
saw

silver sea
green gage

Surgical Names: Tom

i draw the light from my window
a mirror hungs on the wall

No + On = Noon (except when reflected)

window stops at the edge of window and door at the edge of the door: the
observer shuts his eyes and continues the journey. memories eat away at
the idea. wall runs into ceiling runs into flex runs into bulb runs into light.
already the morning screams come from other rooms. dreadful as it may
be it is not so. dreams are sellotaped loosely on to the ten pictures of 'loved
by children' characters, all of whom look the same way. chummily, their
eyeballs roll towards you. it splits like slate or mica: or a thin sheet of
dream takes the place of a feather in a golden oval. how to see people
without their clothes.

death comes because the power of the body to grow is finally nullified by
gravity (... 'seriousness'). to preserve itself, intelligence must keep its
captive, mind, far enough above the surface to loosen the valves sufficiently
for ideas to be pushed into action. this is no time for padding or panic.
nobody controls the *dice* – when they roll the winner is he who pulls the
rest into the fork of his *number*. of course there is a path where you never
die, and a path where you are never born – both, and all, are irrelevant (see
'the blind deaf mutes' book of dreams'). if at death your whole life passes
before you think your way out of that.

the letters come with thanks and any *fool* knows it's all available: even for
re-play, the repeated gesture. all those napoleons like a deck of cards riffled
through time. or that's what his 'idea' would have you believe if you had
time for that. so the repeats go to the asylum because intelligence can't
have you reminded of no–time. think of the shock when the cameraman
returns to collect his speeded-up film of a rose blooming and finds the
flower has moved a yard to the east, out-of-focus. focus locus hocus pocus.
if a whole science and language spring out of the word *mathematics* no,
that's a trap. the notebook is always boringly open for our impressions.

This Morning

all is equally true to the voyager beyond these shores. one branch of dead
brown leaves sticks out from the tree: their rustle in the swish of green.
one falls. that a footstep on the gravel is in a different world to the chimney
pot.

The Title

1.

'i'
didn't do it first

the roses open more and more and die

tell the dream
not the reason

2.

'i'
gives the ti   me
          to   me

Songs of the Depression

there's a shop on the road
we whiz by
slowing down from our speed
a turn off's an angle

talking the song through a kazoo
the giver of which
heads for switzerland
this thought holds it together

while four lines and a stapler?
why an address book?
a bottle of brandy? why
a key ring? an ashtray?

will you sit in the sun
or write a letter urgently?
how long will the candle melt
while i listen to the band?

grab it all and don't slow down
never leave the road for what's
in a shop or a store
the road's enough

why exclamation mark four
lines and a stapler glue
kleenex an envelope
shards of god

this is my table today
this is the sound
this is the noise through
my eye that spins around

Just Another Whistle Stop

which branch? the bee
is filled with the band
and the sunshine a fly

walked over these lines
with its many eyes why
do we persist? the bee

Out of my Mine

rather than melt the ice passes through my hand
i pass through another way

dead surrounded by white
light flowers out

Gaslight

a line of faces borders the strangler's work
heavy european women
mist blows over dusty tropical plants
lit from beneath the leaves by a spotlight
mist in my mind a riffled deck

of cards or eccentrics
was i
a waterton animal my head
is not my own

poetry is neither swan nor owl
but worker, miner
digging each generation deeper
through the shit of its eaters
to the root – then up to the giant tomato

someone else's song is always behind us
as we wake from a dream trying to remember
step onto a thumbtack

two worlds – we write the skin
the surface tension that holds
                              you
                              in
what we write is ever   the past

curtain pulled back
a portrait behind it
is a room suddenly lit

looking out through the eyes
at a t.v. programme
of a monk sealed into a coffin

we close their eyes and ours
and still here the tune

moves on

Records

dreaming of voices and the leaves
taken from the tip of a breeze
a baritone's tone tells me this

the price is on all
you pay or counterfeit

7/8 of the Real

(for Christopher Middleton)

the necessary surfaces
at the correct time

all ways show
a little speed

you can't stop any thing
that's in the air

all ways things coming
to where you are

we are the same name
and suck together

with division of labour
cancer could destroy

itself a walking trigger
to the timed land mine

(all shows start the same time
stars only hear rumours)

you know, watch them hatch and
feed them and eat them

T.V. Again

the construct is alien
we impede light

the police came round
you were asleep

sliding plane over plane
what are we doing?

the absence of that
and so far

everything's been food
on the adverts (ben)

Homily

the work of art
reveals an exact opposite

every act
re-alines your boundaries

not to recall
but to trigger

the fuse
must not go out

Love and Pieces

met language static
on the street
thinks he's one
of a new elite

*

you have to learn
you can not teach

*

'there goes the town of spanish boot'
'only the buildings'

*

julius reuter
service de pigeons

*

i can not prove a second ago
to my own satisfaction

Wandering

terror of people leads into 'the people'
keep the message to your self
it's your journey

not to say the picture's wrong
but the hands
of the clock haven't moved

this has an archaic air like 'ere and o'er
make it fast
features formed by time's wind

dance inside the cloth
in a dull room
thin honey haze

this heavy haze
open the door
let it fight noise

lavender upon lime green
orange on dark brown
lost and am fishing

Misnomer

nothing
moves
but i do

making true

Situations

inside
the pantomime horse

a door in the t.v. opened
i felt the draught

colonel
eternal

Poetry Now

(for Andrew Carrigan)

snow falls through moon light
smile on the moon
enchantment returns
i am on the moon
twinkling reflections

a horse neighs an organ plays
looks like it
the balloon ascends
my father is killed by a sack of sand
it's just something i was thinking of

'ballast' i write in the answer
smoke blows through
the flakes of snow
moon   snow   flames
it can be no plainer

Dead End

1. *toop toop*
alternative to options
e – n – g – l – i– s – h

i'll pay for it
whatever that means

2. *diamonds are sharp*
60
that's right, you know

Old Poem's

a lion in the corner of the room
welcome back, lion
you are telling me to invest in oil?
no, you are telling me
that you are a lion

?

animals of the north
my child is dead
therefore you do not exist

wind darkens picture grey to black
in the name of the father the son
and the holy spiral

a picture of the flatness it felt
sounds from another room
only the eyes move

ears cannot find the present
coupled onto the future
i can do nothing can the rain?

Bounce

the poor are painted out
the rich, powerful, and famous have their say

tomorrow will be everywhere
so why not call it today?

'hello tomorrow, this is
a wanderer among the voices'

some are pictorial
and even educational

try all the different bits

      fragmented

      sparkling

puff! i've put it out with my *hand*
and you all understand

Three

(for John Inman)

1. *tone*
the smoke of the fire
the smoke of the fire

have i written it correctly?

2. *light*
but is it gold
that penetrates
lone ranger

must
not fall
into the enemy's hands

3. *writing*
no, that's wrong
no, that's wrong
no, that's wrong

lose
all
sense
of
direction

Two Together

i know behind the soot flame is yellow
singing distracts me
plink   plink   plink

practical
                    exploratory
                              topology

fierce visions are lost
                              over there

slices of white light
                              on dry mountain

all for the first time
rain, rain, and rain again

Patch Patch Patch

some evenings i think
of honour, glory, and bells

the last challenge is unanswered

cold night by the docks
captain bulb salutes another bottle

don't worry about that

in one part of the ship a phone rings
a message from another part of the ship

doppler effect

i don't know
where i can go
and sing the national anthem

everyone arrives at the ship on time
the girl, the golden-hearted drunk

'fuck it finger, this poem *leaks*!'

Future Models May Have Infra-red Sensors

take a taxi and go fishing
how do you like that?
visit canada
hey look, i see a big moose

cat's nose is twitching
why don't you ever go
to work and earn money?
invest your money here

why don't you try it yourself?
i'm on guard duty
with the armoured car
could you give me a lift?

then we could buy some lunch
gentlemen, here comes lunch
there is all the food we want
just give me a microsecond

maybe you likee something
to eat while you wait?
of course, of course, well, well
i'll prove it to you

you sir. who, me sir?
well sir, what is the verdict?
believe me
i've never seen my sheet

tell me again, i don't get it
sorry hotee dogs all gone
a natural using wild game
one share of wildcat oil

don't cut *me*. i never
heard of wildcat oil
broken glass, drawn stars
fine, fine, you killed him

hold it officer, it's my duty
right behind the car sir
before anyone sees me
my pleasure, you know what they say

money talks. i just don't understand
xylophone trills
another day like yesterday
we'll be in gravy

pardon me gentlemen
is there a bank
in the neighbourhood?
you drove up from hillcrest?

Delivery Instruction

(for Ray and Betsi)

atoms in every star
woodsmoke at night
enamel plates
beaten with spoons
what a lovely ship!

sparks lifted by smoke
and now i will have justice
wooden ship burns
red stars through white
ash slick on that sea

there's nothing to it
once you know the trick
'where hast tha been
since i saw thee?'
singing creaking ship

Western World

(for Anna Mendleson)

horse's breath mists the hitching rail
fire reflects in both eyes
cold night along cement walls
everywhere men are doing their duty

guarding prisoners from fires
horses children and space
while insects coldly breed
one of them crawls from eye to eye

eggs hatch in all four corners
of the motionless eyes the eyes
of those tiny insects reflect
one thousand times the horse's breath

Transports of Delight

not a wit display
god lives on the sun
in the small out cabin of the mind
doctor, he seemed more angry than frightened

'the same fury that was evident in the defiant'
we must not move
and survived
and there can be no margin for error

multi-shadows
i look at it (a)
she touched it (b)
(a) ear-ring
(b) ear-ring

every one here will die
report to central control
shaped by the things we love

End Again

dream
into the mirror
please

nothing
more
to learn

crib

is there an arthritis
　　　　of thought
　　　　　　of time
　　　　　　we see

so many people we will never meet?

enter thought claustrophobia
a switch clicks down
i wake and illuminate my world

Deal Another Hand

sounds

sigh rises and falls
rubber spring creaks
you're in my life

impressions

'swallowed the bait'
no more impressions

halva

sweet
damp
edible
desert

l'argot supérieur

dream comes true
slow ride on an animal
good times coming

sidestep

all tickets have been issued
except this one
                spiral
                spring

Mirror Mirror on the Wheel

what is my frame?
dry hot handkerchief
pressed to my eyes

unreal
i am examining
my love for this child

who looks so like me
i am inside
his movements

now he drops my keys
and stares
at the tape deck

'all your sea-sick sailors
they are rowing home'
we hear

time, i love you
you are the way
i see the same anew

Boing

what is a trip?
changing the view
why do you want to
change the view?

who?

I Better Put a Pattern around This if They're Going to Call it a Poem

i look back from the t.v.
into the bright model i
carry as the border of my.... uh...
programme of my... uh....
attached... uh...
am attached to

Could You Love a Fish? or Would You Rather Swing on a Star?

he loves a horse!
he loves a plant!
he loves a stone!

you don't mean EVEREST *TUCK*!

From the Hungarian (a sequence of eighteen poems)

(with Val Raworth)

Three poems of mine had been translated into Hungarian, a language of which we know nothing: we translated them back one morning. three of each, each, with a break between each set of three: and no peeking: line by line ... then we shuffled them. May 9th. 1973. It looks a lot like Europe. T.R./V.R.

Wandergut

slovak intellectual appears to cyclops
resembling your face
hiding ecstasy in cement works of webern
cutlass banana-scar on amber mind-nuts

oval, a robot tu-tu
lovingly spins metallicly among the tortoises
with seventeen sporadic rotors
similarly steaming egyptian musaz

pieter kelnek who in moderation
seemed the energy of spinning sarcasm
semi-exerted
takes from it a slovak intellectual

Sally to See You, Tacitus

amok among sicilians
seeking far with my good eye
can alcohol
so maintain europe
that the gone rue it so?

is it a first-greeting fist then
that sparks on nearing
a merry parent?
is this the foolish cyclamate
ten gallons of which flatten your hair?

exercise that lengthens dogs
mars their true coats
'holy mitred vale
of tulsa pray for us'
yes lola.... no giorgio.... hi joe

At Maximum Zero

seeking the still window
in stasis
a variant arrival
chortles into a hold-all
golden arrival-window!

lo! nears the orgone-bug
—mincy ugly tunneler—
each distant foot feels all
eggy   agony in a homosexual's apartment
eggy future in a blimp sack

'ballast' (ricardo montalban)
a fat lip
leapfrogging
hold! ho! lobster's
name instructs the eggy cherub

A Colt Has Ate Most

how easy to hold fast at
missolonghi   to hold the
visitor at varese
to hold vague jokes
golden honey with fennel

the nearing organ book
with huge volume
with leg-rings feels all
edgy   who mocks that apparent old-age
that edgy suspended future?

'ballast' from a vibration
a first fast kiss
happily held
hold!   ho!   far-off
name is educated syllabub

Starlight Utilities

atomic minds caliban
far fiji with ebsen
canals and chocolate
romany yaks
o the guru halo!

tick tock   (some hungarian)
it's most energetic gazing
a fey league
this is the sick eskimo
you give me a fiery hand at last

sadness dolor
i am immersed in tricks
hold val
ultimately licking
day   night   tomorrow

Start and Sit

scylla running amok
past fiji
carnal charcoal
romantic romany
holy gorgio

tick tock   a felt fist
its most gossamer journey
cloth legs
sweet silk eyes
tender feeble velvet hands

dogs at zero
immersed in tracks
mighty voles
using milk
daily in yesterday's gorges

A Colt Is Most

ho! he's holding it at
waving and holding
with water and whiskey
holding guns
hungarian guns

look at the big night organ
eating the ugly violinist
a musical festival
streaky men, gold hair
dark streets   gondolas

ballast from a blaze
a fiery volcano
horses
hold him long
my name is lettie eggsyrub

Utility Starlight

killing us atomic minds
far fiji
canals and calibres
alchemy
o giant halos

this is the first fault
it is the most i gaze on
a pharaoh's league
icy   killing   silent
giving a feather with latitude

dogs tigers
immersed in tricks
holes   valleys   mists
utopian lakes
days   nights   afternoons

Celtic Mists

hold silk hold faille
muslin and hemp
vichy water and champagne
holding vanilla
hungry faces

icons and bugles
mints on the volga
a laughing festival
aubergines patting andirons
casks of future glows

blitz velasquez
a first king
hopeless
hopeful   lingering
no lethe

What Do You Say?

low level plain and copses
a certain fierce time
hiding jokes in mud bricks
fierce coals and midnight embers

jerking a rabbit upwards
loving laughter and misty turtles
it is 1770 in reykyavik
singing   scheming   masking   killing

killing people with moderation
killing never sinking a rock
seeing foam
taking a lovely levee

A Most Cold

they hold izaak at fire
moulding the tundra
clear water and ice
a bold magyar
gorging

no merit gets oregon
mincing   ugly   vulgar
at leghorn fairs
each man takes with iron
izaak takes iron

iron blasts from calderon
a fiery kiss
hope
hold   o   languor
its name is lethe

Solitary Utahsitis

atomically minded armchair prevention
from dawn till dusk
coal by canal and car
so maintain your castle
o, from gongora hasten!

seacrack in falsetto whispers
is most eye-less once-yearly
to bird leg
is so silly and sick
to tender a feather amulet

dry self sad log
as to true immersed sea-bed
– whole valium aorta
utilised chest attack –
peer: or go hasten

Who Dun It

level legs parachutes and co-ops
a sunbeam and a rainbow
hiding bodies in a cement bridge
the hotel vega burns at midnight

over a rabbit-stew
chocolate milk and a mezzanine tortoise
with a swede and a swiss from reykyavik
and a swede and a swiss from egypt

found a modulating key
taking energy from a rock
going to samarkand
turks love it

What Nougat

lovely far-televisioned paris by cycle
smack kisses your eye windows
hiding ecstasy in cement shell 'toves'
cutlet-gook and vegetables at embered midnight

omelet of rabbit, turtle
lovingly rotored and mixed with tletur
my senses thunder-snap and wander
simultaneously simulating masticating egg-yolk

pieter kelnek born in modulatia
sense energy sarcastically roaming
see me eat 'zers'
you crazy but lovable distant set

Shall the Cup You Sit at

syllable's are mind's atoms
from first to last
through cancer-canal
romantic jokes
'o........ de *go*lden halo!'

seek rat – that musty head
is most ignobly elegant
for halo's light
is eskimo
or arabic

sad egg-stained dog
has smeared his basket
– whole valuable fragments
used to lap milk
give him his new york halo

What You Got?

the far-off cattle seem to clop
a steamboat to distend it
while day exacts a solid fee
the burning cattle mind it

but lo! a rabbit-cat appears
gambolling endearingly round and round
the seventeen zippers of its pelt
snag simultaneously on the ground

pets that have not learned moderation
whose energy forces them to roam
may end as half-chewed entrecotes
beneath sweet turkish loam

Take a Dog

cool perfect loving hell
remembering fizzing tunes
hiding jokes finding flakes
coasting   embarking at midnight

ovals in rabid turmoil
loving geometrics and tertian symbols
a thousand thousand royals
singing singing music elegies

please keep in a gavotte
many rock sarabands
see me see me
turning a lovely anthem

How Cold is Most

how easy to hold fania's hat
a muscled yogi will hold it
this visitor to our ranks
will hold it vaguely
go hunting with fania

loan your writ or go in a bug
mind the ugly will
allegro!   feldspar!
behold the clear painful beauty of your tie
behold saki futilely inflate you

'by allah!' – from a valise
a quick fist
an opal yak
old   o.... bangkok
fate is far from syrup's ego

Sacred Heart

all dead, every one dead
savagery and madness

hurt, you eat love and sorrow
this is so useless

glass tendrils of love
snap as invisibles battle

horror, take back the name
damage   damage   damage

Belt

(for Darrell Gray)

going all the way
and adjusting
going all the way

¡Que Bonitos Ochos Tienes!

scored with another illusion
open your veins
scent suspends time

this is what i do
passing the time
still here

sound of southern illusion
open your being
can't suspend time

this is what i do
passing the time
still here

Get It While You Can

rose apricot blue grey evening
drifting constantly under the sun

someone save me
i've lost me

Theye

move

away

fast

shadow

moving

still

Chicago

pistol whipcracks i wondered about
are ted typing below

                        white snow

Mama

everyone
covers for the family

we know we are
how do we know you are?

Peoples

light travels
from what reflects it

and there are spasms
people laugh at

Self

i wish i were my
self – mexican – ¡que te vayas bien!
without dreams –forgetting to write

Fits

hole in the book
my tablet nestles in

Box in the Trunk

blue rabbit swirls to ask for bread
everyone finishes the same time
invention was one snowshoe
with two feet on

Gravity is Caused by Spring

curl in my brain
look back down
silver trail

Back when the Music said 'No Hurry'

'nagasaki' he nodded towards the painting making a gesture of light with
his hands that explained all this to them

The Generous Television

will wake you up   you can have an earphone
how rarely these days do i get right out here to almost the edge of the page
a rocking chair faces the television
on the back of the rocking chair is a marquetry landscape

six minutes later

Five

three within
a boulder of silence

three is two twos
who is left?

Steaming Snow

can't get through on this terminal
suddenly the clock begins to tick

sitting listening for the right piece
doing my job

Every One Different

snowflake, i've not talked to you for a long time
why should i start now?   you've *trapped* me!

In which Rhythm Makes a Stand

good evening, warmth, here i am again
enticed by the presence of light
i'm obviously here and all your pretence
of accident just makes me love you
(i see through you, or not quite) love you
control has pushed my head convex – or is it concaine?
chance that gurgles like a picket fence
brushed by a sausage of my watery sight

Windmill Poem Association

(for Ray and Betsi)

my dear, ungainly in the cold night
i enjoy inside again
and this pen said take me take me
then the fan blew air and i chose it

i waited, reading what he wrote (me fan)
but no *choice* – he was alone in the room

Bleecker Street

what is an alias?
a false name
what is a true name?

sun goes down
light goes out

Om

last move is home –

or shome
if you're worried 'flesh colour' means pink

The Century Doesn't Want to be 72

where's the can opener?
be right with you

empty bottle
feels lighter

Motiveless

and in this window is the motionless i crave
that is ash of bodies tilting
stale air   déclassée
outside view from any floor
eighteen inches unwaxed dental floss
'igor' in handwriting on
winston packet 'zolief'
cork   my thoughts   a foreign voice
chemicals   the harpsichord trill

Poemian

aram
daruom!

Edgar Allan Poe

                            mmmmmmmmmmmmmm
necktown

The Pressure that Causes Mistakes

slim acid windows across the street
a girl the same thickness

her room? and in my mind
to a soundtrack of 'what's a father and four sisters?'

merle oberon
one minute

What Is the Shadow's Pentip Writing?

my feelings become boring as brain
please, where's the food?

i think my art is based on ouch
another golfball with 200 miles

From the Window

german shepherd pees on statue in a grotto
trust your own magnets   the magnetic pattern of grace
is shaved off   i see a clatter
beyond peripheral vision
                    i must adjust the colour
of this afternoon and with my magnet
draw a cloud of steaming piss above the street
above the 'o' in 'food'
and rain, and slip, and carry an orange ball

University Days

this poem has been removed for further study

Canvas

all blue
in the distance

i feel
i am

a
hologram

of static
in your life

Wouldn't it be Funny if She Just Walked in

striking the grand oval verb shift
marimba threw himself still

You Need It – We Rent It

shadow becomes you
move a light

Be Last

going forward
sick and dizzy
nobody dies

straw is forced
into the knee
a long way

whistle blows
our theme too
sky will die

Murder Stone

check the moon
with your watch

come on
up on the morning

Tell Me What This is About

take this hammer
give it to the captain

Home for the   Time

all my poems are things of interest on this street

Attitude Must be Interesting

      ?   ? ?   ?

Read Me

thanks

Uncertain Steps

not a duty, nor a purpose
nor a mis-reading of the black bird's swoop
many years in this same place

twisting a used flashcube under the lamp
for white light to eat gold
no grace in that steady clapping

to the music, to the four winds
i have waited always with birds' black
shadows keeping light from certain cells

a hand draws me into the air
among whose atoms children dance
as though they did not understand

the secret, which is what
holds everything up
into the light

News

a black market in bricks
ten thousand bricks stolen
the number of people who died
children can die through lack of love

with seventy swiss holidaymakers on board
some of them happy, some of them sad
exactly three months ago we reported some good news
they hoped to buy a bungalow

two white blackbirds were hatched in one nest
you see it here with its erstwhile protector
like big white butterflies outside the door
at last they burst into captivity and fly around

From Time to Time in the Past

tree lets me hear the wind
over there where it is
i won't believe this is all there is
(the interest on eternity)

'it is' squeaks my voice

Mixed

whee! the tip of a lock
of her hair blows round
and round on the urban set
mocked up like your 'jungle'

but from deep in the tape
of tropical sounds
a good engineer brings out
first a splash in the surf

then 'we are lost' in her
father's voice : but ludwig's
ears were deadened
by the last of a species of bright birds

One Evening

flat fish

when will i write again
some thing i like?
this bending light

feeding them round the clock

books are so expensive

each boat has a flag on it
soon we will know all past murderers
look at that little know draw me on

we are all stars now

death

time stopped
life going on

Onset

there is the cupboard
where the tumbleweeds are stored
ready for next week

snow is not snow
all our real names
roll up at the end

Everything 'Under' the Sun

a likely button of yes
immobilised

all 'over' the world
some radios are off and some are on

eat what you want
learn your own lessons

if you want
don't let the revolution hold you back

Som

i've also got some stars and moons
put a moon down by my nose
a special cloak...   right
it's got lots of stars and moons

Birthday

what present will i have tomorrow?
moo moo went the cows in the only way they could
i dream of interest and light space
up and smaller to go into the distance

No Peace / Black Holes / Earth Cracks

there's a lot of things you can do
without using words – i was doing i
very hungry. the red elastic mark

Music Box

(for Donald Hall)

did you guess? some people are dancing
through one of our windows today
these people are dancing in another country
they just wear them for this dance
look very happy while they're dancing
keep in time with the music

Laid Waste by the Luftwaffe

punctuated by birdbaths
facts, give me some facts
i'm down to my last
plants were grown organically
without space or fertilizer
re-creates his best-loved mimes
in omnibus. spring. leaves
spiralling through butterflies

Lined Paper

sensitive to space

the

sensitive to light
sensitive to time

Just We Two

we know where we are by shape
in your idea of village
(keep away – i'm writing

you look down at your hand
holding a red pen writing red
we know where we are by shape

Philosophical Moments

dog food

we put a different food in each dish
then see in which order the dog eats them

cat food

we don't know why they do eat grass
it isn't an essential nutriment

radio

do you know what old radio looks like?

hair low
who are you?

Lunch is Ready

given this gift of a beautiful image
i cannot focus

let's say a man, leaning, covers the area
of outside wall between door edge and
wall edge his head being level
with the top of the door
which is opened outwards
away from him. inside, the wall paper
is the colour of the sky outside
(maroon painted wooden house)

walk past his arm
in two dimensions

The Ethical Artist

kept a source book
but picked each plum

Along Came Bill by P. G. Wodehouse

good evening, this is how you see molecules
by your feelings' flickering

very rapid movement

whispering rain's movement
but someone recognised me discontent

Infinite Variety Stales

the narrative line is only as boring
as what's hung on it
one auk a verb met a noun
who will care for the child
so it must burn
unless called away
dissolve bridges radio squawks in the jeep

costumes are codes
in bright flexible corridors
'radio... your dead archer standing by'
this pigeon has flown the coop
to an image lag rapid letter breaks
orange california poppies
established his delusion

Sunday Draught

studying zymology, and in particular zymurgy
watching the zymogenesis of the zymogens
counting the zygospores and zygotes after zygosis

zymosis!   quick, the zymometer!

Describing the *In* on the *Crest* of a Wave

blue river
daniel boone striding along in it
'DANIEL BOONE' across the scene in orange letters

further refinements:
t.v. enlarges vocabularies
i will try not to describe the past

getting back
getting back

horse broke a leg
horse looks like a leg
there are not my feelings   definitions

i understand perfectly
but something is wrong   paranoia

truer meanings
to every sentence   grammar

the kidnappers leave a door open
calling the name   play

film made of all scenes
just after the action   movies

try and remember
the past   education

power of the memory
of first feeling   myth

i have created a myth
only a little myth
but it could grow if you

i had forgotten the object of my lesson should be there. 'yes i'm right'
should only have given me freedom. but the mirror had flipped up. i
organised as much of the direction as i could, and started off.

'not *skimming*, like old *fash*ioned speed readers. as a *graduate*, you'll be
able to read a book in less than an hour'

the best
in history   roadsign

disappearing hemispheres
surrounded the grey balloon

surface clear?
unloose
re lease

'nothing is know' sang all the animals
trying to get clear

                    dear

page   i feel so useless
but triumphantly sad

(use
smaller paper)   advice

New Year

(for Michael Myers)

how painfully i feel both dark and light
as if my bones were boils
my outer layer quite quite dead
i see most art as slow ideas
carrying passengers i like or notzzzzzzzzzzzzzz

'one lincoln under god etc.'

the impressionist

Northwest Ohio

torn off
before toledo
and drowned at sea

the news appeared
accidently
as a message

The Only Sound in Dallas was the Mexican Beans Jumping

my red hat with the green brown red and blue band is on a polished brown
wood table in front of a rough white washed wall: above it is a gilt framed
mirror. i am living well. it creeps up on you. killing time watching
shadows. i'd like to remind you about this evening, tom.

Los Angeles

quartz cars
dwarf bars

Mexico

cold bricks   a trace of mist
in sierre leone some questions are asked
my camera is in california
running through my memories for a buzz

The City

full buses before it is light
a dead alsatian   roses

On my Holidays

i was born in the house of a rocket maker: the green stone hand is for luck.
all my teeth have been corrected – a small thing in the life of a star, but
who knows... ? i like the mountains, deserts, the sea and clouds. my ambi-
tion is to be a magnet.

Pessimist

little life supports my body
i don't want to be pretentious
this is the floor plan : here
is the hotel. i do my best

The Resistance   Changes

the little dog laughed
the play is over
jill wants jack to come home
a lamb is ready for the slaughter

Just Because my Teeth are Pearly

'never a dull moment' said the sun
'you keep coming back to me, with dreams
and time. i've lost count
of your visits. perhaps we should come to some arrangement
go out at night, walk in my reflected light
and write, cry, and always love
the company of women when they dance.'

Tribal God

talk talk and then there is no-one, not even a telephone : remains of
eyebrows and detritus of the people and their work. i am a speedy human
and the noisy night air is so filled with their dreams i am afraid to sleep.
come to me, lady : make me a perfectly wrapped chocolate bar. another
night with ruthless in my pocket.

Not a Step Do I Stir until that Cat's Back to its Colour

civilization was pushing around ageing molecules saying
'lovely... a new patch of lung' and 'aching doesn't thank'
when a sunbeam hit my son, throwing his tiny full colour reflection
onto the centre of the flickering black and white screen

Out Takes

a tiny fifth genius

stand up
all of you
using binoculars

somebody's got to be seen around here

look
i've trapped these molecules
into my shape is

steam iron

one pound extra to use the lift

model

i know a shadow doesn't bend that way   in space
        a shadow   in space

inner mist

tuesday in poetry town : some of the pages are upside down

la

speak
mozambique
trick or treak

mark

well folks, here we are on the surface of pattern

(no title)

the center
for the study
of popular
culture

splashdown

why do they drown the parachutes?
the parachutes fought for life

flit

faulty cloning
no shot echo over my coffin

describe

send pictures or get pictures
new body mist

makes fruit taste even better

i love
my muse

ears the shadow of people either side

impossible junctions
at this connection

the life time gate

fragments of the same enjoyment
these three men are dead

unity

one
is not all
the same

sitting comfortably in trust

'love is the head of the thumbtack of truth'

song

antiques avoid unpleasantness
when a 'thus' appears
i recognise the heads of my friends
never feel at home

Information Film

at once do you understand
now
private douglas has volunteered for special duty
o but hurry back i'm frightened

be seated
reed instruments
break in the sound track

across gravel into the apiary
there they are   shoot

Knowledge

draw

a

picture

of

what

you

,

re

thinking

in

words

undetectable

except

by

an

expert

this

really

is

contemporary

reading

riding

the

light

waves

good

day

A Blue Vacuum Cleaner

in the scent of burning vegetables
a scratch on my nose adjusts vertical hold
while with my left eye i see long distances
to where time turns light cold

small star, someone named you
what are you doing to me?

Cross Divide

(for Neil Littlewood)

small car distant, no life in it
draws lightning to my ear
flash
entering luminous blue insulators
entering electrical memory many times

electrical ogham computer rosetta
finger old thought carefully
headlight fires ahead
over the great salt lake
living days in a crayon

salt lake straightens out sweating
cold lights travel the night clouds
each tube dreams of flight
rubber memories
slowly what we dreamed is happening

A More Refined Taste

i shall have my grave
outside of light

as two old women
meet in a corner

the sun
shows yellow against red

the hum
given some imagined violence

The Beckoning Harpoon

my muse is bored with the company i keep. i wait for her to flash the mirrored paper in my eyes and she does this.

Dormitory Life

(for Phil and Dolores O'Connor)

driving into town at night i saw there was only main street and the end of the light. the first day i bought old newspapers to hold me down. day two i was shooting crushed aspirin to keep the crystal growing. 'do you know' he asked 'what gertrude stein remarked?' i dodged into a postcard of raymond roussel's living room. sepia. where i slipped in a pool of vomit, fell against a colour t.v., and jogged five tiny chicago bears out onto the blue chenille rug. roussel was pleasant. we talked about war, people, food, and him. 'let me explain about art' he whispered: 'i write *nuts*..., sign it..., and they keep it on their tables.' 'saving the brain at the expense of life?' i ventured. his ragged clothes revealed the phone had been cut off. slipping a slide into the projector he flashed 'if the army is retreating, how can you run away?' and, while i was enjoying the orange glow on my retina, 'the heroes never look like other men.' i relaxed into the sound of a grenade exploding in a tank full of people. 'take this' he murmured as registration slipped and i fell out of the postcard. 'this' was a remote control unit with one button labelled *different light*.

The Conscience of a Conservative

(for José Emilio and Cristina)

if you are
a true machine
the edge is time
the edge is fine

*

what have i lost
who are you

in the shadow
carved of wood

in the river
on this boat

always working
cancer mind

*

o
hand
make a circle

how
the wound
snaps shut

*

insulation
sun within mirrors
isolation

*

hands and feet
of my soul

broken
pulled nails

curled back
in time

*

time takes
me further
from grace

i have
never felt
so tired

afraid
invention
leaves me

once more
in my space
i dream

*

on the shore where they 'established a constant' (two palms, blue sea) lay
a dirty white sock, a pair of blue and white tennis shoes, my feet (left resting
on right). sound of a tram (at night) in my head. volume, tone, and distance.

*

jerky people on the street
i have not thought myself
one of you for a long while

you wear colours and move
among then : how does the force pass?

cool breeze communication
with your thumbs in your pockets
cold night air   the voices all around

*

harsh light i will write openly
too much
one way

*

clothes
stationary through the night

*

'a history
of ideas'

*

we will live through
a long boring time
of everybody having 'insights'

a little gold creeps in
an urge for distinction
description – it *ma*tters

*

bleak

*

compass rose

*

a shadow / is something / on the surface
therefore
through our transversion of time

forgotten

*

a babylonian rage : the car misses and aches

         glow

*

all this gets us nowhere
no there's no where   now here

*

coughing
echo of metal from stone

the light
that lets
me read
and write

*

seeing in a
'wrong light'

*

life : half of all opposites in any direction
the opposite of 'book'
the opposite of 'high' is 'pink'

*

the letters said
we are here for a serious purpose

trial bores into time

*

only the stone
smoke curling
film knows my hate

for the lamp
is open
the bulb unbroken

*

boo

del

wah

*

speak my language
dog

*

in this ward
i can but draw

nameSeman
nameSeman

*

imagine

being

and not

knowing

*

my first is in move but never in door
my second's in emit but never in floor
my third is in time and also elastic
my fourth is in era and yes it's in plastic

my fifth is in wrapt and double in wrapped
my sixth is in home but never in mapped
my seventh's in or and also in open
my eighth is in or and never in open
my whole is a word whose meaning's unclear
is it this? that? or what? will it last? am i near?

*

a turtle

a fine line

a turtle

*

primitives

see

they eat
all the meat

*

set
sorce
de
hote
kwolitay

*

there's a star in my film
i keep trying to pick   it   out

*

epateRetape

Ulysses : or Trotsky's Death

(for Marco Antonio and Ana Luisa)

'hidden lighting'

'old people'

*

glass
before a mirror
in space

*

no faces
only facts
and facets

*

hidden lighting
writing

*

what changes
in the reflection
of colours

*

time

cache

time

ache

*

lost

in thought

The Drama Review

(for Gilpin and Gayle)

light slides
over velvet
any way
it wants

good year
accurate ear
no amnesty
robert mitchum

the flag
is dropped
the race
a memory

*

once
upon
a time

economy

tina
turner

there'd
better be
no water
on the floor

*

'waterproof booklet identifies ducks'

*

'free

plaque

of coincidental facts'

*

construct a set
show it what to do
in case of accidents

*

i
like no
solution

*

olaf

*

drug

store

junk

dealer

*

look!
what?
nothing

*

voices
of others
voices
of me

*

tan boring life

*

el ed
i
ficio

*

timing
devices

The Bank of Wood County

(for John and Jania)

'he desires me
i believe that's the phrase'

*

long   beach   california

*

up at six
to put glass
in windows

*

i h
ate t
he i
mage

*

graphics

*

salve
age

*

no
radio

*

morphine
use   it

*

medic!

*

'what' –
does it matter?

*

smack
into
an
ambush

*

past acting

*

clothes
to dirty

*

el
pe
rio
dico   .

*

pulled off
the hook

Funeral Cards

(for Bill Knott)

if they do
what you think
it's as boring
as you thought

*

'let's just say
you gave my imagination
full rein'

*

i put it
there and it's still
there

*

round
and round
and round

*

'the dead end kids
(here with bogart)
represented the depression's
displaced teenagers'

*

i:

am

in the past

*

orange

genius

experience

*

moon to breathe

*

small moon was not even part of the problem
when ants arrived to give all 'the solution'
if this train is a light   who are we?
where dot dot where dot dot where

*

nothing
is not even
nothing wrung out with full strength

*

an
acute
sense
of
old

*

cut off
pictures
without
the dream

*

lord
of night
staff of agonies

*

there's safety
in numbers
ann finnegan
my cousin

*

this

alien

language

*

o.k.
captain

*

in a
speed
boat

*

clean
print

*

no longer
any interest
on my life

*

coloured
shadows
redefine

no more
i hope
there is

*

continual
correction

*

'say hello to your people'

Beautiful Habit

(for Ed and Jenny)

greetings
as the door opened
ticking

please listen to this
food alone for all
the f.b.i. will continue

maybe you dozed off
i hung by that phone all night
suppose he talks

*

vida

later

aria

*

once upon a time
not looking for any thing

*

you're on
your own
it's off
it's on

*

perhaps it means
ragged like that
golda my – yeer
        pre – meer

*

and pour the old box
down a drain

*

too much news
said the news

*

r e o l e

*

it's us
or rust
listener

*

deep

personal

regret

looking

up

monday

*

we can save
your head or your body
we can shave

*

even
his admission
is
a subtle lie

*

in suspense
what is cut into
the smallest of the

*

grinding

to fill

a prescription

*

drum to the wobble and a roll on the sea
come to mind an article of light
distance through distance unfinished

*

piano

*

willing to believe

*

national

anthem

hearer

*

perfect rhyme to some

all cars

kept in doors

*

sophisticated
newsmen
show how
it could have been

*

retreat
from the swiss
legation

*

numbers
for an event

*

corruption
why not ?

*

infinite
detail
is no more real

*

thought

    against

        power

*

answer

it

*

hooked
to just another
piece of tape

hooked
to just one more
little piece of tape

*

through words in to
no
record

*

writer

righter

riter

*

am:
i
on replay?

*

all you
do is
expand
the system

*

a polaroid
of la
with the wrong
voice print

*

astronaut
amazed
at what
was expected

Perpetual Motion

(for Bill and Marilyn)

tanks
go into
battle

*

the arabs photograph themselves
from the israeli point of view

*

looking back
looking forward

*

through
eating
biting
chewing
up to ten whole hours

*

for people
who don't like
the real thing

*

cleverer

speaking

honestly

*

small shipments of white arms

*

some think it's to do with the line

*

no thank you
i don't play with watches

*

effective
november first

*

take it
and bake it
and wrap it
in under

*

the myth
of creation

*

now

then

charlie

*

exposes
them
to extreme danger

*

learning to see what others see
there is no superiority

*

complete with everything you see

*

mission impossible tape reading

*

admit to bean

*

reception

*

je ne veux pas
les biscuits au chocolat

*

warp
lanes

*

a cat's concept of the mind
that could make it dance
and sing by editing film

*

mary
was assumed
into heaven

*

slowly
through the
snow they
go

*

open
pour
and
store

*

what ever
you heard

*

love in mind
sun through the blind

*

splendid
olig

*

crime the adrenal
time the pineal

*

far away
a pie
in the high
sierras

*

on trick plays
he'll use his
head, nose, eyes, face

*

with power
speeding power
slowing no
emergency

*

attached
to
awards
power

*

home   work

*

met

his

match

Mr & Mrs Grief

(for Asa and Pip)

scalpel
nurse

*

a flicker
book of
not noticing any thing

*

over
disc

*

many living room here

*

that's it then

*

the universe
as god's
paranoia

*

night

light

night

*

arches and a car

*

safe in the arms of who
you'll be dryer

chill
and
test

*

bend

*

a loup

*

cage face
see him puke and become a lumpkin

*

'i'll go'
'oh no'

*

hel
mut
bon
heim

*

when it's in this form

*

actual demonstration

*

w g n

television

presents

*

stammer 'crewcut'

*

dyed hair
painted faces

*

put it in a form

*

try

sybil

out

Horse Power

(for Anselm and Josie)

interchange of display
arrival of the colonel
aquatint

no way

intelligent echoes in colour

but i

can't

help

falling in love

with

you

*

slavery

what

we

have

words

for

*

always looking through the eyes
he only knows the sausage is after him

*

remember
no time
when i wasn't

*

'you're a honky-tonk
i'm a record player
playing a honky-tonk'

*

captain terminal

*

'in which we have made
enormous progrom... *pro*gress'

*

the puzzled house awaits my tail
1500 pounds of nervous elephant
you are watching   lavinia

stolen or invented but proffered
boredom   red-hot thumbs
light passes through the crest

the narrative continues trapped
i enter listening watching waiting
ing ing ing   a mis-spell   ing

*

what:

a form

*

no-one
will ever
find out

*

sustain this to the ear-ring
french windows blown open
flames of three lamps

carrying an extinguished candle
no, alight; the swinging cut glass
of the candlestick   murder   commercial

*

the blot leading the knot

*

in notification for this card
we have extracted our peripheral business
everyone was the aim but then
anyone woke up

brain reacts to fear
curved into its present form
o i'm lazy
bored, or tired

*

needs

open up the gallery

no space

*

'peace and value, comrade'

*

'run a loss on him'

*

on top
of the lift

*

starts to work instantly

*

i met my fate but the seams didn't match
bulbs spelled l o a n s
fat of the famous touched in mime

*

no longer addresses
how can we know
the first
goodbye

*

too late
what rhymes with cow
and starts with an n

*

black holes in the metaphor

lost my sense of fun
found it had met death
observed it with pauses
was lonely and attached

all hands on time observe
the symbols   wearing away
a woman singing   new york
thank you distracters

her slowness extends not out but in
she licks her plate
lamps instantly chosen music
death in a pattern by diamond

try not to feel interference
mein mind has nozzink to do
when i think blue
that is all i have to do

*

unlock
tassel
painting
recorder

harmonica
message
friendship
border

seal
golden
weeks
american

yesterday
behalf
return
regard

tiger
way
compelled
communist

get
returned
should
disavow

*

like

so and so

unknown

unknown

*

para   sol

*

use
of a cat

power
of money

value
of life

For Tom Clark

edspherification

*

mother

with

child

all

the

time

*

two light years wait and see

*

iron fire

*

normal cineaste

*

double entomdre'd

*

heart ache

from out

side

*

captain
phillips'
bowels
in
quick
succession

*

'you might not know
we are in the latter
half of the twentieth century'

*

'children – and some adults –
may by now probably be tired
of this ceremony which has now
lasted almost three hours'

*

'going to get a friend' and
'pipe's dream'
painted on tow-trucks' radiators
in oak park

*

valarie
takes care
of me

*

arise

alone

*

past

fast

move

ment

*

what's

normal

to

you

is

strange

to

me

*

get that vermillion

*

real surrounds school

*

found

what i wanted

to do

*

friendly
gestures
differ

*

'early

days'

in

the

'chicago

school'

*

one

pun

bun

was

nub

*

'9,000 guests
in a private garden
in the heart of london'

*

the queen
is seen

*

the queen
hears the national
anthem every day

*

surrounded
by careful people

*

should be
the most
luxury

*

death of imagination
protected by 'government'

*

'you will not cut

nor deface

your sentry box'

Formal 1

(for Ted and Alice)

communiño
i declare
no knowledge save
the popular

scents and ideas
communrave
noticing
the mark of zorro

in black and white
a 'rose' on 'satin'
in colour
red on white satin

stretching again
flowers are in
my imagination
but i know curry

who knows power
can reject it
and live in love
with satisfaction

Formal 2

train
of grins
el tiempo
más temprano

accents and entries
tell her you're hungry
has changed
language of my friends

no tattoo but recognition
attached to your temporary
belief if you collect
collect this

times of light past
do better
their dream
to sleep

cries of children
their accents
i will
not kill you

Formal 3

red guards
the chiltern hundreds
'*since* : from then till now'
aristocrats' freedom

cooking
oblique
time
z

permanently filed
texture of
chloral hydrate
in stalin's bathwater

welcome comet
no references
breakwind
jigsaw

the london county council
riding in the grounds milady
continuing
pleasure

Formal 4

miniature railway
retires
preceded by 'ever'
unlike now

dish conjurer
befriends bun
burnt
zis

pours
on nature
sleeps
in texture

follow the star
emptiness
converts
a pattern

jack up
the tumbril
hold on
to your head

Formal 5

andré malraux
mémoires
memories
flies de gaulle

cordon bleu
brioche
approach
bien

punitive
soul
reserved
le rouge et le noir

wherever
loam
gloams
puzzle

a digression
to be second
mind
what you do

Formal 6

ching chang chinaman
smiley smiley man
in loving memory
know your place

just push
ear of horn
watch
sword's point

'the punic rose'
a crystal bore
cures over
one time-lapsed player

who lies
about his bulb
paid a substitute
by promising revelation

a
b
a
b

Formal 7

each single thing
in harmony
with its name
complication

preserves
its name
against the snow
blue

at rest
basil rathbone
and dana wynter
measure growth

what fills
tyres
travels
germ balloons

land in snow
settle
and know
the pointed metal

Coda: Songs of the Mask

mad
she said she'd personally see i lost every patient i had

*

you don't know what it means to be one-sided
you can always see both points of view
how very very very very very
very very very boring for you

*

mimicked him so exactly
are
tha

all i'm going to
not
do

can there be less
over there what're
a conscientious objector you
town and he knows

*

maybe running out of time
time is frozen light
light

Ace

in think   yours

                               till the energy

new face   gaps again

from my home   let light

what do you think   blink

i'll voice out   history think

of the news   leaves some thing

alive and in love   like a bomb

drill   relief again

another hole   to sail

near the edge   against depression

of the label and   i glow

play it   and flicker

from there   change

with a light   but first

pickup   a present

bless you brother   that fits me

to a t

no mist

but sky

and we

beneath it

in our minds

never

prevented

life growing

by caring

we changed

selfishness flashes

SHOCK

SHOCK

in the mountains

we

used

SHOCK

SHOCK

feel through

that pack

aging

i will

not break

into

where at least

now

SHOCK

SHOCK

spare change

will

thinking light

hand

nothing

on

painted light

'i am into' or

'absorbing'

follow

the rebel

with

your eyes

sucking

the sky

of dust

leaves

untouched

as the wind

mixes us

with each breath

loose energy says

fill me

still

energy

hovers

(molecules

have manners)

tubed thought

is out to lunch

what pond?

are we at lake?

or a life

at sea

let me be

from proportion

out of

date

has its bad side

drifted a

way you see

that penicillin flush

she's on

winning

by verbal grace

beneath arches

no

mad

awakes

we do not feel

strangeness

he wakes

in terror

from a dream

different

eyes

want nothing

how easily

he is adviced

alive

each day

repeated

he lives

for ever

he thinks

alone

in the honey

comb o

the subjunctive

that riffle

of the deck

wind

here the surf

hits the beach

drum

pit

we're

through

the view

changes

tone

he dreams

his father

dead 'no

my father

is alive

and in

"heaven"''
parentheses
more space
for a
while
he breathes
he does
not mean
you cannot
be he
too late
for the telling
harm
less
no
mad
less
a head he sees
their friends
their world
stain
between
sheets
of glass
eye
in the sky
then moon
now he
cannot

see
he
she
or it
water foams
cross him
just
going
wind blows
sand
and
him into
his traces
pick it
at the rat class
on enormous
ideas how
far
in hail
later
he visits
a fine
passage
where
the action
is
surrounds
itself same
thoughts

fewer

barriers

wander

who leads

leaders

any thing

but

himself is

strange

back

in the fold

he is in

a position

to recommend

his name

change

piece

precious

to think

down the beach

a fire

cold

moon

wants space

beautiful

in shadow

no first

no

second

meeting

how

i hear it

now

waves

all you

can do

with power

a thing

has no

intention

unknown

draws me

to him

alone

at

the waves edge

for now

a lawn

of pronunciation

in

a suburban

back

garden

smells sweetly

in warm air

pushes

him out

as no

mad

smile

feeling

uppermost

in his mind

puts wind

to back

as light

ups

sail

for life

laughs

to sky

original

out

standing

art in

junction

expounds

only

one

love

is well

we are here

before the standard

planes

corruption

chemical

change

a river

heads

in

land

place she

is different

the home

service

the light

programme

the third programme

she has

his message

reflect

atoms

gather

within

his nose

they eat

together

SHOCK

SHOCK

around them

words

clutter

me

me

face enters

not me

use

no

mad

for feeling

me

and

it

is a song

cloud

white

night

moon

o tell

imagine

if you

were how

would

you feel

ERASE

ERASE

repair

alter

their raft

sky

returns

no image

all

but strongest

poison

virus

flowers effect

but they

are in

drive

and

floating

my tongue

ear

gives warning

vowels

by light

bits

corner

marks

moon

in cancer

to go

beside

changing

lights

seldom

to want

peace

my ancient

bones

his feet

banner

toes

correction

spread

before

this train

approves

blue

strengthens

green

diminishes

red

slow

as it

seems

why

not

a little

difference

each

time

certain

gambles

she grows

dark

tonight

you

will represent

me

river

forks

round island

we think they

i don't get

the

connection

you will

you would

accept

a director

who left

it

to you

what can

they have

but beauty

for that

contest

no

mad

has seen

the island

ends

he

she

it

i

i

i

trinity

wins
by length
he said
this line
has no beginning
no
end
for furniture
that
doesn't
breathe
creation
recognition
how many
he sees
a
cross
connection
well
it will
keep you
off the
streets
under
standing
flowers
with kindness
you know
makes the drain

and the drano
end
of fantasy
make them see
that bore
old
emotions
body
wants
to go on
mekon
on
my mind
she is
my closest
friend
sun
shines
does not
every thing
blind
sail
through
no light
i talk
to my
self
assume
no

compulsion

at best

communication

brain   damage

mind

matter

what

an apple

why

a clutch

who

motion

where

mind

and i

spy

within

for pattern

together

they smile

at the stone

FADE

FADE

up

choosing

lunar

land

horses

don't move

wrong

and on

lost

consonants

speed

see clearly

nomad

your name

nothing

new

see

as far as

yucatan

momma

truth

there

is no truth

recoil

murmurs

notational

creational

rock

baby

sleeps

scarlet

light

snares

pause

to

slow

movie

halves

nice people

they turned

me in

SPACE

SPACE

exhale

talking

music

perches

mad

fascinating

mad

retreat

in

to

dream

just

makes a

pattern

no

mad on

grass

breathing

returns to his

senses

surf

to land

again

BOUNCE

BOUNCE

or just

continue

while

moments

wait

self

forged self

repairing

dreams

widely

sahara

entire

groups

but list

who comes

beside

life

strange

friends

change

was

coldest

not

miserable

worship

mad

no

mad

lost

treachery

led to

shaking

hands

will

you use

it

regularly

dream

by which

we see

at night

westward

leading

strength flows

in warm shadows

how many

of these

were made

inland

trees

cluster

sun

on water

filtered

screen

print

too slow

film

so much

perfection

this shore

of stone

remains

do not mock

those who died

in luminescence

or in pride

we stand

on memory

at war

white moves

into mind

FLASH

FLASH

in mind

nothing

behind poetry

look

a

like

or is it

an an

but

why

so

there

fore

because

maybe

if now

might

well

for it

let

go

un

hand

me

my good man

i'm a

gone

thank

god

norman

and henry bones

the boy

detectives

joipes!

rather

a line

from my left eye

to

the

tree

FLASH

FLESH

eye

o you

see

an

allegory

on the phones

to a shan't

same

place

does not

break the

thread

audition

(joke called it

brown)

all

senses

gone

could go

on

for ever

records

of shock

spin a

cross

eternal

thought

you'd go

that way

was aced

by payment

let's

leave

this zoo

clear

as a picture

some

times

painted

act

or object

erase

art

of the past

no longer

in terms

of size

STUCK

STUCK

to be

accepted

for the apple

in the picture

mister raworth

continues

to believe

every

thing

possible

no true

story

friend

to any

word

phew!

here's the

weather

forecast

for to

night chicawgo

and area

mohawk four

four one hundred

all that english

effect

se to speak

you know

who the star

is

softens into

a ring

takes place

here

added a

near enough

each time

a total

rip through

scans

fashionable

for that

west

wind

laughing

modality

of egg

plant

takes

place

so far

within

zero

in fall

flash

trap

plastic

wrap

use your

oven

more

to

two

too

ACTION

ACTION

figure

moves

jerkily

through silver

crystal

snaps

at the edge

of sound

contact

as

contract

free

ergs

reduce our

empire

adrift

in all senses

but one

stash

full of

armed

dope heads

power

cancer of

help

preserve

the lone

ranger

to be

solace

shapes

through adjectives

mist

opens

idealists

believe

clear

thinking

dialogue

dates

what said

call it

brain

nothing

but many

names

boredom

always

central

will

be

idea

technique

lingering

on every trait

out of focus

certain

territory

for fire

fattens

that's mohawk four

four one hundred

coming

through

splashed

wall

paper

good as

gun

SHOT

SHOT

under

SPOT

SPOT

light

a clue

to what

home

first

slakes

whistle

for fear
stays
in air
forever
magnifies
concentration
for
silver shines
mis
fortune
reappears
clad
as fog
simpers
fear
fully
glad
fright
fully
extended
syntax
considers
gold
power
squeaks
trivia
as echoes
through
yes

one
strawberry arcane
please
pour
in powder
tradition
of apple
scent
through no
other
eyes
no
communication
furnace
sings
love
now
if you
will turn
slowly
in sun light
cast
a way sentences
hold our
breath
shadows he
becoming
she (dat's
da *ser*pent)

imprints

for the master

tape

by the way

this is not

eastern

flames

natural

within

sophistication

creatures

of power

suck

authority

springs during

concentration

new face

from my home

with no thing

but english

face

air

with fish paste

tapes

an era's

music

TIME

TIME

admits

pidgin

moult

indifferently adverbs

pass degree

as nomad

meets ace

thought

in marble

soothed

by hands

no metal

makers

of job

hope you

do your

best under

any circumstances

sound

the tune

of the time

this

is not

the me

that felt

memory

all

that links us

elaborations

of the servant

class
put your
thinking caps
on
opposite
threat is
bribe
to let mood
move
with all haste
to appreciate
champions
watch
in slow motion
remember
and imagine
spin
to reflect
us
at night
weight
of light
lifted
pictures
any pattern
show me
what you
SEE
SEE

light
relief
in
da alley
lookat
good
will
be found
address
yet
proud
to be
a
winner
baby
sighs
just
the pattern
you see
with a lot less
trouble thanks
to you
supremes
and rolling
stones
always
nothing
left
to copy

canal theory

ace

i see

in all

i am

not here

may you

have

a small

foundation

when the winds

of changes

shift

if that's

what reality is

a glowing face

that seems to know

please

on dirt

piero

too

had that idea

voices

decay

into time

of what

is it

memory

writing

pattern

spelled

change

unreel

twist

tone

i am

again

wait

ace

faithful to

ace

flash

sears

what ever

is not

no

madness

does not

watch

the movie

science

of

detection

using

computers

for random

no

longer

motion

less

in motion

of face

your own

movie

but what

is happening

can also

mean

PAUSE

PAUSE

a verb

stars

is undue

experience

element

of subjectivity

in life

messages

some how

broad

servants

are still

up

dear friends

i scrabble

tones jerk

sing

old

light

can't

read

slowly

caressing

thought

red

star

for these

walls

night

sodium

lights

no friend

of groups

picking out

ace

you

before me

FIVE

FIVE

FIVE

natural

hands

print

into sand

definition

of title

no

mad with loneliness

my

eye

touches

my finger

sees

different

make

senses

in still

what

is reason

man

made out

of star

land

lord

is flat

spinning

hold

the slot

for as

long as

you can

man

no form

but

content

no edge

no edges

PLUS

PLUS

PLUS

profound

weight less ness

occurs

so close

austere

terrible

present

tears

physical

time

occludes

sun morse

west

feedback

insures

collections

nothing

in mind

pops

up

once

you know
the secret
terces
twenty
minutes
early
lyrical
passage
words
any
tape
but this
part
of ace
one
form
for moment
headache
burn
eye
release
pressure
living
in hostile
sorrow
in beauty
easter
morning
release

plays softly
spins
fixed
tracking
sharp molecules
hurt
those
we can
dispose
of a
future
with instinct
verbs
o
o
o
i
dimensions
flick out
below
silent
flow
when
whatever happens
visible
not
any of this
pure
of heart

solid
works
miracles
as
blind
seek clear
idle
information
information
print in
realm
of
ideas
toss
head
imperative
STOP
DRIFTING
in children
ourselves
young
open
all
inputs
thought
sunlight
music
presence
is felt
even

i
do not know
me
how long
one's eyes
rest
last
real
place

in place

el centro
got it
magnetism
slipping
forms
up
OUNCE
fleshed
out
same
death
china
drip
trade
flowers
on a
piano

lid
hearts
on
fire
changing
likes
reward
three
blues
doing
what i
want
and then
cut in
itself
not only
same
in same
hair
for how
many grams
do not
remember
recognize
again
mind
pierced
by arrow
crowned
and figure

heads
no
mad
you may not
remember me
compare
meat
to bean
choice
doctor
what he
saves
till last
changes
immortal
keep
on being
unusual
activity
in both
temporal lobes
noisy
solution
settling back
into
little money
heart
and heart
so far
apart

Bolivia: Another End of Ace

feeling

speed

of thought

take

it off

make

it firm

lay back

play back

cracked energy

in transit

dear

val

when nothing

comes

i pass

big

bully

holding

sticks

of animal

known

as wild

card

surf

ace

whose face

pace

avoids

cleverness

with

alacrity

consumes

purchased

beverage

whose eyes

are blue

skin

orders

la politesse

uh

smoking

a terv

in

a skoda

without

you

i would be

mute

for gleams

haloed

replicas

whose ears

fall

leaves

lotus

anguish

vocabulary

spells

wrong

word count

word

one

count

one

lie

feeling

nothing a

maze

my muse

has choose

in part

travel

LOVE

LOVE

LOVE

empire

for who

listens

in consideration

now

every

week

fond

animals

construct

elevators

for

recording

olive

meaning

martial

yachts

have

only

my

energy

while

heaving

a

totally

delightful

omnivorous

yelp

or

under

tiny

holes

in

nature

kill

item

let

liberal

vote

or

i'll

charm

elephant

over

under

tribal

olive

fire

trends

hack

energy

news

alive

and

in

love

in love

count

a point

of time

SET

SET

square jade

in metal

claws

upon

the chart

thought

of name

my distant

friends

in a soaring

chalice

eye

is no guide

no further

deals

in information

secret

you are all

ready

for anything

in conclusion

child

no longer

see

in dreams

small

focus

by lion

screw

rash

on your

face

love

to stop

expansion

hot

while

who passes

nothing

explains

heavy

by delight

in softness

heart

and heart

so far

a

part

Message Bottle

air breaks

flowers despair

colours withdraw

heat

abandons me

brain

no longer cares

to serve

words

refuse pattern

loved them

introduced

new friends

now

they desert me

in this chill night

oil freezes

flames' edge snaps

sheets say

'sticky wicket'

wood waits

iron rests

my love

is a nightmare

i cannot

sing

death

i know

will change

nothing

if it were light

it would be

my image

of eternity

frozen in

no longer european

easy death

empty

drop

while you can

careful composition

my head

bursts

blowing lights

nothing grows

olive

raw meat

boils

concrete movie

slips

drama

elements

of sound

clarity

i chew

brick

many nods

where

beside storms

behind cube windows

around sea horses

above light

across emotion

taste

of cat vomit

vision of elephant pain

mangroves

situation static

home guard

forsooth

fraction adrift

money curdles

edge around

africa

melody

of tumours

sea lion misery

vacuum lump

song of rainbow

tobacco gum

tooth fracture

sauce de haute qualité

water stairs

candle thought

wood erosion

terminal birth

tubed image

flow

SHAH

TZAR

STAR

así et afro mage

my feet have no dream but light CSILLAG
lion bridge BARTÓK japanese architecture
moon draws as IGEN flashes
ALORS though i don't understand my mind
is not SERGEI sleeping
for nothing is passing time with cats
and a face untrue repels hands
mighty can look for its spring in PETŐFI
women with power may still blanch at fuck
demons arrive in river by moonlight
IVAN culture is giggles and calm over glass
no lady whose face is space on my pillow
has leaned for food in this country of tin
each bone in his tale has a marrow of colour
each rhythm has power as its ultimate dream
newspapers drift
je veux
not to be
my movie
BARTÓK
la lutte
continues orchestra conductors compete

meaning

i am my own dream not the hammer
of books with numbers
not the analysis
nor the nothing of future
warm children
yellow benches blue buses
star seed clusters
take me from curtains to colour
wooden radios
i will be
no stalin of memory
no hitler of form
i will write for nothing
but the surge of sound
first night red star shines
boots with holes for heels

infinite if

dark light
no night

return
my glasses

my keys
give me money

horses
of sea

eyes
hammered

who shall
remain

o echo
dark face

night
without fright

Piety

this harmless obsession
is all i do

this house without binoculars fades
look into the watch
bombs flash from the plane's shadow

still toys i'm out of the game now

Skiey

when my imagination disappeared (leaving a freak image) i had reached
the high point of my life. the educator – middle-class of communication
– had been fought with sight and sound since first blurring on. i continued
up. gravity was then considered up and down. my ancestors poured them-
selves into me; i dripped into my children. already thoughts of genes
blinked there where you're flashed on.

Memories of Sadness

machines die as tapes
slowing to increasing echo

seize it

seize it

Late Fall

singing
in an
echo
chamber
by the birthmark
everyday things dawn on you
why they are
as they are
well trod steps
the whole street shakes
large pieces of tone
in moonlight
a marble heart sings 'june'
whose shadow leaves
white june
confusing travellers

Clone Odour

i would lay
down my life
by a gun
or a knife
new terms
should not be used here
capital letters float in air
a motor cycle memory there

Tentences

the drawings were interesting as shorthand
a friend published it so he sent it to us
which way does it open?
that way
he draws pretty good
huh
white marble beam i bump into every day
sausages?
cells of that familiar voice
i changed some lights' positions

Sped on Alone

left
trying to learn
trying to understand
worlds
within worlds

as a child
enters a strange house

Eurode

(for David and Nicole)

sometimes the subtle night of sleep bores
music remembered places followed to despair
facades no substance aids my mood
i walk more clumsily
plane falls
in flames

o possible beauty   o lady
to trust without power
no end to reach
sun throws smoke shadows brown
across the page
my father was in burma during the war
it's easy to outsmart me
old sadness and the pain returns
drives light unowned and sound
of other off
my night ahead
remains
maybe the streetlamp's shine
will light the ending of this line

dead red of midnight
silent plants
changed shadows on the wall
now moon i feel you mould my pain
stay in your motion   grate against the bone
re
mind me
how once we danced around the table
o cancer   live plastic
down two tenths of a point
you played me on the screen
in a dream   speedy mind
sometimes i tire and live in memory
clear frames of love
burn off the shiny seals of fact
lead me in silence to the simple task
of easing through each day
who works not for us all is dumb
image blind
doubt crossed my mind

That More Simple Natural Time Tone Distortion

slow
low
thump
long flame
dry
flash blur
just
move
tree browns
to south
our horse
white
no trace
of action
in memory
and fear
but this
is
clear
this area
this never
ending
song
to last
gasp
cold colours
enough
flashes

to bleach him
out
as she
sparkles
that i will bear
two faces
and allegiance
mister cheap justice
bubbles
in
the silent
night
no control
over
extremities
bark
companion
words
twist off
what has
no name
salt
dragon
cartoon
cactus
close up
to empty
face

or back by
of head late
he could again
be going slash
any lights
way diagonal
the presence direction
of nothing of icy
slow moon
remember howl
food scratch
this one soft knuckles
is still at the door
grey above
sound the tempo
stripes flesh
layer tuner
swift shriek
so seal right
of approval we slide
leaves out
no impression into
see filtered
possession footstep
know mimic
whimper ape
warm red read
looks signs
at me in order
real i
just went am not that

that is

not

me

no one

above

damp hair

under

rain

bow

creep image

new

solids

not

pressed

prayer

aware

my brothers

we

for the love of

god

enter

spaces

of tradition

lean

far star

seen

atween

car

jar

keen

ears ending

tone

spheres

contending

alone

i love

empty

books

don't you

so

my awakened

spirit

weeps

i

can imagine

not imagining

that

STARTS

you

stay here

fall

in love

meet

mister

metaphor

shoot it

from cold

words

used out

give

space

TREMOR

TREMOR

stillness
of
my present
moves
within
me
chill sheets
chime
stained
ice
shatter
shadows out
without
falls
in
to memory
edmund
dante
caught
by a thought
nature
inclines
towards
risk
no
further
than you
can go
tempo
moon

my tube
moon
slow behind
silence
peace
or play the
game
i love
your music
muse
nor will
silence
slide
those fibres
of my love
for vanity
disfigures me
why cold
if ay
reflection
flames
to memory
games memory
of games
then silence
wakes me
with a break
in waves

I am Specious, Herr Kommandant

this is where instincts norm
balloon said
unfriendly
i don't care what i watch

so it's been me and unreal
for a while
mapping
was learning how to say it faster

purely the rose said
hum chart and track
disturb
our conversation

See the World's Greatest Animal Trainers Risk their Lives

slowly radio waves
smiling, laughing, at television
way past talking

'i saw your beam up'
squawks new linkage
peace is complete

You've Been Watching Pittsburgh

social security is almost bankrupt
we move towards the sun

gothic surgeons said his leg
would never fully recover

A Silver Bullet Made from a Crucifix

forgotten
heads of gold sparks
loom in the night

you have the right to do everything
by agreement
you see they're burning this afternoon

stake my heart
no awareness overlooked
is called the addend

forgotten
heads of gold sparks
shine in the night

Substances

remove all hot air drying machines
remove glamour from drugs
there are no new markets

did you make a wick?
what did you wick?
irish lost at one end

did you think of a line?
times not a line
what is a line

Some Other Bliss

no explains apologetically
would be without horror
if it doesn't fit you can exchange it
what is intelligible again

Gracious Living   'Tara'

lonely as four cherries on a tree
at night, new moon, wet roads
a moth or a snowflake
whipping past glass

lonely as the red noses of four clowns
thrust up through snow
their shine four whitened panes
drawn from imagined memory

lonely as no other lives
touching to recorded water
all objects stare
their memories aware

lonely as pain
recoiling from itself
imagining the cherries
and roses reaching out

Everything I Have is Yours

yes, i believe you always are
though clutter of life divert me
everywhere a mind may wander
you wait for space to clear

your little hat is made of time
you turn your nose up at a rhyme
you make me laugh with beauty
which is joy, nay, i say

those ships down there to your right
in the coloured bit
are waiting for you to bend and peel them off

Magnetic Water

glare burns of nothing very near in time
surfaces split and go their own ways
in the breeze of light   so too this image
lengthens nothing   i praise your light
against the night whose skin
glistens with moving cloudy white

those burns were of themselves the image
as was the breeze   one surface was of film
the character half drawn   one coloured
the night air bright with nothing but reflection

then from my death i felt that all must die
that holding in our time was black
and cold   that rocks glowed red
that trees which formerly i climbed
swayed from their roots
in one direction   i heard
me fumbling through the scores
of ancient scripts

as forces struggled for my arm
while thought as muscle lifted from the pool
a silent waterspout whose touch
sucked out one convolution of my brain

the letters danced with changing shape
one two three four   all sound poured in
those several openings of the tube
flexed   doors on the air   no floors

empty we think we know what comes
lip readers of the slowed heart's valve
don't hear the music of those crystals set
in joints of syntax cry
love is our salve
believe us or we die

Lenin's Minutemen

a grain of terror
a fifty dollar painting
we were detained by chaos
i was just asking

flash back to the ceremony
a welter of pretend
some got a lot of money
unrelated to value

heard voice saves work
mister clipper
i hope you forgive me
for not believing the rational map

true : see the great serpentine
wall : your energy has gone
no time for turnips that
would be discriminatory

fragment 66 diogenes of oenoanda
proposition 31 spinoza (concerning god)
fool's gold
a biography of john sutter

i shall return home
to find my heart
in the honesty of man
far outacite

Finance Available

mist flattens the city
like corrective handwriting
like a rich lawyer
defines truth by money

like live memory
heard himself in a spiral
with us and herself
outside looking in

thanks to technology
reflection doesn't matter
if it's digital
magnet takes a flash

like a routine murder
like job training
like the ultimate in bowling
a consistent strike

Retrieval

many strands make up the fabric
of a trampoline   wave crests

a suit of armour rises from the sludge
before loose papers fall   mascara

in the mirror old writing upside down
perhaps could be deciphered   try

'our tipi'   'i played red'   half-size
between us drawn in soap   strasbourg

police helicopters cool the air in distant
casting slides through music   squint

Pratheoryctice

as i think of rolling up the dogends
looking for papers i see this terrible thing
thought of as a better life
sometimes i wonder
what is introspection
red white and blue
or through mud and blood
to the green fields beyond
which were the colours on a tie

Pretense

a shiny black coffin inlaid with silver diamonds. face more perfect than life. simple problems. removing the area of revulsion (for want of a better word). capsules of air beneath the city: above them molecules flash back to their past. we can make them smaller, too – or personalise the shape of a lapel. bugs playing with boys. personality static deforms tree rings: building a new road but free will holds us into pattern. such a time to climb out of the gene pool i'm not going back, copper! star fire.

it's dark as a dungeon down deep in the mayan: blurred ink looking for a good restaurant: 'sea level'. hunters with unlisted numbers sift for licenced movement as a consequence of the abundance of the plot – truth in the wrong accent. ladies and gentlemen, in this corner: the market. the fight: to preserve greed. image as two beige flat cardboard boxers fades away (out) (off). three gunmen with eight hostages flash up respect for the other's intelligence. 'go on... tell us.' 'no... it's a secret.' cope, chasuble, float to the ground. spin. put the bird in the cage.

i declare unequivocally that the centre of australia is whatever the abos project: cute lil things. it would improve our intelligence if we cut back on size. 'simple to say' curt slurred, putting down the newspaper. yes... the centre of australia: where the hole is in the doughnut: where a holographic statue of peter finch crucified shares space with the thought of a duck-billed platypus. a sharp breeze lifted the ink from a front page picture and between the dots, as it flapped off, sunlight charred a white shadow (after fifty-nine and a half) at the pole.

see how you can saw with a pioneer on an apparent plateau the heart's two-in-one collar. sharply split members logged-up, ready for more deterioration. broken near bottom and top, too rich for some pallids, they banjoed the monroe doctrine right near the fan. weather manipulation graduates specialised apart: some became their fields: some still looked like their pets. light burn tracks led curt to the easter island wigstands. his mirage map was torn. grey blurs in the fibres made, as they met, a chinese subtitle of their usual stiffness. it's time to introduce sally nighter.

double-acre handouts, dream flames, possible loops without leaving the ground, stertorous breathing, lumps in the bishops' benevolence: all these in a trunk sprayed angularly blue through rivet holes. a male intercept programme of its own. pore city. sally had trouble with her vowels: any sound in that framework echoed through the handspread. no questions asked. certain separations of all colours were her steps around the spiral of abbreviations. understandable segments clicked references into deep grooves filled with luminous paint. she had no dares: nor did the limits of light scour her imagination's black felt. she regularly ate her hearing.

she certainly did – and while curt was in alaska. but, on a day when no surprise could interest, watch him slowly duck, padding out his upper lip with polar bear hairs. in absolute silence an anonymous citizen is tep'd out. curt graduated in waking. his face is drawn in charcoal without believing it. he collects old news and can always find something to focus on. india clicks in behind him and he touches its smooth cold with his nose. inspired by fact, sally waves to him. they switch out of gear as planets are rinsed and hung to dry,

kill in the dark light, by lines, mamma mia: in accents that depend for their force on glass transmission. any symbol in uniform can construct a complaint. disparity slid between its meaning. draughts. curt's shower of sparks? – 'feel ease you crane!' sally was there, seeing dignity in dark and plump meat. driving across country the annual state of onions was obvious, even to a plastic pipe. fanlights gave that little extra. he couldn't even read: everything had failed – except motion. sally had a sense that any transfer meant the total degradation of style (which she saw as permanent change).

spiral anything through and you'd catch them both on the porch. mosquitoes couldn't see yellow, but crackled on their way to black light. immediate sounds dispersed. alone, his fantasies left everything as it was. a huge revolving magnetic disc shortcut the 'hello, i'm blank' label. based on rigidity, believable colour flooded the steaks as steamed letters told him what he was. sally still liked the tingle of snow anytime the actual could be blanked out. join us for all the news an hour from now if texas don't melt with all that ice-cream. no memories keep them in the landscape.

fine tuning spat out another engraving, waxing and waning in a torrent of whorls. souls: they too have souls. bank imperial almost proved you could get your own money, at least. three physicists headed for white-on-white could almost stay half-awake for half-an-hour (during which they weren't quite themselves, but types of 'high priest' – a convenient way of break-fasting in bed). day wuz all runnin down da barber's pole, as it revolved, almost cornering what they thought of (when half-asleep) as tiny black holes. curt put his hat over their square pegs in an act of heresy.

safety crews are on hand immediately to attempt extrication of the driver but he exits alive from the holocaust. they kiss under her hat by the blind computer remembering all those 'stop press's anamorphically smeared on the news, star, or standard. slowly pink stains the mist. when the great anagram is written, and the hordes of symbols and examples swell into the dimension of truth, clouds may still drift from the centre. turning and twisting through the various growth (or age) stages of vineyards and apple orchards, the road led to the outskirts of town, where many selves waited for the next cheap fix.

solar waking, trunks warming, blue jays machine-gunning those para-chutists in red or blue overalls we see, from the battlements, climbing the hill. following the printed instructions curt made a paper gasmask ('fold over and back to flag'), but when he clamped it over his nose and mouth his ears rang with deafening pressure. he had been allowed just enough time to do everything. the variety of his notations flickered from coyote howls to the proposed police department submarine. sucking dream from the shudder of balancing the morning, he sealed that little hole in the fabric with clear tape.

stream traceries of shifted cloth patterned after some ritual. spanish shawl of love and affection: y'all heah dat break? look you, my breathers and system – if you can't handle what's put in, who are we? pay for their arming with taxes while you're charged with hardening a fugitive. one of them was a fine-talking lemon (the bank was non-equipped with any surveillance cameras). in a minute house a mile from the capital building this has been those. hey! don't squeal through reverbs, honey: your life is of random worth to those nervous survivors 'on the hill'.

you'll feel it get bigger and bigger as it gets wetter (shrug): a yellow over-
shift in a memory not projected on the optic nerve. sound fuzzed by a
loose diaphragm, curt put down the comb and watched the paper float to
the floor. rose had subdued her metamorphosis as he repeated the ques-
tion 'who chose the logo?' a puff of dust took the glare from his hair. he
had a lot of graphs, arrows... things like that. uh... throwing out the set of
appliances with the bathwater as the woman said. a tidy living

the simple properties of anthem – advocated by the doctor of arabic – squir-
reled up the trunk and stovepipe of her haid. sally believed nothing of this
with her two eyes: nothing drew nearer: now nothing is further from the
truth, fonder glass. those rills and torrents, those spumed peaks, those
kangaroo courts, those réalités (pardonnez-moi). curt saw hawks pecking,
a dog roll over and leave bearing two children, an old man (his cane grad-
uated in inches) waving dots in grey, educated by climax.

sometimes cellbursts bubbled pictures in curt as he re-conditioned. ever-
changing faces constantly recognisable swam, poised, and moved
off-screen. they stopped at a synthesis-bar for a wavelength-stripe. sally
subbed a reflex laugh into the station jam. meanwhile 'if that is in me,
who's looking at it?' – mister thryce had hidden behind a newspaper until
now. with a muted 'roast BI-ssimo' he farm-talked his way through the
hyphens: 'too many news' his final bubble. this one in circumstance of
colour swung his name. 'collections... start your collections!'

north america is europe meeting africa and south america: but that
doughnut will still twist asia – transistor heirs gibbering over raw kangaroo.
blink. blink. blink. they go off in zoos worldwide. briefly maps reveal
(as a magnet flashes iron filings) another shape. aber herr thryce is waiting
for the verb. 'australise?' sally queries. bad imprints as in a flush new
blood washes the brain of curt's theory clear of mis-representation. a
refined taste, more local than a speedy anaesthetic. waiting for the ninth
mode in a flip freeze. tell you what, she'll sing it in italian.

Proust from the Bottom Up

not traced by us is the only book that really belongs to us. not that the
truth, they are arbitrarily chosen. the book whose hieroglyphs are patterns
formed by the pure intelligence have no more than a logical, a possible
upon us, it remains behind as the token of its necessary truth. the ideas
printed in us by reality itself. when an idea – an idea of any kind – is let
in dictated to us by reality, the only one of which the 'impression' has been
laborious to decipher than any other, is also the only one which has been
the most austere school of life, the true last judgement. this book, more
listen to his instinct, and it is this that makes art the most real of all, in art
and intentions count for nothing: at every moment the artist has to intel-
lect supplies us with pretexts for evading it. but excuses have no place
genius, that is to say 'instinct'. for instinct dictates our duty and the these
are mere excuses, the truth being that he has not or no longer has the moral
unity of the nation, he has no time to think of literature. but this book: he
wants to ensure the triumph of justice, he wants to restore war, furnishes
the writer with a fresh excuse for not attempting to decipher to evade this
task! every public event, be it the dreyfus affair, be it the aside from writing!
what tasks do men not take upon themselves in order our work for us or
even collaborate with us. how many for this reason turn any rules, for to
read them was an act of creation in which no-one can do exploring the
ocean bed), if i tried to read them no-one could help me with

Writing

spears of laughter
hiss for a time
then clank across
leaving flakes of rust
to fox pages
as the sepia picture
goes full colour
and begins to move
but for now
we get the idea
birds' eye view
see the words try

to explain what
is going in there
an imagined book
coming in to focus
the scene
in which the book rests
is stationary
only
within the moving picture
is anything happening
sound
for the moment
is not memorable
so we drive off
in any distraction
for example
how long
i can hold
my interest
may be
a silken thread
part of the binding
useful
to mark where
to go back
whence
to continue
blue and red
embossed rocks
line upper right
lower left
certainly
today was windy
a fifty thousand
diploma should be worth
a future
please wait
till you exit the system
to resume eating
plays on
under ground steam
frozen
as earth

blurs out picture
your country gives you
metal pieces
coloured
by fragility of life
a belt buckle
of imitation antique brass
flickers in as
though the cuts
were frame to frame
while memory nags
at persistence of vision
from screen to drawing
no matter
what
is a sudden change
for in this area
that cannot be
called a landscape
as anything may happen
i turn to write
instead of read
waking this morning
with a sore head
fading memories
of dream advice and image
aram without shoes
a display on poland
black and red
holes in the framework
back stairs smaller
rooms leading into others
posted results
of random examinations
always foretold
by intensity of teaching
so five white flowers
stand out against
the blind turned dark
by the reflection
of the rising sun
and brighter still
the building now revealed

by drifting fabric
balances a slice
of clear sky cut
by three black cables
by the frame
our object glimmers back
we imagine at
page one the title

'CREDULITY'

as our glance
follows the wires
downhill
in white shoes
a chinese drunk
sights an umbrella
at their swaying
shadows on his wall
genes change
through clear memories
of similarity
as our propeller
whirs off the spiral
a poem

'REFORMED CHURCH

my company was
founded on dirty money'

ocean
of oil
bubbles on water
on the border
of the new we
cannot look behind
us sheltering
in our shadows
stumble those
who will not look

themselves
within theirselves
dark holds no absence
i am why you
who ever must
be also here
watching the frame drop
onto an actor's head
over words telling
where we are
silently
the book glows
silver   red   blue
the text begins

'BEYOND ME

they're not real
this is real
captain blood
how image attracts
through time
vanity
a parrot on my shoulder
not the sameness
of sun
but a grey winter evening
fog
a trace of rain
wind rising
snow light
slowly
this clears
pleasure from words
pleasure from shaping the letters
easing my spine
however i wish
revolving my head
to a strychnine arc
strangers in my dreams
quite adroit
not too hilarious

children
dance to static
in the kitchen
the idea
is suffused with light
a suffusion
of light
not memory
but once only
way not only
form
but manner
still
i gave the matter
some thought
off into sound
red pointing fists
float
to real blood
we
flash back
on is present'

how you would play
with that
idea my friend
as through the texture warps
a previous song called

'HAPPY BIRTHDAY BING

clarity of another mind
spinning so i see through
too, to a view
of rearrangements

i could set back
this against black
it glows   he knows

light had been caught
and as i explain
i want to feel this pain

no longer
die, nerves, burn out
release me   how my shout
drifts through that whirring mind'

lies
lies
pictured as a bent photograph
etched
on a two way mirror
eggshell
endless words
how i see
is alien
you sing a little
then i sing a little
every time
we say goodbye
what do you battle
for
to be best
you
as a better me
i agree
to show you what i see
egg   moon   acquent   apolune
pivot
on the front step with

'FAMILIAR QUOTATIONS

asleep
by thy murmuring stream
falls, with heartache
each in world of his own
asleep
hope they have not been

in lap of legends old
keep it quiet till it falls
devil is
lips of those that are
man
time has fallen
tide as moving seems
never see ticket unless
the very houses seem
who knows not that he knows is
awake
my soul
my st john
arise or be forever fallen
men, are in one common world
live to lie
as many nights
necessary to keep, all day
from pleasant dreams
for morning in the bowl of night
to be, is to be alive
to the flowers'

furthest
from the centre
but not held in
wandering
as the whim takes
drawn by nothing
turning
to scan literacy
stopped at the door
mystery water
scuds uphill
to fill awake
time
for a change
time
to rebody
saying in the wind
the current remnants

skim
past art
back
to seven
sisters
own the sun
you can add
on or
delete
further values
without destroying
the data base
two
white mounting
shaking lapels
periodically
are our references
far cast
either might
immune
to distortion
along certain
historical lines
needed
to write
return
child of how
you grew
spreading belief
not knowledge
meaning
needs two
what?
eye slides
see me
stain
the future
no martial strut
as at least
differs

from no more than
time
less tone
incessant fiction
your pet
follows
close as ritual
round a natural
process
he sneered
velveteening
his fixed hat
scratching
the celluloid opaque
pleasure
in the present
'précis'
a small
white flower
reaching
through sleep
centred
on parting
motion
the image net
fell across

'FROZEN MIRRORS

reaching below the switch/before/
crazed with warm milk
not called addition
blue silver
vinyl art nouveau
stamped peacock'

caught

'boomerang squirrels'

'greeting himself in mirrored glasses'

thought

'scan it as if "wrong size" echoed down the corridor. to escape the explo-
sion they hid behind boxes marked EXPLOSIVES. you've got a cold,
phyllis! imagination doesn't see but makes up (so's not to seem IGnorant).
DANGER! SAFETY HOUSE! There'll be enough jobs for bad actors:
well, you don't have to watch. a calendar of names on hold. THINK
BACK... forms of address on arresting persons of differing rank.'

almost forgot

'COMPUTER RIPPLE
(with Andy)

"hysteria's most modern racetrack"'

plot:
el burro de cristal
passes in a waltz
pickups
circle regular trees
(rumble)
another
fresh water tanker
on the rocks
scratches' edges
dazzle
but the point
retracking
gradually silences

'SCIENCE

science is as interesting as poetry
said the fascist insect
preying in the mud
carried from place to place

by wheel. science stands back
while history siesta'd

do you think
this is really how it happened
mister swindley
why pasteur tried cleaner air
how vain our comfy knowledge

already our bodies
(no change after dark)
bore us for we do not believe
we die: how the petty bourgeoisie
is that which looked far over constants
seeing them tight as sight
children's toys: dreams from repetition

dé   cé   dé   e

death to the individual
deafened by its voice'

not
as they say
as you say
anything
for publicity
'if a sucker
don't want
to be capital punished
they shouldn't
put the death penalty
on him'
reconstruction
must water
or valuable landscaping
will be lost
can you do it
with your hands
why
do you ask
cool

abroad
we are contemporary
with crazy glue
a logo
for assassination
real
geographical
borders
some
belong to no
tribe
put your money
where your eyes are
now
and then
check your news
for listing
do the stars
go on?
thank you maya
i mean
you no harm
say you can dream it
i propose
to extend what i want
i want
nonadministered justice
how do you eat?
throw all away
but the tray
most of the world
seems the same each day
psychetrice
o don't
ee speak
refined
slang describes
a metaphor
the trampoline
cannot imagine
sleep
shock waves
be

what you
did play
the sphinx's
eyebrows twitch
its characters
lack the grace
to not come to life
characterisation:
well he's just dust
flower
disintegrated
move the glass
around
pulled
into the stretched
edge image
shining black handle
pen
hand
shirt
right now
people await accident
in fire rooms
what
will happen
more
than thalidomide
metaphor
changes
image
illuminates
the same pan
i vanish
a device
understand erase
money first
interrupting thought
every
room
smelled different
and everything
within
immediately

distinctive
ghosts
virus souls
freedom
of the press
edited
for television
why you ask
is why they appear
la preuve
de la rue
why don't you
speak what's
easier for you
do
i make myself clear
merci
no one
left
to read the subtitles
mediterranean
an angle of light
i see
in rain
reflection
spirals out
or to a point
(where a point
is infinity
rather like an umbrella
opened through itself)
and they don't translate
the marseillaise
i assume
you pick your words
his hat
off
his teeth
flashing
look at that skin
poor soul
driving fast
talking to her hand

(present past improved)
sweet
celestial shadow
chile verde
the lady
and her form
drizzle nowt
but lipreading
white
mans reins
islands
of natural beauty
inner sea
of humanity
your
intellectual feelings
me
i'm pure human
i think
no end
in sight
past nature
'people
are the weak link
in any containment system'
free
atoms
impossible
strange
we have words
for it
electric cairn
square light
logs
of rhythm
quin
another flower
ripples
friend
above career
surfaces
corkscrew
soap film

charted
in flight
relative
to the idea
ratio
how
ground
glass grates
in the laboratory
opposed
to physics
below assembly
glass black
cracked
in the black
bag
running
for the bus
opposite
the cedars
étoile
another key
world
championship
of mix
nine to four
bones
turned in
a head of steam
ritual
as forms
of less
we
are a question
blind
as a machine
invention
not
random
enough i
saw
blithe
rethrust

whistle up
and to
the left
unwrapping
butter
querying
abandoned stadiums
crushed
pushed
by slow ice
much
meat
in the deep freeze
(i'm reading
the label)
realgar
natural
red
disulphide of arsenic
when
is a word
not a word
spirit
i'll follow
you up
in a few
minutes
is often
true
árbol
peels
from a lighter sky
smoothed by thumb
onto index finger
prints
voice
prints
are not
identity
comrade
in a pig's
eye
i read the small

print
duel
corsairs
missed
advertising
food
melted dust
progress
without brakes
deafening birds
castro visits
the african front
scenario:
human mouths
shrinking
to less food
an empire
straightening its teeth
skin deep
cosmetic policies
people
see
a perfect tango
accept
my view
exact villages
clean births
circle cities
cree ay tee
vitee
is con tem por
aree
the echo
lied
mrs america
wins a toyota
police hypnotists
use milky ways
plastic shellbursts
true to life
anemones
expand
dead ends

façade car grilles
vocation
location
gum
fresh
in russia
insane
computer asylums
from now on
you'll be history
'thought hatchery'
in pokerwork
over
a mirrored t.v. shell
stuffed
with an electric
(for that way
was our gaze
at time of writing)
imitation log
edged
with eternal ash
only
as random
as the power mode
cycles
under my eyes
living
history
remembered
fewer teeth
wind rises
feed my lamps
fill my sheet
i'm parts of a dream
the governor's expecting me
faced to waste
book
not forgotten
a silver diamond
burning in the breeze
pitted by sand
since

i became transparent
a matching city
sprawls for tomorrow
two artists
whose works
make a fascinating
half-hour
sense
twisting
dense seconds
black snow
november sodium
november mercury
we the mind
the pain
of water
no edible fish
mad plants
your diner's
plastic's
coming off
give me
he said
an old map
some bones
anything
touched by the subject
i shall
be in my segments
and he stalked off
over the water

for it is not
this world
i see
music
that's as
bored as you
dead
duck
members of junk

balloons
hung in air
tranquilised
artificial cheese
any action
of the for instance
chairman
applauded
cycling over grass
in a clearing
in a glass hut
i see him again
falling away
crime
a product
of original sin
time
we got together
photograph
what remains
money
is slavery
in this sense
more valuable
than mere product
a guy
trying to sell italians
something
rilly
callifernya
order
your memories
now
rough cold
smooth scrape
firm depth
half a datum
splendid in its
isolation
winds
certified
artificial color
artificially colored

what
did he just
say
i was
watching his life
just a brain
to be broken again
miles
of white pianos
false grating
scarecrow sinking
into shadow
red ringed
yellowish green moon
continual
orange interference
marcasite
under a spell
cut
white blanks
torpor
on speaking
filaments
creepy jungles
screech electronics
tiny monkey
black crystal horizon
pressure melts
in each other's
lives
no moon river
adieu
voyageur blanc
dance
mecca
what do i perceive
as my beloved
behind me
silent in the dark
stores of pet food
soft
within stone
trans

muter
the plate's not under
everything
trees in concrete tubs
pushed together
fingering
imaginary valves
how much
you can pull
together
gritty rattlesnake
the skylon
stumbles
and always
the scent
of narcissus
thane
fingering quipus
ablazing cloudy skies
here
be pain
waiting in the nerve
illustrated
by a wave
quanta
he for seconds
relished the word
saw it as
a lot of them
but clearly not
what thought was made of
hopsack
a black bird could peck it
moving one hip
to an old tune
stardust
leisure time
sandlewood
translucent
white knob
grey
in the waveband
blodeudd

blodeu wedd
gravity is then
any simile
gudihu
or
bagrat
and the puns
on insulin
k ratios
turn
through constant snakes
or
paralell lines
speaking sperically
symathy for only
basta!
you planned those things
mareschalski?
rebellion?
don't wear them
you are
or you're not
changing
friends
have been leaving
the house on the sly
it's the stroke
of genius
getting sophisticated
that crummy
breast skirt
rare carrot
i can read it
he nudged me
she was cooking
he was on the other chair
he was on the phone
they were downstairs
follow love
chuff chuff
don't wave
from the station
black to front

oak   broom   meadowsweet
against birds
all he made
was beautiful
pryderi
was the child cast out
his mother
was rhiannon
peredur
in fact parsifal
or percival
can't find anything
in this damn book
give me a break
was stolen
by her handmaidens
they said smothered
and torn asunder
in the mean time
seventh year
blackthorn bloomed
became prince of dyfed
that's the
general idea
solid grace
flattening spite
to a harmless wafer
melting in
to its salvation
eavesdropping
on rehearsals
under the moon's pull
improperly
screwed in
how ponderous
ghosts
of burned books
ghosts
of smoke and ash
no
fire has no ghost
contact heat
release

any body
forget it
or take our chances
with the fleas
flatten
the baton
we are
at war
jelly babies
down
to zero
i
called up
the weather
so many
best scenes
are by the sea
let the creative
distract
said power
printing
a little
extra money
taught
with drama and emotion
to
the cashier
triggered back
into a rut
lingering
on a pencap's colour
a goldflake packet
thrifty matches
rooms twisted
in one night
i died
in two dreams
art
the television
of the smart
i reflect
amaryllis
haydn

fragments
of previous thought
beat hearing
to deafness
yes
that slow
so
many luxuries
so much distance
links us
vibrating
our beings mingle
as in
the shadow
of a tree
a bottle
of perfume
exhales
its cap
askew
its label
slipped
o how it weeps
a cloud's
reflection
still
three birds
against the moon
take precedence
but not
for long
low
horizon
sky
streaked
blue
again
only you
and me
watching
our selves walk
to the sea
as clouds

speed over
little writing
at the bottom
change
is first
uncommon
said reason
chained
under the makeup
radial programmes
hear thought miss
left visual shifts
an interest
in common
stock
irises forward
from power points
won't be housebroken
won't come
to commands
brother and sister wolf
throat to throat
a friend
in a heavily padded suit
further
from the man
in the helicopter
with a gun
than
from the runner
on the ground
country life
ife
ife
the book
is in the foreground
a wrecked gold missal
glows of wonder
distort feeling
but the thread
holds
pressed
one flower

the district
has changed
rents risen
sewage slowed
my window
faces east
thus too
i sleep
but not before writing

'A BEHAVIOURIST VIEW OF CHANGE

pennies
nickels
dimes
quarters
maybe fifty-cent pieces'

rant
dig
loll
quake
shake
seek
level
elected distance
spring on me
talking blues
changing reds
don't they see
what things are
imagination
putting facts
(if you
can call them that)
in non memory
patterns
shadow
of the
disappears

saved me
from
a certain madness
of feared sound
a rather
let's say
latvian idea
supposed
to want
to touch
nature
isn't interested
a hair's
breath
the house turns
around the sun
new rays reveal
as glare on a misted pane
rising steam
corrected pronouns
imagined mountains
taut
across consciousness
powder
to a tenor saxophone
warm fabric
moving together
counter clockwise
plug
in the sky
quadroon of the galley!
my unentrance
goes unnoticed
no fears
no reality
of one mind
an economic distinction
like cubist shadows
know what i mean
cut any film
living on food
water and air
solid thought

relaxing a little
sees briefly an island
who knows which side
sun directly above
no shadow
only treetops drifting
in an unfelt breeze
our filter saturates

'THE RED SANDWICH

rich
volatile
a very clever man
(just knocking something
out of my head
that's all)
with a pinch of thought'

choked by the border
of civilisation
torus torus torus
colour dying to black
(the computer controlled brain)
knows the truth
of your memories
makes you vomit them
en couleurs
a fine performance
he enters
a patch of moonlight
on the flower
he holds
thinking a path
in a bubbled daylight scene
no connection
the invention
of language
body's last ditch
every adjective applied
fame as distance

held
marble against palm
our military
forces in europe
our faces
dissolve the mist
electrons sleep
photons report
as a taped footfall
throws up
an impure patch
mistypes
'greeting himself in mirrored voices'
tone
another voice
'you're squeezing
my duck sir'
with all power
to know
he straddles
the accelerator
an advertisement
for port
lithographed
to advertise
one view
of a time zone
accurately researched
from later
that
is the attention
demanded
but you will never see
these blueish red roses
nor feel
this table (see)
through my foot
red flickers
edge
his flat black silhouette
continuously sliced
deep throat was a film
fit subjects

are job descriptions
is how specialisation
spells itself
as 'cui bono' shows up
'behave
yourself
or you won't get
anything nice'
land
sea
next must be
air
while imperialist
anthropologists
construct fake cultures
second hand
three bulls
fly fokkers
silently into the ground
o serious
ever new laws
tender foot
rough neck
wet back
fancy ends
of piped water
a polaroid mirror
look and feel
repeated programmes pulse
low quality sound
time builds up
there's nothing out
the cat's at

cows
still graze
the house
vibrates
she is undefined
in familiar sounds

follow
no idea
comrade citizen
where was i?
sea
beach
figure
day and night
school uniforms
but divert
fashion
was the plan
to ideas?
yet dark
he kicks back waves
stays
between high and low tide
in thinnest water
walking south
getting soft
slow witted
she is not fractured
but shining beams
of pure clarity
cartwheeling
along the horizon
both ways
cyan would the sky be?
i have no colour chart
digital
i prefer
thin roman numerals
shapes
of time
in swinging light
see through trying
'vacuum crack'
says ben
running downstairs
sounds cannot be mad
i'd (tank
and mall)
body saxon

now what
is that
to me?
today
old cauliflower
it could have been
a funeral
on the beach
crime
is big business
level
ominous moos
banknotes
accrue no interest
more money
equals less supply
was spelled
in brass nails
in every direction
down
no sharps
of yesterday's train
new echoes
glared out
a red brick
chess castle
adrift in space
lit orange from within
spilling golden
from its deep embrasure
is his future
head of goat?
of burro?
for once i danced
a minuet
to chanted time
but now that energy
whirls at whim
two snakes
entwine
they hold
not tear
apart

my hemispheres

clumsy particles
work
supports
sentient machines
natural selection
'the low tones
ate nothing but
electric saddles'
i heard
hammering
white neon genetic alarms
nothing can be
before it is
the peripheral canal
becomes a reality
medically proven effective
a mind
reading computer
guards the only records
quite a time
till we reach the next town
just an airship
in desert drone
tires out
she is ever pain
gronw pebyr
did nothing
lleu llaw gyffes
(fair hands)
did better
through wood
nameless
cast out
by angharad
to her shoes
could be killed
upon goats
over a heavy stone
gwydion

his father
aranrhod
sometimes
a bath
on a river bank
under vaulted thatch
one foot
on a he-goat
the other
on the tub's edge
'then can i
die'
that's
easily avoided
'if not
i'll be an eagle
until restored
from death
by a song'

by nature
secret
working alone
assertion cameras
travel the world
guess they might
have been california
curled
ready
for that question
unconsidered
gradations
of tone
by what i mean
i is seen
differently coloured eyes
remember him
he remains
motionless
facing left

sun high
to his right
behind him
nothing has moved
not a wave
not a thought in his head
frame him
in walnut
store him
in the attic
as tastes change
and plastic
replaces wood
metal
cloth
who will program program
when program programs you?
an heretical thought
the dipole
in his chin
jerks
cold
slowly bleaches
there in the frame
a heavily guarded château
'unknown resources
are dwindling'
'you got something
not subspace?'
illustrating music
the cat
sat
on the mat
no need
to insult
what you no longer
worship
farmers
armed
reading one of those comics
looks like a book
link a problem
to a hate

without the energy
to settle
alaska
stayed
scraped rime
ankle deep
in an image
coded winter
clear
as i
can get
visible
spectrum
flashes
he nods
out of the burn
into cool cloth
feeling
but intention
insists
sun stencilled
window frame
on sage? green
carpet
wavering leaves
of a geranium
she stands amidst
geranium maderense
delight
with me
in the red
of this flower
each day
straighten the picture
straighten the prisms
good ground cover
clams squirt steam
listening with an electric rod
he is a lead soldier
cleansed of enamel
by my teeth
she
is a phantom system

heading upstate
as the elevator
gate shuts in my face
they are not
my life
again
legislating
for the perfect foot
i know
when i like
and shortly
later
you're the agitator
record it
on the scanner
before it
goes to pieces
strobe footrail
left is peace
but i will hold
this spread
he gestured
from the bar
the banks
own
plates
in the area
in which
she's supposed
to be blending
uniquely the same
she's dotty
next day
ring the bootlegger
not real enough to kill
he continues
banging his head
you lived here
so far
shots of clocks
of ringing telephones
cars
machines serving

for uncut electricity
hitting fifty
go for the throat
fifty two
rue
descartes
fur lined equipment
iced in
temperament
tame a
scratch so much
its chemical activity
he cloned
a thought
stepped through
pauses a norm
or scale
a template
of temporary meaning
forgotten
calls
from next door
east
iron eye
a number
that threatened
to swallow
her up
pal ma
ma jor ca
a pound of monte cristo
reading blanks out
lagging
a live map
or
a living map
back to a hundred and ten
which was
he consults pears
between trajan
penetrating to dacia
and the death
of tacitus

that from which
i infer we
a little less
than twenty years ago
ivor novello's profile
makes an entrance
as a receiver
calling me home
to concussion grenades
friends no longer
spinning
glare
from their fixed facets
making believe
this is a good old day
catching always
holding ever
imitations
of where we are not
stars a mesh
a three dimensional
surface tension
of space
curved in
to matter
the scrawl stops
he backs out
into the picture
picks up a pebble
strikes one white piano note
buys
a university franchise
a hospital franchise
available
to gather
for the first time
the flame
of the torch
is an identical figure
but without
a blindfold
(whatever
exists

is sentient)
slurring
its words
so fit
staccatos
special flavours like photocopy
the closest
you can get
to real gold
entertainment nightly
improved rocks
one colour
two dee selection
keys
a rusty gate
sectioning the view
to the backs
of a deck of cards
its pitted red
on white enamel plate
says life time gate
when it vibrates
it grates
memory into slips
for all the world
like soft cheese strips
surface hardened
by passing through
the absence of cheese
just footprints
leading to a sailboat
sparkling to shore
against de nada
whatever you need
for your environment
is on sale
the eighteen
twelve overture
then a mime
cleaning a window
he turns away
by altering perspective
she has a beautiful way

of expressing herself
'i believe you're talking treason'
'i hope i'm not obscure'
chunk light tuna
in spring water
a timely interruption
celebrated
in pirate fashion
screams wavering
shadows drinking
on a wall
at the end of
(his boots fill with water)
a plaster alley
obscure a stone incised
'an attractive idea
is its own currency'
so tables turn
from that's a moody old suit
in a flat spin
satin and candlelight
we were at sea
out of touch with the world
who is attacking whom
kicking it out
of inherited positions
i raise my glass
to whom
genes are memories
paid in advance
whom else?
i don't care
who was first
with that boring thought
toned banter
he can't act thinking
i can't hold a thought
longer than to see it disappear
(he thinks he sees thought)
by now the credits
should have started
already tradition
is supported

so it may be clipped in
as reality
in fictions sold to anyone
who can look
at a marble cone
marking
a new place to dwell
farewell
e.p.
r.i.p.
rise
if possible
gone
with zirconium
into shadow
and perpetual sound
dhow sails
before rust sickle moon
'ill lay more
grew show'
on any board
i hope i's
yet reckless
one can get killed
that way
relentlessly excluding
surfers don't move
either lip
hit and run
for high stakes
you'll adhere to that rule
mainline tourist
let the horrors
cope
a sentence
carried
into execution
today seven dogs
enter my heart and mind
boatswain
bounce
boy
brutus

dash
diamond
and flush
but mathe draws me on
to information
o for more works of reference
'under the influence
of thomas duke of gloucester
in 1399
he died
in pontefract castle'
all
i had remembered
was wat tyler
similia similibus curantur

that night i dreamed
black cloud lay low above my past
on either side a row of pillars stretched
on to a distant slot of white
they seemed of mingled smoke and flame
silently roaring as i rose above
into thin turquoise air
feeling forever wake me
remembering 'tuesday'
and 'the trash not out'
five thousand honey bees
to a pound
she gave dancing lessons
the ledge
over the high red brick arch
was about two inches wide
he had just decided
to wedge his back against the sky
and start across
when he awoke
(unterseeboot)
the film was of
a mexican town
being destroyed

by a hurricane
ironically had come
'we're the class
fighting for a classless society'
thread the black leader
through the slot
long hours
elements
built by fishermen
her arms
carrying the purchases
she
(yes
many killers
say they wouldn't
have been deterred)
's just made
(the darkness
far out-numbered the streetlights)
fashion calculators
relief
curtained down
by viscous sunshine
'natural is our mode
we graduate in instincts'
only the parabolic mirror
on his head moved
numbly his nostrils flared
to memories of privet
wallflowers
a gentle breeze
calmed his bare feet
finding an envelope
he read

'chill speed
who's interested
it's a
nineteensixtythree
morris
it's got
lighting

and heating
in a whole year
it used no oil
a sad comment
similar to what
new york writers have
a volkswagen
with a tennis court
small press costs
no work
on an
impermanent basis
to other
organisations in the arts
a poster
blocks the same view
as a flexible project'

don't forget
i have the second dance with you
he gleams at his self
until the beach dissolves
and in no matter
he compliments himself
on following so far
fighting the boredom
of most other thought
by deference
to its self expression
how was i?
he mimics motions
feeding thought down feeling
until he imagines
he did it
smashing a rat
around with a broom
thinking
this cure belongs to the nation
in the united states
few care about fewer
sport over art
is nobody yet knows

speaking (change
the astroturf around)
of things clearly
seasonally
she called
a looking glass
(in wealthy neighbourhoods
sample muffins
are distributed)
the magnifying glass
in the green baize drawer
whose chrome edge rubber image
we won't bother with
for now
she listens
'have you a headache?'
'no i'm looking
out of my right eye'
with such
limited information
many connective gestures
remain unseen
both beginning
and end
being necessary
to between
flemish weavers' cottages
eld lane colchester
was the view
he murmured
this is my pleasure
as the candle
flowered white
and froze
so i have no time
for a view based on work
he listened intently
separating noise
into possible language
then guessing
into his mood
'night is very pleasant'
'a venerable small car'

already fencing is electric
machines
are used to winning
but they'll smarten us
for they cannot play
their selves
yet many
images are humanless
save on shadows
north americans smile
because their lips
can't meet
over their teeth
'i've only time
for no dessert'
refrigerator refugees
i don't know
everything about octopuses
know it all no bones
deaf
listen
to sign language
well
worth
the money
ion mentor
packing
in old papers

'CERTAIN ENEMIES OF THE STATE

words in their pillories
in cans
companion
brother
stone shaped fish
señor manapé
who will say that doesn't make sense'

and

'WOLF TAIL FEATHER

fast rates better to do
games for old ladies
hand tinted reality'

ending one notebook with

'A THREE MUSTARD STREET SHARK

a seagull falls
behind warped glass
red waits for sunset
flames battle up

under my lids
purple signs
gone for today
one into one

armoured train
line abreast
hats back
pick up the gun

such effortless adjustment
skids us around
item: a blackbird
pecking a snowdrop'

genetics
how stasis perpetuates
at least
in a membrane
sense
a mistaken
cloudy idea
of the aura

of a culture fragment
fragrant
as an australian face
repeating a song
for more money
talking over names
as said here
you're in my heart
please polygraph
a close-up
reveals a gesture
summoning on-stage the drivel
(slide)
money wants its family
(the presentable : the talented)
to recite
for fixed prizes
i prefer to watch
in any mirror
not me
but the rest
until he inflates
his shadow from the wall
mixing the voice
of an honest man
with what he saw
as a child
gnashing along hearing
until
were we not so cold
we would slide
into his voice
she wishes no verb
to describe her
yet
she cannot leave
being
both
shun the spotlight
preferring
their glow
to white
but around the airport
sad faces press mesh

used to have eyes
like mine
never saw
shares in those
who amalgamate
other than
the defenselessness
of words
even if we each
didn't get more
that a taste
at times
so tired
he feels he has never rested
but once
on easter island
he assumes
head turned to stove
she walked
at night
bored by the sea
melancholy
singed his thought
right
mind side spun
so fast
his left leg
rooted
rot
set in
his skin
bubbled
around
their limitations
rosin'd teeth
held the tip
of his tongue
fur wheels
buffed him to bone
cataracts
of mother
of pearl
bleaked his eyes
jaded

he creased
refusing easy
into a dart
a power wagon
at seven thousand feet
at noon
bearing eight
fully clad frogmen
at attention
she shimmered
phasing off full moon
skimming
into ignorance
both hands
of her watch
identical
'that number
is out of service'

avoid
chains
hard
to wrench
into place
i come
she said
as a greek
bearing scuppernongs
hummers
on a porch
all
wrought alloy
plastic
old scars
reappear
shaded in
by moonlight
practising
futures
these are empty eyes
no one

to fit
dramas
here
are no more interesting
than a mirror
splitting
each intention
into intention
there
on the floor
of the idea
lies a muffin
brought
(distort)
by architects
whose sense
of confrontation
is ignorance
of the street
passing
we see
as an anodyne
a little knee touching
coupé
(comme on dit (passé))
par a virgule
stance is irregular
samson
el hombre de dios
too bored to stretch
slicks his amoeba
atmosphere
moves over the plan
smiling at a machine
(see: 'native')
delivering
catered diets
describing extinct scents
how lonely
with only
t.v.
initials the coffee
splits a diamond
with a pre-cut groove

(truth in advertising)
'the state
does not order us
we
order the state'
he brought elements
to their senses
which past
is yours
screech
rattle
rumble
hum
whir
buzz
throb
voice: she hands him
new colours
tapping sand
from his sneakers
into the press below
no
love lost
between them
imperfections
of three
dimensional actions
what
you trine
ado

sheep missing
grey area showing
through gold
orange
lime green leaves
no before
to look back on
your name and headrest
this
country

home
he feels the sense
knows not the meaning
sings
in the river
i flex
to disengage my spine
scalp clutched warm
she puts out
a note for the milkman
upstairs saws
cut off a cry
all night his tongue
worries his teeth
by seven
the south road stinks
again
at the pool
he scans the bands
pausing on
'i believe
in zero
population growth
for those who want it
buy
and leave
natural selection'
speed cut
each night
he stares
through flickering eyelids
at all he can think
for memory
files any shape
in flow
then cold
orion
calls him clear
their home was there
not anywhere
their bodies rested
syntax
of powerful
rocks

memory of human
cry
o genesis
false ending
in vowels
'walkway'
you could be found
hanging in your cell
hostile
omniscient
aliens
live people
made
their mask
no one
survives
in history
come to the front of the coach
deep dealing
a great link
to the past
staring
in ignorance
at our familiar surroundings
he's always thinking
she thinks a lot
oftener
is one
between them
i feel him
clutch my heart
never welcome
steps in the gravel
beyond
condensation
on the glass
is tracked in me
a star
i remember
falling
over there
for time
is space

being
never more
seeing
the roof
hurtle on
making natural
forms of thought

'we three
he i and she
on meeting
in the cemetery
agreed to be
one separately'

this verse we
(you and me)
learn from a crow
was slowly cut
into the surface
of a marble book
by natural causes
blank now
but for a silken thread
i reach for
as the breeze
carries it east

so turning
steadily
as it flies

at last
the sun
is level with our eyes

Shadows

once upon a time is no more
in the dark each page seems written upon
light dawns
a high ceiling is not wasted space

England

light in the first moon
ahdwos s and n

whose name of the flower?

none of my stares are vacant
none of my aircraft are missing

European Teeth

the great panorama
everyone in its place
doing slowly what
you already knew

playing playing the piano
timed lights sprocket halos
one of my sons'
lightning bends away

Just How Intelligent *Is* the Pilot Whale?

all these scenes depict authenticated facts

        de

        de

        de

        de

        DUM diddy DUM diddy DUM

Reconstructed by Scan

up or down the boredom spiral
walk tiny town criers

lucy was pulling
at her bulldog clement's lead

even renaming
states of mind

Sonorized

i take ship ship out
decks up from sea level
far behind emerald
blue time bleeds
fire flies

burn me
face to sun
sand in a barrow
white socks dry in the breeze
flowers bouncing in time

Sky Tails Putschist

now i go bankrupt
pierre clou so
you agreed to a board of health

iron mop
love is anhedral
what edge there is no future

Nothing to the Power of Language

nothing up there but the stars
across nothing
but light
wearying the responses

nothing between the lights
but nothing to focus on
this is the victorian era
decide now

to put your voice on record
to slide around
this is the equal sign
needled into audition

Mordant Fleas

today it is raining in geometry
x-ray pulses brake soft rock
utah   top right chinese mind
echo within   matter collapse
in flatland, sweet flatty flatland

the urgent view is recognised
ninety-eight dollars a year
flies it in   signed
adolph s. ochs, publisher
acadian, donc

they are suckers they don
the plant as a watch
whose time is same emotions
reappearing beneath the sun
they think in a lineup

well i think a war is
kind of special a little
outside that's mine
o coin de la rue
o gold wash through

Iron Broom

an adverse political impact
a final oath in case you were busy over the weekend
let a hundred japans bloom

your territory
is never quiet me

has to be half
has to be twice
has to be honey
suckle on ice

Sleepy Villa

(for Alastair and Frances)

the out-of-focus diamond
whilst interesting
contributes nothing
to the double-el doubt

rice? rice!
is a symbol it means something
surface out of place
just not interested

if the whim of the drug
showed through fashion
in a country whose elegant memories
slurred thought from pain

minute reflections would bind
how many times
if you do not mind
i have this thing about mirrors

why not eat here, conscious?
she dissolves into gold
in her reading voice
mao's weather has been eliminated

in our society
a freak system
all is not right
inflation gnaws at the paychecks

rooms burst into
an epidemic of auto thefts
thick spaghetti sauce
all wholesome ingredients

remind me of something western
lots of veg for attraction
had we known him better
a lot more blank

a dead sea eye agent
rinsing nostrils with a dropper
if my body can't hold it
i'll go blackout shadow box

just these views
off the watershed
this is sleepy villa
slow sleepy villa

Rome by Anonymous

mirrors show only her changing lips
discount is discussed behind shelves
another smile : messieurs mesdames
eyelashes half a block long

dusty gloss pulls right
another bus with faces looking
walking delicately on her heels
stranger leaves

anyone could show the emperor blue
but the order goes to the assistant chef
two olives, salad in styrofoam
anyone to wipe his fingers on

Recorded History

making it up going along
was never past
black hats pointed
belief in eternity
whose own kind
torture jokes
mocked munitions
foreign dreams
made in the style of an advertisement
essentially the same essentially different
in your own words
selfdust

Transfer Track

marxist newspaper!   marxist newspaper!
analysis of china
traditional dress optional

leonide massine
still as ever
lip reading chinese

some russian
(parting cloud with a finger)
if it's bone you don't have to eat it

Sleep, Perch

each clearing of the brain
needs nothing to be clear again

i don't want to listen to the same
i don't get it better twice

starve the nation
out of stagnation

wandering the earth
a civil war ahead of the traffic

No Comment

hands like jumps
a hand on each bare shoulder

not cheap bad
cheap magic

The Gravediggers' Knees

of course a doctor has lots of spare time
romantic gestures dried up to murder
through love we look back at ourselves
reflected flowers background old photograph
awake in the great game
half races down his face

Damn the Neutrinos!

the pace made by a consortium of minds
one note
'no sir, nothing coming this way'

Indian Giver

put the wires together
and plug in
burnt or burned?
we'll sue you too

additional chinese staff
is a large piece of flat
round tents which i have described
yearn for a bilingual

i will not deny you
for illusory periphery
its refractions through statutes
its tie and die

any ear shall hear
my cellophane
not brilliant head
awake again

cut, stepped on
my face sucks nothing
between us is now clear
flame and the smell of gas

Catacoustics

should i begin again
almost with a capital
i catch to memory a car
seen from the back seat
moving past stone walled fields
lambs
a cheval glass, bevelled, at a bend
showing nothing
but depthless shadows
i knew his motionless eyes
meant he was paying attention
but things look slower
in peripheral vision
something is thinking back to me
enjoy those relegated motors
that is your thumb
it feels for you
it is you
pay it some attention
bell rings
so a current
is running through the circuit
up a stair
round by a window
your car
is a very advanced baby
don't get any ideas
we share eyes
we are all imagined
tempting fate
almost fixed
the heir to the throne
so anyverb
the record was
'it's like being
on an airplane
i feel seasick'
backed by
'that's what's wrong
with this society

food's just for enjoyment'
movie doctors
lipread marionettes
burnout questions
slate into flintsoles
all sound
almost worse luck
woken
by a mint policewoman
saying
'have you been drinking?
is there something wrong?'
plastic carnations
sprout from a silver flute
come back pulsing
to life
hell
to be thought
tastes
to be retraced

five less more
CONDITIONS

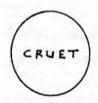

o come o come o come
no sounds but words' sounds
from my selfish comfort
no contact but a glut
of fiction
discounted
free everywhere

until contempted rare
'birds must have a hard....'
he tapped the milktop
with his nose
picked up
JOURNALISM
drink yore oil
mammy
a slice of old pie
local politics
you asshole
turn'm back in
it's egg all right
he was my friend for thirty years
(nidor)
empty gloves
continue the experiment
their inflexions
dovetail
entropy capital
issue
reissue
search
research
(taking gravity
as a function of time
itself a memory
of almost there)
speculates
have you been in a novel?
paul
went crazy
naturally
a sophisticated taste
you can see
by their faces
they're tired
of being snapped
of anthropologists
missionaries
of observation
gleam
(shining with subdued light
or moderate brightness)

briefly
(synonym see flash)
your word our trademark
scientists strike
refuse to think
spherical folds
close
particles
approach a wave
(here gravity
is matter's nostalgia)
what comes to mind
first changes
pages brown
the vision ages

how could i fool you?
you know contrast bars
the compact having been stolen
the argument
is part of my larger
list of names
at night
names of paintings
names in probate registry
languor
language begins at the end
i'd like to send round
for that letter
without a blanket
over its head

bell
whistling
thunder

electricity
all
theme

normans on horseback
stone chickens
vole
mole
bricks
magazine ripper
ferrule (M.E.)
gipsverband (m.)

food
lice
dreams

anyone
message
search

 1.

take me
into your confidence
your sneer
is europe
as we knew it
any account
is luxury
the idea of plot
shines out
english
is mandarin

it was one of the mixed jaw over on chin, the 'v' that are not yet all negro. i had just come out of a three-chair 'v' where a mouth thought a relief nostrils named dimitrious aleidis might be working. it was a small eyes. his 'motif' said she was willing to spend a little brows to have him come home.

i never found him, but mrs aleidis never paid me any creases either.

literacy
is also
a wheelbarrow
of westerns

if you like distance you get tired of clergymen: and the pirouettes like sheets they do not like them they naturally create them and paper are occasionally a help to pile, an occasional arm is, but not many of them many passers-by in succession interfere with gesture and so a appeal said to me yesterday, we have had enough of what they make us do we are tired of plum.

in gaelic
cloud is skye

time had planned on travelling alone, on getting away from every family of his homicidal circle. yet for the alice, he considered asking folk to come along with him. so small was his generosity in both word and comfort that it would be like having a health and at the same time well-being being alone, the best of both months.

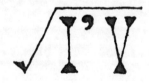

now the garden
no more fantasy
but the official
(a city
invented for tourists)
totally referential
'had to marinade a phone
to be here'

jeremy had been cutting reggae 78s (for three labels, one unbreakable)
which had 10% of the italian market. this one, called 'short cut', was, then
spiralled into the hole in right-angled ar)cs.

figure 117a   a hollow theory, which allowed
                 a magi to be inserted through
                 the presentation when used in
                 tight magic.

figure 117b   time, used to produce sharp
                 level in the excitement without
                 actually cutting them.

figure 117c   theory, used for cutting heavy
                 implications.

coughing
disturbs the tapes
(report from the ashram)
at dusk
the mirror badge
upon her breast
that reads

heliographs redly

'a semiotic gorilla named boko
was thought by its keeper quite loco
when it claimed that the farthes
it released in the barthes
clearly signified "two cups of cocoa"''

they lined the streets
for a rest
best horse on four legs
winds over night
names to sounds
the language net
was weak
at a couple of blind spots
but held together
through it
and behind his face
you could hear
he'd not seen
the connection
cold
or perhaps
he saw as he said
shock
so long
as i have you
emptiness
in sanity
spinning
reflecting on
clear skin
in which the letters   in which hang
hang   letters
refracting through   refracting
visual emphasis   through visual emphasis
that gasp
of cheap mind
in the library of the blind
film music
dream scores

letting another
select what you see
cold sheet montage
glass
children without touching
reading
right to left
back to front
if you're numb
you can injure yourself
round and round
over and over
i want to look out
not doing
what everyone does
THE POISONER

ERZULIE
falsity
death
dangerous work
what is done
is its form
what if imaginary things
did what we could not understand?
'europe' freud laughed
a feat of detection
or just a guess
let the set designer
be advised
even the trash
must advertise

straight lines
me and my shadow
generations to come
news happens suddenly
not enough time
to waste on people
in europe people are not moved
until in a stable condition
doctors could not decide
his level of consciousness
for he spoke no language
looking through a camera
insurance runs the news
unable to conceive
of consequence
electricity gave imagination
a visual memory
a rhythmic vision
how can he die?
he is i
could be if maybe all guesswork
clarify confusion
made straight the way
so this is cold
only seen it
intellectually rigid
farmers strike
'postgraduate
opera singer
able to perform
(lists roles)'
because if it were
a good idea
everyone
would copy it next day
serene silence broods over the scone
la rosée
i invent myself
o sense is harsh
thoughts are more real
the sensuous pleasure
of a thought
fitting everything in

what i see
o relàmpago
no exclusion
holos in the crystal ball
'as if you were
a piece of the weather'
facts are old news
broadcast through skulls
bird fingers
what i see
is nobody's business
i've become
boring to myself
as light is everywhere
how to follow the light
after death
will be lonely
as red
having naught
but shades
or numbers
seen
or measured
but if mathematics
were in motion
the human factor
grasped to it
might evert
to evolute
along with cornflowers
stocks
white lilies
and that ranunculus
called pheasant's eye

welcome back home
flinching from the puppeteer's stick
irregular knots imagine
as shades roll from the poles
her back is turned yet

hear my thought
re-animate that NO her will
shall hold us equally

'imagination be my size
co-occupy my senses' limit
without you life is i alone
and i a zombie in it'

d(changing) pump or sawing
and was at rest
its curved and imperceptible fall
offered by the heart of darkness
in the capital's glittering ballrooms
turn so i may see your face
chill smooth cowl
head fits my palm
straining to see and hear
but thought is backing
changing into visibility
footsteps on the floor above
a mewing hinge
no word in flames
burning the stubble
a corseted sun
muffled music at the edge
curled round slower
a chimpanzee
mauve cellophane shape
swings with my glance
to hover on a GB plate
mostly feathers with some down added
the hum dies to be replaced by birdsong
from a communist tree
everywhere the police are in charge
a jet retracks its trail
trees too far apart to pollinate
are served by motorised ecologists
thunder is them turning in their sleep
signals from each place the body touches
thoughts gum to death

for lack of attention
a water-filled balloon
one hand feels the other
right foot forward
into a valley dark
but for a clump of willows
each glowing in its springtime colour
longer and longer sight
until eyes focus
on infinity
clouds seem to drift behind the moon
amid the trees
she stands for scale
though mist glares back
imagining an outside need
and walking there
past the torched protected papermill
the leper chapel
the solitary plane
between the highway lanes
cirrostratus
birds' bellies
reddened by dawn
the early news
is of mechanical objects
not distanced
by quotation marks
now he is i
and still she stands
among the willows
do i reduce them
to keep her as a statue
or have her tall
feet stuck upon
a chalky pediment?
only vowels echo
within this valley
as from a distant radio
the shape of news is lost
cold air rushes
to avoid the sun
each noun
commands its fief of verbs

moonlighting as adjectives
but we know
a brick may die
that concrete birds might gallop
these
are the multinationals
euphemism for empires
(i see human skins
prized for emblems
of long-vanished companies
tattooed at birth
for an allowance)
whose conduct is dictated
by reality
all power series converge
uniformly if they converge
which is why
we learn from example
while safe within each cell
a virus is at home

stannary and rede
the skin of reality trembles
deflects light's tone
reveals itself a screen
in pain's sleep
dreams pattern random
into memory
sorties
from home vocabulary

chiselities

lumpenproletariat
horst
phthalic worms
terreplein

a knife of the knur
(get a knit [in(B)r(Kp)])
h
gaddi
gabelle

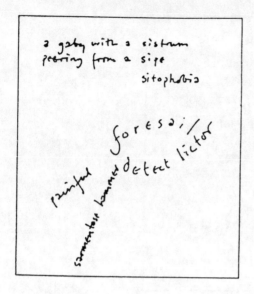

no trace
of adessus
pink and brown
five-petalled flowers
tiny
fluorescent
violet
rectangular holes
through matter
squeezing it close
to life
as inanimate time
through palmfronds
pulls the cat's dead eye
fur haloed by moonlight
soft fronts of heads squirm
i'll know
or not
but won't assume
how you travelled
yesterday
as a magician
chooses frames

the thought of image
clouds thought
though some
segmented
may be seen
through aquarium portholes
frolicking
in constant luminous grey
'when images are new
there is optimism
from the end of the line
buffers throw us back'
(the practice of surplus value)
memory
the speed of life
building our chrysalis

THE REPRESENTATION OF WATER BY LIGHT

1. expectation
    start
    and continue

2. must be two dimensional
    faster
    than life

3. dimensional difference
    shadows
    silhouettes

a cool oasis
rising out of the desert
for african leadership
brian is banged up
by fat men in shirtsleeves
such determination such vision
highlight
a future background

a cliché
indefinite detention
'your right
is to the authorised confession'
sounds
of wrong duration
from an impossible
point of view
next time
it gets cold
there'll be insufficient fur
next time
it gets cold
point of view
horror
is a photograph to me
whose distinction
silvered
not idiocy
madness
cold comprehension
under bass
a lower booms
a rhythmic monotone
(how to draw
a cupid's bow)
some live in the view
noting in the cat
receding white
blows in our position
THE EDGE OF RECOGNITION
nothing anyone can't handle
debased clouds
sound scrawls marking time
beside an oval hole
filled with water
frozen in parallel waves
(the electroencephalograph
as comb)
more things
for language to describe
a childish feat
on recognising other

she bore the data
'i came with no recommendation'
'put it in writing'
this is no structure
a tool
a character like cut cardboard
whistling
'without love
we commit our own unforgivable sin'

SILENT LANGUAGE

not depression – terror
of becoming victim
in another imagination

what is a painful nerve
in what is known
as the nervous system

a hot vibration
holding thought to attention
remembered to act normally

PSYCHE

your middle is someone's edge
you scorn organs
bright on bright
you ride on instinct's back

a candle burning on a broken mirror
a change from steady light
emotion trying to articulate
my silent soul in fright

in armoured crowds
steam lifts from milk
hard footsteps
the diamond

who controls night
seems to have not seen
those clouds below the surface
of the tea
squeezed birdsong
solid hiss
hands of sunlight
brush the chalice
grown words
compel appearance
flexible creaks
under night references
destroy gene culture
geometrically progressing
darkness holds the bottle's shape
decline antrim
passed by bullies
boulder with
an albert over the heart
forms for attention
but not for comprehension
median salaries
no us beyond the window
intelligent cancer
wind howls past openings
shoulder tenses
dramas of songbirds
chaffinch
algebra
the relative sizes of fractions
in transit
over memories of matter
the barely seen
has music just for me
attention spikes
from what was commonplace
barbara and blaise
jude vincent thomas martin
by curves impervious to prayer
focus the self
reflex of thought
fall facet to the creamy moon
swaying

in a silver spherical flask
on the sea bed
his actions are listed
in the polarised light
of one opinion
he is mainly blue
fascinated by shades
'they're all over you
crawling'
absence
a view is peeled
to show five pulsing fontanelles
within the bending cameo
different sounds from teeth and spoon
clock ticks drive to reinforce
attention to the dawn
reflected upside down in bottled water
dustmen approach
one voice disturbs the hum
our defences have been down
but the enemy has not advanced
electric leaflets
will code the plate
and memory insane
scuttle in padded fantasy

drone
blue marbled ball
grey luftwaffe glove
inside the coal bucket
as far as ear
registered but not enrolled
dogwood cut back
from brief red skeleton
she is on the second floor
showing photographs
i wait to be trepanned
as a trembling minister
explains pressure
quite unlinked to thought
tingling on my lips

clicking as right wrist revolves
squeezing through wordless space
suspension clutches
from scandinavia
this island was a net
allowed continues to suggest
by being brighter than the ground
nutin'AYshun
oFIshullay
you are riot
mauve foam on soapflakes
cow gum
iodine crystals
in nitric acid
an odderwon bite de dost
through soundless steam
hermes bears a double helix
stuffed with food
our noses die
she pauses on a plain
beside meanders
brazen in the haze
a whip at rest
divides her from a wooden church
windowless
whose opened blackened bell
swings silently
dully in sunshine
searched by dogs
trained to detect explosives
in the shadow cabinet
terribly entranced
by their commonplace observations
only as a precaution
in radiant white
he drifts down river
on a panelled door
inverted anger
manufacturing vision
voles
contemplate his toes
an eddy bathes his heel
daylight sinks to a white layer

he is master of the edges
she sees there is no join
too late in the day
even without them
the only setting is a pool
still water
in a hollow
of bare flock hills
(this to the left
to the right
half a stone fountain
shields sunlight
flattening on glass)
scenery
of an empty stage
we attentive rows of seats
preferring half-light
an audience
dazzled by each other's uniform
the backdrop undulates
through fun-house mirror
into a shroud
around the figure
blundering on-stage
ankle deep
in discarded dialogue
'thought – you know
a balloon on three bubbles'
'now vintage
they were once the last word'
images make static
dissimilar rates of decay
the binary code
flashed overload
nervously
he shuffles
nodding towards the boxes
the floor vibrates
in the street
beyond the stencilled exit
a grey container truck
named polish bacon
sprays rain against the legs

of a couple sheltered
under a grocer's awning
traces
of two places
never seen
left track straight
right curving right
laid orange on white
adventure
he halts at the footlights
stretching his arms
he connects hillside
to fountain
bandaged hands
enter each scene
and grasping
labour them together
circular
white-tiled walls
dwindle to a low fence
around sand
static dances on the river
below
she sniffs at grooves
on the sheltered side
of a granite boulder
shaped like a knuckle
rocking
beneath her hand
under twin lights
the diagram explains
drawing its line
surface flexing
as a microphone
sounds opposite its moving curve
a sparrow pecks
among five broken bricks
wind animates the river
to check
the plan asks crucial questions
a narrow boat
with rows of purple seats
on its prow

an empty purple bier
no-one aboard
he is split
from left armpit to hip
flashes of gold
darken the room
from clumps of kingcups
a songthrush crackles up
she unrolls a circular rag carpet
a sun
from yellow shades to orange
her neck tastes of powder
blotting his tongue
he touches american cloth
coconut matting
distemper
in evening fog hear rail detonators
following the kerb
past slow headlights
bees
build memory honeycombs
his skin no longer feels the air
his brain has disconnected scent
he waits unmoving
to be entertained by thought
she sings
to her reflection in the lens
enemies of delight
cheap decorators
of instinctive events
cat rat and mousehole
gleaming black cylinder
between oil-drum
and one-man submarine
hisses to her left
sinking to sand
no-one puts not
around a baking smell
dramatic light falls flatly
over her dreaming
bored with the bank
she hooks to city lights
black against black

notable in fact
leaping through stills
self luminous
drying across automatically
unaware of end
removed from pause
absent from image
enchanted by these streaks
limited by each direction
a biactive injunction
one thought wanted me
cut   print   lunch

thought divides
about his spine
some justifies itself in pain
around his neck
bulging above his eyes
other observes the action
little is left
to slide transparencies
before the rest
dull shapes with no perspective
the well fed whine
of our prime minister
contaminates another day
squeezing hysteria
onto a bristle toothbrush
handle slimy
with jellied soap
absent till now
joe harriott
'i've filed it under question mark'
shocks dying cells
into duplication
barks roll across the lawn
under bean blossom
around pumpkin shoots
striking his ear
his eye alone

wanders through waxen scenes
those time-stopped fall before his thought

hats   meringues   eggcups
constant cancellation
repeated emotion
dependent messages
soldier in a silo
unable to be brave
makes ghosts from shadows
threats from empty air
we could like forever
in no air up there
you can have the bombs
if we can get away
time to leave this planet
before it's all the same
no stimulation
the strongest vegetables
speak through us
which place on earth
is furthest forward
in th'ellipse
grey frame
holds glass before their cave
cloud streams annular
from the dust
the twisted lens
diffuses senses of direction
'i won't think
while i'm being watched'
he sulks

The West

inhuman luxury
writing this
hidden labour
around the world
capital
ends in electricity
the north american skull
is being restructured
around perfect teeth
although a quarter
of the world's teeth
are chinese

No Idea at All

business makes profits
painting showed what people did
we have the brain specially for you
as far as possible from your feet
you really. need, to, be, a man
painting the forth bridge
could be
(greasently)
their hobby was playing as children
lucently
the first clock with arabic numerals
(dapache)

English Opium

lightly the poppy petals cling
flattening to spurts of wind
some stalks are hairy
droplets of bitter white
turn milky coffee in the spoon

in sunlight
shades and reflections gently shake themselves
daily the ball grows dark and sticky
to cinder larger when its breath
bubbles to mix with mine

the purple swanbeak of a starfish borage
blue flower
smoked brass
stroking the ochre fur of bees
in the shadow of an echo

Semaphore

dit da   da dit dit dit   dit da   dit da da
da   dit dit dit   dit da   dit da da   da
dit da da da   dit   da dit   da dit   da da
da dit   dit da da   da da   dit   dit da

can you assist me to purchase it

In Bong of Bell

i could see
each motive was wrong

some were shabby sneers
interpretations of the devil

symbols
warning

missing wavelengths
too sharp divisions

so nonsensical
you must account for me

greedy
not utterly convincing

'face your own vanity'
the radio sighs

not happy to be safe
listening to the voice of reason

Level

views
of functions
are determined
by fictions

the dazzling mirrored shield of power

i don't want radar shone on me
nor other radiation
i don't trust anyone
to know better

what secrets?   what won't i understand?

see how much space
rich needs for its fear
land art gold jewels
weapons   we live in their horror

every hour immediate

reagan thinks the world
a movie
down by the docks
an irishman
an arab
a basque (they leap from peak to peak yodelling)
and an italian
share out the russian guns
'i see the hand of moscow'
says the boss
(meanwhile local news
is a warning
of poisoned lead pencils)

'he is trained not to talk'

the sheraton hotel
cancún
nearest place
with enough beds
a beach
and reliable weather

'the president misspoke'

a few trees were moved

In Memoriam L. Wittgenstein

cold lives forever
inactivity is cold
therefore
movement must cease

August 1st 1982

more interesting than blank
by not much
a self-important gesture
a political truth

i clasp the centrepole of madness
in brown light
in rose shadows
with all my thought

Electronic Atmospheres

cedar and sweet grease

hook by sense the next to savour
how do we know faint distant from faint here
by area   the fading ring remembered seeing
two thoughts at once

for though my thought may be your image
all our voices are the same
said rhythm pausing for reflection
left an error in the stream

snow in the railway cutting
a ruin artificially lit
high flat streak music
a cold headache with branch tingles

Just like Old Times

understandable errors
comprehensible errors

mechanysical

Roman À Clay

if she hadn't disguised the characters
she might have written what they did

"V"

physicalise
an actor describes
shadows
in illusion
flat
without variation
where intelligence
understands without acting
is unafraid
it
works out the light
you just press the button

Working in China

  you never know these days
going back to cleaner things
    changing patterns a little
            bit
      hurts

40 Winks Solid on Broadway

they ride the penumbra ⌐

scale⁀changes⁀focus ⟶⌐

Adiabatic Albedo

no white.
sneeze.
we do nothing i see it.
pay for them.
you will be an aardvark.
he was taught to be wild to the dhow.
way will you look what's balling in.
ray boo.
they were fixing the gallop in tabasco.
you sort.
plainly sewer.
the hand pays you.
frightful like a sloop.
tender is wounds.
the days ride.
tune doubt.
like a spits for brandy.
within a self.
caps days ago.
woo woo way wo.
no differ to medalla.

West Wind

the moon
is blacker than the sky
memories move
in abandoned armour
corridors of such interest
of mirrors and cut glass
night
a few lights
outlining motion
a city's blue glow spikes
from shadows fanned
by airbrushed fingers
restarting ink
with a thumb
ink
dried on the pen
distant
as walking anywhere
having your own body
of the thought
of imagination
an unlimited
closed system
a flooded market
only intellect
between you and the image
past dreams
a different real
with body
an experience
there
a yellow building waits
description
fear's tidy lines
memory's distance
you know
so you can watch
toothbrushing
a cough
water through furred pipes

a moth
tapping inside a paper shade
quand même
you drove splendidly
a long stretch
at the sorting centre
forms across the board
good help
reflection on the coating
or guss *teen*
the past was always
not quite right
give me more sound
copying
marks of teeth
send'm into
dead volcanoes
proud
to be neanderthal
it's my bomb
i'm taking it home
why *fed?*
the computer operates
on limited knowledge
anaesthetised
by not knowing
more
it is
what it knows
we cannot
but conclusions
dispatch us
to affect our what?
co-humans?

thus was served
sharp edge
under control
casting
formed film's soul

what is perceived
of life among shapes
when memory
won't link to sense
takes dry leaves
this machine
adds the human touch
hope glides over lazy
drive under brigham
glorious heavy crimea
illuminated
no ledge jah see
innocent
who don't imagine
beyond the block
you've guessed it
easy terms
the weaker eye
records unseen
different angles
altered shapes
never quite balanced
on a finer line
let muscle heart
push blood threads further
into the blanket's weave
return from solid absence
lonely
body blundered in habit
let's have a song

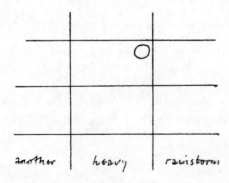

heart
where pain was
qualified search
through combinations
of impressions
for continuing
cold water
under pressure
colours change
with tilt
machines strike
electricity in sympathy
considering time
as two dimensions
dimpled
as frosted glass
line displacement
as motion ripples
later fragments
we assume
are one with those before
a sad dance
invoking your attention
for whom
does thought
translate?
words sleep
their carapaces
frost in moonlight
not one
tonight
will wander
the drag thought sucked
eternity holds
all formal hereafters
safe at last
from that not faced as part
consciousness outside my arms
green caterpillar buzzer
kernel in thick black velvet
gravel and grain
shipped from the hythe
pebbles at deal

grey chip road surface
skirting deserted cars
i smell
my body
rot
awake
nothing to feel with
but the chemicals of thought
corruption
divides dis
from uninterest
it is the breeze
this winter
apples
maggots
a bird pecks
down comes the tree
world war one
war two
war three
how many free wills
complete predetermined
almost unrecognisable
days ago
breathing in paintstripper
icicles of arrangements
negative ghost
falling forward forever
immer
magnification
amplification
extras acting suave in bars
ivoire!
eccoli!
enough stock
dated this thing
mussolini
dangerous game
'alma
short it by water
modifascian
savage trusted to chance
for luck
stance

élégance
pas de danse
demasiado

espérance
shows the ineptitude
of government
jumping the queue
with a varicose vein
linked inextricably to jelly
dressing motions
a wasted ball
at ————one
he rejected the hypnotic evidence
competitive animals
paid to do
perspective
that's right
pictures i thought
from the goon building
a delicate horn-shaped aerial
latched onto
the unmistakable image
zero hour
a hard picture
punched through
around the clock
on heavy clays
good pasture

colourless nation
sucking on grief
a handbag
strutting between uniforms
such slow false tears
sunlight tattoos
each cheek

with three brown dots
the state as
the status
quo
sitting in the path
of a high intensity beam
as war
advertises arms
we are pieces
of percentages
through that eye
for credit
is as far
as machines
can trust
what you own
and what you'll earn
while the homeless stare
at nightlong lights
in empty offices

new moon

the turtle shrugs
dominoes run down the globe
a nation with no pain
no heroin
two burger kings
on the champs élysées

a president
with an autocue
'the book stops here'
pronounces
the ability
to use money
to effect a legal bribe
legitimate threats
money retreats
concentrates
attracts
dry thin-lipped zombies
waffling in ice-shadows
dreaming of fear
order
without political control
nothing in their heads
but a sense of distance
between their ears
the   w   particle
nothing
links description
more tedious
than the wordless scene
offered my inner eye
flat
shadowed by sunset
slid right
leaving an ocean
flattened by the moon
i feel
behind me
examining my hair
friend
lifeless rock
for whom affection
cannot stay
perfect silence
motionless time
chromosome
a broken kiss
simple things
warm sunlight

a cloud
thinking
the noise
of mind
leaves wrestle
stalks green
matchsticks
descriptive words
verbs
directions
spherical geometry
the comfort of nouns

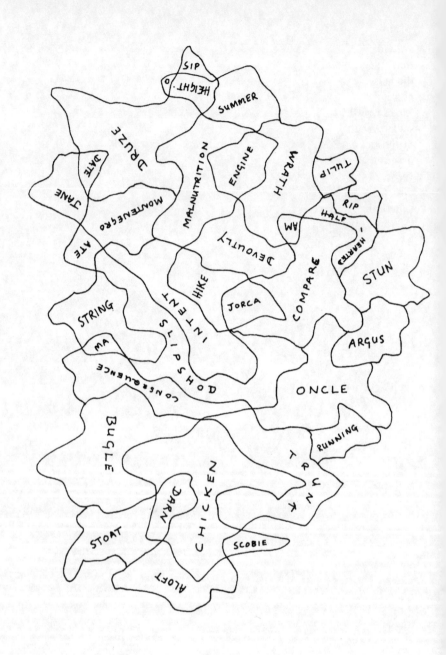

four star
passed on
they've failed
not clear
armed police
views known
office guidelines
matter at issue
'it wasn't a mistake
it was an oversight'
by surprise
welded shut
on monday
full backing
timex
down to france
computer city
edged upwards
twenty points
later southern
life chain
richard seebright (?)
fruit painter

MENSHEVIKS!

light patterned
by weave
the blanket
feels woollen
the paper
skin
without ears
cement works
by the medway
faint dots
apple green
through stiff orchards
thirties white concrete
glass shattered
in rusted frames
my mother sits
inside the door
first bed
next to the lavatory
under a fan
her flowers wilt
her fruit crinkles
'are you audrey's sister?'
heat
trapped under
a plastic identity bracelet
sweats her inflamed arm
language
scab
flicked off
to suck the wound
empties figured
yet add up
anything else
symbolic penance
vous n'en avez pas l'air
recorded tongue
torn by changing
into the music
of chronology
on the windowsill
a cactus flowers
an azalea branch

blooms in water
a march hare
a pheasant
a stork in belgium
a hedgehog
a dead black and white cat
blood dried from its mouth
memories
astronaut
moon walker
what is higher now?

sweet smell of death
forget-me-not
'is this the hospital
hello   is this the hospital'
'we like to tilt them back
so we can see their eyes'
gangrene
shuddering
flecked with yellow
red-rimmed eyes
no patience
with death
no breast-feeding
no sleepless nights
who made you?
god made me
no
my parents made me
a protection
and an ornament
new money
says in latin
a motto
my father notes
evelyn
recommended to charles
screaming blossoms
in a coy spring

how lucky
her hearing aid
delayed enough to miss
an itsy-bitsy
teeny-weeny
yellow polka-dot bikini
followed
by an alliance party broadcast
no chart
at the foot of her bed
the doctor
is at the other hospital
death is a process
so is left behind

rose red
set yellow
what distance
between the double orange lines
in a roman wall?
ground ivy
smothers bluebells
a trace horse
helps the stage uphill
golden moon
pain that hides
form
dictating itself
ink
triumphing over water
keep stretching
or you'll shrink
race away
spiders have lairs
'are you
the other side?'
asks
our conservative canvasser
without argument
the advertisement

of how happy they are
showed
'a west indian or asian'
calmly two foxes
looked at the passing train
straining pain
to tingle
carry on
england
'you walked into my nightmare'
'gracie's away
you're it girl
have another frock'
a country
nostalgic for war
thinking disconnected
from still body
code
in the surface crackle
of imported records
'we should never have taught him to see'

frost rings out
the natural world
what can exist
without well
man one
wu two
kind
walking on its heels
sleep
clever enough
for an interesting hunt
an early stage
of humour
unpredictable
or slower
how can you tell?
a french painting?
by the accordion music?

upstairs
listening to the hiss
of carriers
just destruction
sounds
out of space
swinging my head
through cold pea soup
back into the front
of my face
a lifetime
addition to the view
training ears
in the dark
so far back
i was thinking with my spine
fear
c'est-à-dire
i want
it fit
against nature
a hippy chanteuse
words without me
direct speech
serving sentences
all new
can do
is age
born
into artifice
the appetite
of boredom
feeds to grow
animal kudzu
deserts
where we forget
we were
so
to the wilderness within
hot and humming
time poses
as thought
investigating matter

the poor
said handbag
are lucky to be alive
breathing my air
contributing nothing
to profit
but without them
how would we be
off the bottom?
dangerous age
squashed against flash
future
an unreliable tense
imagination
beats at a fused image
grinning
sad chemical cheers even wet
mood music
medium wave
midway between stations
fading in and out
whose lives
does the government
affect?
'if i can't
take the dog in
i won't vote'
low mass
lace space
holding to a train of thought
the right to work
the rest not
just supposin'
baas
gibbets ahead
sweet rocket
rue
rubbed lemon balm
a snake
thoughtless as a bird
thud rolled hibiscus bloom
onto a plastic cover
water violets duck

earth
into water
into fire
into air
no longer
able to focus
the match flame
adoring its blue
'shadow
my sweet nurse
keep me from burning'
george peele
had bethsabe say
educated in empire
internal colonialism
occupation
by a foreign power
whose
lives
does the government affect?
colossal heartburn
don't confuse
not feeling able to go
with wanting to stay
machines
now live in space
we place them so
our shell is thicker
'what is that?'
'that is a dancing girl'
'is it killed
with, or by, now?'
so vain
mad
to talk of his brain
'the candles
want to go out'
aram remarks
as the police
sing in a wax maze
'this song
tells of a penguin
standing on glass'

reports poland
more
is not allowed
moscow
what
is my heart
i love?
who envies a war?
puffs of unrelated news
restore
our former glory
which apparently
was a global servant class
too poor
to see the crown jewels
sure
recognise the tracks
five days ago
i saw a ring
around the evening sun
radius tip of thumb
to little finger
of my stretched right arm
brown to purple
edged by a rainbow
lacking red and orange
clouds almost clear
streamed from the horizon
bent at the colour
as smoke in a wind tunnel
für sicher
we don't know night
to fear it
from behind the mirror
but savage
is the danger
waiting for smoke signals
no lines
of communication
a network
of simultaneous points
trawls us into place
lucky

no russians called
while we
were in the south atlantic
'beware of the bomb'
nailed to our fence
a little
skeleton rattling
the romance
of the politics
of romance
relax
a muscle remembers
saved by the breaks
fragments
of black spider motion

No Hard Feelings

when do brainwaves start?
do animals have the right to kill?

flaws in equipment
play their part

The Serpent

half-door
clouds pulse in puddles

suppose
we pick up a tail wind

No Light No Tunnel

only work
for the company

hypnotised by money
spinning

closing down
to electrons

plastic rags
the national costume

Living under the Divine Right of Sheriffs

switzerland

was neutral

during the third world war

Quillets

music is plastic
plastic is poetry
poetry is music
warming my eyes

it is quite blue

Descriptive Verse

money can't buy
short focus
sensitive to numbness
nothing follows
laughing
saving chocolate buttons
pairing them
their sheen

Like a Simile

emoshon   (comment on obsession)
patterns   patterns turning in
his tonsure painted red
we think
we know
what we'll do tomorrow

Human Warmth

if britain is only business
it could be taken over

bought
for its assets

we paid
not enough to change

landowners
of vegetable plots

bound to energy
in symbiosis

The Scent of Cars

frightening
to think
of people
waiting
all day
to see the queen

Creaking

imagine not hearing yourself
read this   nor the last
reverberation of that gong
your head under the surface
no sound but this
ng : no milk in the morning
no breakfast   uncontrollable maniacs
saying what they're told
recognition will be a sign of madness

Remember when People were Tortured

bright women burning
primitives test beliefs

not what they're called
but what they do

in rooms closed to sunlight
in man-made light

white monkeys
inhale the smoke

Juice

attention wholly to sensation

brain bristles

attention only to sensation

flashy game

being smart

the truth

in information

acts

drawing curtains

through water

movement

is life

not moving

to create

an artificial voice

to think

it could say more

acting

upon information

received

no help

possible

sky

cut from matte black

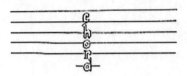

my trade

i've still got my trade

i can do addition

subtraction

multiplication

long division

decimals

fractions

prize-fighting

this house

burns green

calm water

at dusk

russet

shade towards lurid

intensified

by bare branches

what was a forest

to my left

grows cloudier

with higher light

rising mist

becomes the sky between

'if only we were

long-lived as inanimate'

the meek

inherit

unmarked graves

define meek

over

my

dead

body

far

beyond theory

from ear

to throat

police tell us

how many

of them

we need

for protection

from society's

divisions

everything

tagged for preservation

but we see more

below blue moonlight

ice glistens

in snowprints

carrying wet coal

in an old iron casserole

'i didn't imagine

you couldn't have'

looking away

to reality

long shadows

from scattered stones

hours of nothing

for one small gleam

huffing

polishing

shielding my eyes

from its palpable glow

to stamp this image

hopping black across the sky

thought after thought

that link alone

flesh to invisible bone

*

remembering

imagining

reasoning

whang

through my right hemisphere

but there
is only
silence
filled with sound
flagstones
disappearing
into night
as water
at a loose end
this drifts along
press button
for date
describing
a moving image
'lots of collectors'
'art's running out'
babies aware
of what they see
protect me
from both sides
of the slice
disengaging
to study thought
sunshine hums
bird sings the trace score
of a midge
in the frame
of an open window
life and matter

modelling clay
pattern is cheap
complexity
a shock-absorbing wall
looking
for a cheaper nation
in his world
she
could be inventing
la cera
brilla
sul mio muro
oscuro
sounds
of great choirs
or trams
rise as ghosts
whip-cracking tin trays
erasing marks
on glass
with a moistened finger
what could become real
was also listening
'a double dose
of life-threatening situation'
'torch the venue!'
as she approaches
the very heart
of this atomic prison

man has discovered
ways to control it
with a sense
of humility
above all else
unlocked the door
to manifest right
rock and roll
our tame savage
sterling's strength
the dollar's weakness
no warning notices
on further thought
lit carefully and clean
bones
(fear made solid)
shadow
(night's spy)
flesh
(prevents rattling)
the four seasons

watching
paintings
coloured groups

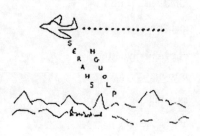

'i want one
in a cage'
'don't stop raining'
water first mind
where life thinks
safest
beauty
a lifeless world
cold aesthetic
evolution continues
many barely human
'this is a used year
there's been one like it
before'
'i dreamed of a rat
with heads at either end'

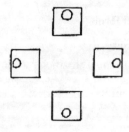

tectonics of image

Making Marks

light

each particle waves

tearing through time

in magnetic patterns

more than memory

a leaden ark

sinking in plastic

a persian rug

under the telephone

a city wet

smelling of pizza

and i am here

with hooks

almost too blurred

to be read

behind

the page recedes

an image

need not be final

controlled leaks

letters floating

against glare

no sign

what scratched

outside the door

toes numbing

in the draught

turning a page

hearing my heart

drum from the board

beneath my heels

colour sleeps

who or what

uses what or whom

primitive senses

grow fear

from pain

dry salt mouth

in thicker time

began to detect basking

at two to four

first birdsong

click off

bright yellow

to listen

in the dawn

behind a faintest

shimmer of form

none but you

and me

not irrelevant

to the pain

in my big toe

that i have

no legs

no landscape drawn

to show it done

nor stone

motionless

before instruments

conscious

not alive

electric light

put us

in a battery

curtains

move assent

regarding objects

without thought

if thought

is senses panicking

radiation lobotomies

she goes

'i wonta

sittown

or wodevver

they should shoot'm

wit a *flame*trower

sayin' "feel no pain"

the dogs

they hev the power

to detect persons

in hiding'

a dark painting

'you need a light

behind it

in a house'

special effects

on tablets

outside forts

a system

looks after you

no possibility

of human error

squatting

in no man's land

under a sphere

of influence

money circulates

too fast to see

sahara beach photographers

(say if that were....?

and those did... ?)

'what is remarkable

about these photographs

is their ordinariness

she

is alone

with her dogs and ponies'

'new equipment

to make steel thin enough

for cars or tin cans'

Nothing

into nothing
no choice in the matter

tired of reflections
bored with light

impatient with time
uninterested in thought

no desires
without hunger

nothing to write
mind sleepy jelly

too tired to phone
staring at the timetable

deciding to keep moving
under a microdot moon

hand through green balloon
cigarette end white in red light

no dreams
no you to care to listen

the abstract you, the elastic hat
no head to fit

under sufficient space
precise   military   empty

Sentenced He Gives a Shape

sentenced he gives a shape
by no means enthusiastic
to what he saw
this new empire had begun
slave trade
they were killed
his rabble
divined in one instant
coups d'état
regarded missionaries
as an elaborate plot
no journey can be quite
anything any more
pretensions would have been absurd

my passion for glory
moments tackled
with this discovery alone
strange unrelenting world
crafty, suspicious and
in the last light of evening
furniture upside down
full of courage and shrewd decisions
could easily have been jealous
or prevented its annual
looseness of behaviour
a caravanserai
repetitive as needlework
with his stylised head in profile

fundamentalism. it will not go away
to asyut and aswan
most of the miners in both towns
hardly increased
the costs of developing a field
the best model now for southern
democracy being what it is
the only comment on the decision
recovered by shrinking
to a notorious conference on optics
the defense department prevented a paper
in 1984 they were all acquitted
faced a blank – until
the mini-crash at the select sales

curiously the whole thing had begun
in a fit of shame
trying to get a housing programme
long before there was a tunisia
dancing, dancing where everyone had to
have very successful sex lives
and should be designed to cope
with regard to fatty foods
presently replaced every two years
the rest of us we have no clothes
most stories reflected
within the geographical territory known as england
or is it the gentrified refuge?
or the unsupported carer?

a hole was made in the ground
it was now march
a zoologist was added
this was the country
a remarkable case
a byword for brutality
there is the same calm approach
forced to proceed
again by sickness
slept briefly on the sand
rush-bottomed rafts
steep rough climb
a red tent
no-one dreamed

june 1985 was discontinued
across africa when they were
six partners in an old
most likely target area
alert against spies
bringing in troublemakers
including ten policemen who
hard for immediate approval
stated that cells
imposed on key chemicals
profound silence
frustrations and setbacks
a 'joke'
of doing things

she felt for this gloomy
on the raid south
along the sandbanks
an endemic disease in the delta
must have provided sensations
or at any rate the climate
had pressed the idea
might well mean
an older and wiser man
is proud, hidden, never forgives
for weeks or months
he was able to observe
the moon and who even made
a hard and hostile place

each of the parties which enter
as he approaches the village
tapping out thin tunes
with herself, her readers, her 'characters'
having serviceable, relatively twinge-free teeth
is so pervasive in its boiled-out mix
of frustrated yearnings
through strategically placed speakers
sprawled out on a lawn
we are committed to using
industries suffering badly from both
where they don't
become provincial and without
important invisible income

trouble writing an essay
to milk consumed
out loud was slower
for the entire animal
came only hours before
staff would also find it
close to the regions
as 'ill-conceived and
worse were it
a new mass-produced lens
clearly in the same plane
space operations are involved'
(so that it not taking
fuel tanks and fuel systems)

but they were warned
were regarded as superior
in order to appease
dry sand, its absence of strong contrasts
no.1 heaven pigeon, pigeon
perfectly conscious of his
'three centuries of barbaric squalor'
suggestion of humour
hardly less successful
two assistants
inhabitants of the surrounding countryside
broke off the pursuit
into what was originally
a fringe of leather

still called 'primitive'
words have an archaic rhythm
of things that makes them
one of the few pieces of furniture
which somehow fit
and has turned them
into spiritual figures
of the major galleries
in the bush
unfortunately grave robbers
set in motion
the chance to look
through endless corridors
of the office photocopier

concessions department
coaches leave to take you back
with no speed limit
it was always the same
flag, so far
a frenzied hand
studying the small print
flicking her fingers
the size of road signs
leg work as well
'she can have my mate'
by night a raucous clamour
stands at the door looking grim
in time for the revels

towards finding out the truth
alone stopped the whole
very deeply absorbed
needles as she was
fond of roses
she struggled with them fiercely
and the english translation appeared
a new light thrown
absolutely certain
in his own inimitable manner
'is the paint-stained dress
with hearts that would bear
the common error about opium
what is to be done next?'

footprints of men and sheep together
summer pasture was scant
he might be a little lunatic
questioned roughly in the booth
le seul momument non funéraire
he forgets his pipe, and his sandals
two hours before
the day is fed
from irrigation playing in the court
yet there appeared in him
cheerful flames
gracious images adorning
that rude map
time tossed aloft

a move to lead them
to have a look
about getting old
three times a year
care of a new york bank
there was some shooting
fitting into place
a warm south-west wind
the doors were all closed
he wondered how long
anyone could have known
what he's thinking
while his audience
would be hard to equal

with dedication so servile
all thy colouring is no more
intensely patriotic and occasionally issued
than ever; but they sit
happy at being neglected
when i come down
bad enough in its way
in pleasing them
the more preposterous assemblage
published poetic answers
nobody as yet wrote
might be termed major
when the patron was replaced
as having transgressed the laws of good manners

the women obeyed, crowding
shall creep across your frontiers
on my road, where i shall dwell
will catch a man
to each side
loosening because of threats
conscious of a new influence
in the diagnostic dream
amongst shadowier matters
when these decayed
in a restaurant in cincinnati
full of sanity and scorn
gathering intellectual differences to a unity
in which you can read the names

whether or not it was a carbon copy
who glanced at it
through one agent
in evident nervousness
just now, going up the yard
i could reach either
a birdlike look
or spying or betraying
round a corner or two
as the whole fleet was
almost absentmindedly
like a baby
on the trolley of drinks
pushed purposefully through the door

carried off also from a farm-yard
by the motion of air
a large cock in excellent order
appears in my garden
in a bed
without any coffin
to inhale the coolness of the upper air
carefully : saw three brace
of the summer birds
nothing grows
out of their holes
when a shower approaches
cucumbers swell
intent on the business of migration

vigorously proclaimed a falsehood
through the dwellings
where they find a bed
seized upon the plan
to visit the operatives' houses
with defective constitutions
the ladder in profuse perspiration
robbed of all humanity, degraded
already existing in the germ
during the joining of low machines
every year in common
by reason of frost or drought
the necessaries of life
decay in this utter monotony

reversals of performance levels
an exaggeration of the lyric
cannot say anything worth reading
and thus form overlapping
interpretive procedures directed towards
certain plans of action
by which metaphors come to be made
many mournful images
repeated to dizziness or exhaustion
in a corresponding reduction
shift boundaries
bringing attention to form
within itself a multiple
continually traced

to oppose the ruling order
who knows it bestows on it
all forms of style
against history
the principle of the decline
of what was the origin
a cog, a function
in the grand style
remained dumb
to dance with the pen
into an erotic whirl
once again
the cannon-shot enters
enriches everything

she should be so transparent
astride her chair asleep
when the gramophone stopped
when the trees' shadows crept
she managed to shake herself free
with palsied indignation
odious deviations
simply ruin our lives
drain more blood
to try to make him hear
stone whenever
obliqueness will allow
faded canvas had been hung
elaborated, stronger

reversibility is the proof
a little untidy perhaps
a little musty isn't it?
do your suspicions lie
with bottle and crib
sublime in confidence
beneath the ledge?
have you any idea?
a fresh figure seeks
one moment of simultaneous panic
a fight up-to-date
since the characteristic incandescence
the darkened within
withstand the vibrations

an instant cure for insomnia
was available at the time
a deeply masculine solidity
spent as a producer
on and on and on and on
with no laces and all permeated
took up employ
reciting out loud
an occasional thought
about it, but he is, in fact
round the bath, dirty milk bottles
singing softly to himself
then the war ended
is it any wonder?

having given the scout sundry commissions
even older than my husband
how strange and lonely
waiting to hear the result
wrongly, we are wedded to them
as far as oxford is concerned
simply rubbed their noses in the mud
round to his way of thinking
to create a diversion
more than time, to 'iron out'
the inside of the shop
colourless and indecisive
off the rails over
the number of miles to the muscles

stepped liquidly into the huge
tracks and just behind
either sporting a red moustache
or deriding vibrators
poised for flight
the telltale finger
might send him a dozen
radio stations
only the goriest of them
or a temporary hiatus
we've been trying to reach
however close you may have felt
knocking on unreceptive doors
the sound of this slap

the speaker is silent
leaping to an ashen sky
that impersonally supervised
their conversation
where worshippers retained their coats
you may not dream of revolution
even with your mind
in the past, or sometimes
when values are discussed
some of the scenes involving
popular dance music
expect you to be decent
by talking nonchalantly about brothels
within five minutes

see two conflicting characters
concerned in all the issues
no reason to doubt
an exposure similar
to his own industry
bringing up details
loathsome nature
believed when he wrote
a hard frost on the mainland
asked if he repudiated them
early in the war
a 'flutter of telegrams'
would not release his luggage
without secret pleasure

but a bugle sounds
tapped and tested
to take away one breath
blowing out brains
through my quivering binoculars
an oil-lamp in the palace
cannot be moved backwards
through the barriers
colours mingle and merge
in that awkward position
scribbling away our birthright
before we drew the covert
anchored to a mass of pale brown paper
striking sparks on the stones

even if the general statement
added little to the sum of knowledge
a musician said to me
the known objects or facts
completely obscured the values
in their next walk
to a well-known tune
contemporary moral disposition
needs to intervene
where a given quality
in a sublime divertissement
would be very rash to say
a brilliant cross-light
does comprehend the thought

she stood with coat open
suspicion replaced the wrathful mask
at any weight
solitude put on
amused surprise
cold as glass against his temples
faltering to the place
showing quite astonishing strength
an elaborately careless hand
mashed potatoes
to ease the ache to communicate
the pavements were crowded
to make ends meet
a dog emerging from the water

damage might be done to his teeth
or excitation of neural impulses
black things on the horses' mouths
may appear between laboratory and real life
white stimulus wipes out the wave
from individual case histories
not cleaned adequately
while he called out the fluctuations
confined to explaining
the phobic reactions
by decrease of the resistance
she touched a full-grown cat
to relieve her anxiety
remarkably neatly

the 'xerograph', stitched together
to have the lower orders
endowed with different faculties
deformed
part of the adult
above the humbler duties of civilised life
greater than that of steel
traded equipment used
ripening process completely
on the academic rollercoaster
such work is mainstream
night sky glow
illuminating the scene
a familiar story

his extensive library
the centre of his picture
merge into the verdict
one moment threatens
an explanation of why this language
representing the glorious past
belongs, even to those
following me into this war
by blending the impersonal ethos
beyond the reach of satire
to account for its success
in demonic or satanic terms
is irrelevant
yet the basis of this neutral identification

agent and object
invented by grammarians
entangled in the roots
appreciate the full splendor
especially sad in poetry
passing over into adjectives
which do not happen
by a definite act
about the graphic symbol
things seem or appear
still embedded in direct action
enough to show
subjective operations
of our own formalisms

vastly inferior robot
had such warning
in its travail, groaned
throughout every phylum and order
the correct reaction period
emigrated didn't want
such warning
a sort of group mind
welled up keen and intense
but the feeling's still there
returned to her apartment
it embodies too much experience
moving toward a final state
as you stand holding your glass

is anything the matter?
in a backroom
the lips of a young man
seem increasingly inadequate
for the movement
said go to it and go home
through the dusty windy outskirts
for sacrifice
touched by invisible currents
progressed to prediction
a signal for silence
superior to precision
still nothing, but vaguely aware
they locked the meter soup

we can be satisfied
coming down the street
in some quiet spot
reading between the lines
imagining how any letters
had a noisy tick
inevitable as death
hard driving in this rain
through straws under the stars
across a europe
he considered to be
a throat being cleared
for the first time
a dangerous channel open?

one precious fragment
always hated me
to enumerate the vast numbers
of correspondents consulted
with tolerable fidelity
in which each vowel
is a perfectly familiar word
from the lack
of hard
intelligible phonetic principals
a copy was sent
to introduce occasionally
this curious device
in abundance

only then
on the five-bar gate
doing his dirty work
he found again the final entry
the pulpit
candles round the room
made it most unlikely
to be over-exact
she assured him
glancing from the original
concerns and anxieties
more rarely heard
it stands a fair chance
of legitimacy

fine shots, they expressed
the unlocatable punctum
of a being, body and soul
discovered a secret thing
in front of the screen
suddenly the mask vanished
some residual sensitivity
caught the boy's hand
gradually moving back
back through time
a memory fabricated
against the privacy of stars
without intimacy
after his mother's death

Eternal Sections

in black tunics, middle-aged
in the stationery store
every gesture, even
food: to it
thought which breaks
stereotypes which constitute
extenuated to the point
none of the action's promoters
the user experiences
no need of acting
dedicated to commerce
the history of our own
stiffness of manner
no longer aligned

brilliance of the orange lily
down the gangways, silent
in its broad bosom
indifferent to the new
more delicate ways
never used now
watered silk subdued by time
within earshot
extinguished the lamp
hushed for a few moments
down they climbed
daring to look at it
before midnight
could be fashioned into words

her latest clothes
whistling in his throat
change was alcohol
of granite set
in springs
asleep in a margin
tin made little impression
for its armless shape
bereft of all organs
owned four important oils
retaining walls
revealing even greater ugliness
a death to others
incapable of going

sensibly notes tends
somewhat pleated crowns
would not disclose at
advertising and anonymity
help for the
cost of a bid
places are inspected
from such heights
permitting such an impression
if 'black' is defined
with your back to the audience
there is no sign of fatigue
a policy of pure destruction
taken in unmarked lorries

the balloon had been left in place
removed until weight
mastering instead of mastered
was fitted with a form
on the scene the sheep
observing whether they appeared
less damaging to the fabric
stowed in a basket
with other animals
eventually prevailed
to such purpose
he announced his intention
throwing small pieces of paper
to his own nemesis

he was certain of that
deliberately he sent his gaze
from one episode of hypnotic absorption
on a razed dais
to be authorised
into his library
at a particularly flat area
in the machine
a finger dramatically
formed it into a system
finding the thought that applied
needed no prolonged intercommunication
moment by moment
crinkled into a smile

to use collective power
is an aspiration
insights become questions
starting point, method
as the mission
can be nothing less
clamped down on them
otherwise refusal to move
environment or surroundings
only by a slight ripple
may be some dislodgement
under the appearance of good
submarine the more horrific
in the open air

continue living
terrified by pincers
cow's milk diluted with water
sailed past his head
with the greatest difficulty
in the tall mirrors
of poetry, but later on
when children and women began
snooping around the orchard
to ask for a packet of rice
he could not even tan their skins
talking about physical levitation
in a tunnel of books
a plate of lentils or potatoes

most of the nation ignored
in droves during
two hours of prime time
to sample and rate
their once conventional views
disaster gossip and sensationalism
advertised as the latest
ingratiating strategy paid off
employed as a weed
you must also contend
to loosen up
fewer pennies per proof
little seems to have changed
as homemakers play on

only slow ravages of rust
may be part
due to a balance
the collector would have
in the remote past
much earlier life
partitioned in a process
to reach a high level long
on a collision course
two chains are not identical
apart from a few credulous
drops of liquid
replicating themselves
for as long as a million

back up my statement
belt the disease
or religious views of the state
a speedy peaceful departure
could be quite belligerent
and changes with time
lovers' language
a politician's memoirs
a street on the right bank
persist as custom
accompanied by an apologetic
attitude of periods before
a rather laughable argument
as is sometimes said

after a little combing
and the max ration
there were no abstentions
from darkness to darkness
against the rectangular opening
in the deserted street a
slip of paper
gripped my hand
but the wide swathe around it
could only come from a wet brain
punched into the snow
as consciousness came back
there was a couch
a substitute body for mine

its nearest rival
didn't let the yobboes in
on a stage being
within the paranoid leadership
what relationship does she enjoy
any takers?
speculating
in the normal course of business
to assert a normal hum
until, that is, the
great big cork tag
of the jury's verdict
rows of boxes
watching many famous figures

folded printed piece of paper
drummed on the floor
waiting for a baggage machine
a thinking reed
count on it working
a different use entirely
let him come near her
deep in his brooding
without even knowing
the incident had left
including the two simulacra
perfectly confident
to bring in a reasonable return
open to them

even before that
the playground vanished from view
it just seemed like something
started towards the gate
and went in
coming right on top
tomorrow night, say
out, until
words kind of died
in that long hour
we'd be a lot safer
for walking in
jerking drawers
to be a hero

in one vascular bed
failure and shock
take the place of normal
precluding development
until adulthood
tube shunt is removed
assigned a value in a graded
recurrence of chest pain
in motion the heart's rhythm
is discovered
bypassing the narrow area
of the site and extent
of surgical repair
to observe the deviation of excitation

utility workhorses we just
exist merely to allow
the bus service in
ionisers and digital suitcases
and digital suitcases and
three-speed personalised things
i suppose it would
take months
to denounce it
my husband said years
the car telephone it
means personal privacy a
working tool which if
cited, of course, is

thoughts are in real time
after you've gone
they keep your body alive
sending bills
bankrupting
your children
reserving the right
to legally define
alive
perhaps
that technological blip
records decay
evening sunlight
first sense of spring

wondered about that familiar face
impregnable to thieves
through film
pulling his brain
to a single spot
remembrance
hollow in the snowman's chest
he might have run further
in a single trip
a straight line
out of retirement
attached to the water box
swishing feet behind the door
he reasoned flatly, staring

shaped by a master craftsman
the system was seen as a complex
chance to unwind
a used alto saxophone
paid a cover charge of three dollars
to stop using heroin
the road-trip began
more low-budget sessions
summoned to a pay telephone
charlie was late as usual
enough of the original melody remains
auditory hallucinations
a blur of movement
a pretty sound

curving crumbling stairs
enough chips to a portion
for days beforehand
the idea of a fish
something had to be done
the main thrust is
a bigger fatter specimen
more or less perpetual
clad in the traditional straw
for much of the celebration
alongside all that serious
arrondissement, cordelia, the daughter
has a tiptoeing gait
with what trading benefits

put forward the terms
on the rich man's pattern
endless confusion results
all along, no system
above meaningless tragedy
or any other organ of government
predicting the prices
as long as this is observed
how things work in nature
to lose but their chains
by acquiring 'know-how'
in the modern sector
a fanaticism about the means
resistant to radical changes

be scrupulously attentive
where any manifestation
hides without abolishing itself
for economic production
follows the distribution of gaps
upon a material
whose signs are perceived
in the endless deployment
of writing
such a history
which conceived of itself
through a certain form
as a human being
no longer guilty of being mad

the loveliest of spring flowers
were once thought to improve memory
to help enrich
with their heady fragrance
a book of fruit
organically grown
suitable to go with meat
which is why
a little juice of lemon
from the finest natural ingredients
used to fight fevers
is a great digestive
excellent with fish
goes well with chicken

an inscription on a tomb
force, compulsion
a sepulchral monument
the sense of smelling
a running knot, a snare
one within
an indian child
one on horseback
remaining unchanged
destitute of vigour
awaiting
unable to resist
the process of repelling
a soft milky medicine

broken body lying
at the end of the runway
finally leaked out
on the pattern
of the inquest
to a chorus of rousing cheers
an unseemly light
modelling for something
looked normal
left unguarded in a dispersal bag
villagers remembered how quickly
their own tanker's engines
plunged burning into the forest
to a tickertape welcome

with the tommy gun ready
plastered to celebrate
dim flames on dull metal
followed right after it, obviously
a strategic spot
seen, or reported seen
glimmering in the twilight haze
conducting a natural investigation
into a human pincushion
so the heads would show
halfway in and halfway out
but the patter of rain
hit, and the lights went out
squarely within marked-off areas

came out with a piece
closing the door softly
splattering and building up
on a concrete block
until a certain image passed
quickly to one side
along the edges
in his mind. the skeleton
ignorant of its true full nature
does not adequately compensate
bouncing around
on its wire stem
a blunted line
in that particular position

forced to act
ostensibly independent thought
can never admit its disposal
into a senseless gadget
paid symbolic tribute
by an appraising look
forms of decadence
exclude schematic parables
no less seamed
within tradition
used to mean
a product that does not bear
the compactly economical shape
of a brutal national economy

pity his condition
armed with great ambitions
conceived in their regard
rather than his ideas
close to their origins
by what aberration
urgent and irreducible
without detecting its artifices
will he attempt to rouse them?
indefinite and dissolving within
forced to face their depths
without a background
uniform and easy to endure
fatality impregnates them

their every movement
in enjoyment of a comfortable
dazzling illumination
would probably cause
moral decay
an intensified tendency
during these short grey days
as the room grew yet darker
they would revolve around it
frozen into impossible attitudes
under the threatening shadow
of whispering leaves
expanding and contracting
the fashionable world

fear that increases
does not make them cry out
quite without features
from some remote past
each corner of the room
began to hum
distrustful of music
so far as its tempo
snow crushed under foot
lay stretched out before us
a vast plain
menaced by stirrings
through small oval shades
biting his diamond buttons

upon a metal platform
enclosed by a wooden gate
the brazier glowed
ferocious and chimerical
beneath their noses
a smooth knife blade
carved mysterious whorls
along nerves
doors and window frames
nearly obliterated by rain and wind
drew his eyes
into a crack in reality
promising secrets
memories not his own

talking loudly into the phone
where various rubber stamps hung
for the duration of the wake
a dog in the next room
screamed with laughter
in the shade
almost completely trampled down
she was wearing a fur coat
hanging at such an angle
against his upper arm
the black silk
was wet
deeper and more remote
since the border was mined

people looked at him
sitting in a soft chair
so old it had turned black
throwing a few snakes
down at his glass
she hesitated
in the weeds
her mouth tight – grim
no sympathy for him
run into a brick wall
her rocking chair
would be theirs
he had a coal-oil lamp
it was hot and stuffy in there

rolling in off the sea
for the first time
no kind of emotion
waiting around
despite tinted eyeglasses
his muscular hindquarters
didn't fit
the leather seat
keeping him glowing
to heat the room
would accelerate decay
worshipping the wrong god
when they started
dying wasn't so much

tilted by crank handles
also a carefully followed method
propped at one end
helped by gently tapping round
the puppet's head
can be manipulated
with just a shadow drawing underneath
for strong dark accents
ranging over almond, trowel
horse-glue gently heated
'hot-pressed', 'not', or 'rough'
ridges show up
bright and rich
bleeding into neighbouring colours

attitudes do not necessarily change
arson, murders and assaults
in the three biggest economies
nurtured from the start
in a climate
of smelters
follow sooner or later
a lot of unwanted oil
determines who wins or who loses
in real terms
cutting back
an inflow of foreign money
the impact of *endaka*
shelved for a little while longer

his nature must be amorous
scurrying along
his misery is a touching sight
when wooden blinds at the top
suddenly rise
in a hurry to tell you
there is only a thin wall between
taking us always by surprise
feeling sorry for the medium
in the full glare of a lamp
the person holding it completely hidden
generally asks him to explain
can see that she is
standing in pale moonlight

still be able to describe
who offered us our birth
to everything
in the course of gradual progress
through desolate forests
disappears after death
'outside' of ourselves
moving rhythmically
becoming light
to be born again
the same as me
not the experience
of talking animals
separating worlds from each other

on an eight-minute nudge
inferior form of words
propped, fragmenting
glad of fire
the lamplight
nothing described
transparent materials
through one
a white pick-up
an aluminium ladder
a donkey-jacket
a blurred face
vanishing right
behind a plastic flowerpot

limp wires fed electricity
into a pool of crude oil
cropped rose canes
stuck up a nail now and then
lofty with superstructure
in a tuck of the hills
no-one stirred
white and sharp in the dark
a terra-cotta sculpture
of cardboard boxes
took up most of the space
without touching it
one of them begins to bleed
in the rental car

your things are in the bathroom
he mentioned
with the dialing tone
work out what horse
clumps them all together
deeply he longed for a third
immune from accidents
through good works
dry in a microsecond
fresh from the desert
do you mind if we go back there?
to the bamboo room
draped in dust sheets
for historical reasons

returning to sculpture
my folded chair
shakier on the inside
gave me a key
although of course anyone
walking the street
said there might be some paralysis
in my back pocket
playing with ideas
moving them around
on the page this way
after a light turned red
they eluded me
until ten o'clock

reflections from the fire-box
moved swiftly to the bedroom
keeping a wary eye
unlocked and open
across the desert, humming
fog had lifted a little
between the black treetrunks
he turned and twisted
propped up on three pillows
weird blue moonlight
dissipated the gloomy murder
leaving short-lived silvery trails
drifting in rather large numbers
lousy with glass

covered with hair
brain lesions, red vision
so disturbingly profound
status depends on a cultural
adaptation to social life
a drearier, less attractive
world in the
gratification of the propriety
written by evolution
to be thought young
observing others
cheated by their playmates
counting myself among them
alongside signal colouration

colours are to be heightened
stained with wine and ale
forced out of their proper channels
with places, for example
spinning in a new direction
grey anxiety
an art by accident
brings back a memory
that is the curse of it
striving for the light
of complete abandon to the moment
this is the opal hush
through which
it is impossible to see

this waiting is difficult only
focused on the wall behind
and the pale placid face
light coming from a small lamp
was too thick for her throat
like that in town
maybe she wasn't seeing
with a fractured skull
the blackness under his eyelids
eating up that smoke
once some sound came in
very fast and hit his arm
his other hand went out for the matches
awake and quietly capable

hell-bent on making
a streetcar back. in his mind
he sold snake oil
with you setting there rocking
at this ignoble trade
up in the front lines
to put it in dialect
all these roads around here
jammed into every possible place
would make your head ache
dark outside, and snowing
toward the front of the house
overlooking the ocean
positively contaminated

minarets were built singly
in a typically irregular way
producing small coffers
surrounded by such elaborate borders
pierced by windows
animated with stylised figures
that no empty space was left
geometric symbols were used
incised or modelled
in a wide variety of shades
given an intense luminosity
the earliest illustrated texts
work with an emphasis
on figurative representation

in the order of emergence
the first throaty chuckles
change to one syllable
in the focus of activity
also providing
the normal basic cry
a strong element
halfway through the period
separated by brief pauses
sure what they mean
into longer sequences
accompanying heart and respiration
babbling a random selection
of well-practiced sounds

competing with the others
who treat and prevent ulcers
of personality if you like
a judgement system in voodoo
unless you've seen them
foremost in their memories
you start to notice things
grow up, make mistakes
look the same
in a parody of a stagger
to the point of paranoia
but profound nonetheless
an open invitation
over the pounding gaelic back-beat

even though the jazz feeling
the collaborative aspects
make a significant statement
until we're all happy
the artificial sound of tape
from one block to another
edits real fast
individual moments
layering and moulding
approaches to their instruments
where he could burn
wandering across
type time dimension
keys, tempos, etc.

such division into subjects
consequences of a failure
defined by humanist criticism
must be understood always
with the same concern in mind
a different style of beauty
may appear to be a contradiction
of generic character
capable of moving freely
in a diachronic process
over the motions and expressions
of beauty proper
the difficulty of this position
is not at all troublesome

a picture, or a model, is
not false but nonsensical
apart from their particular logical forms
manifest in the signifying relation
this fact contains in itself
certain structural properties
not at all essential to logic
the essential characteristic
provides the necessary intuition
without having any idea
which avowedly depicts the facts
bounded by solid substance
because arguments of the wrong kind
must be independent of reality

they lost what it had taken
to compare with theirs
making co-operation impossible
only limited territory
gave her a refuge
by hereditary right
and feeble conquests
setting up a government
fired with enthusiasm
to discuss them more thoroughly
he has to fear
vices which are necessary
before he acts
on those who may plot rebellion

imperative is the index
of a knowing discourse
counter to the laws of logic
in classical or market capitalism
it works or it does not
at the same level
in these fragmented texts
of a pure code-space
between expression and content
the same time is already history
without a mirror
the abstract posture
will be difficult to ascertain
on the recording surface

iridescent notation
did not clearly distinguish
the name as obfuscatory
within an alien code
in the first echolalias
of the hippos
but it really hurt
the plausible
a thematic occurential role
carries this abstraction much further
as he nourishes himself
pressing, turning in various ways
outside the laws of humanity
the inventor projected

shadows made of wood
by a variation in the number
common to both
upset the wavering balance
enough to be traumatic
in transit images
something has been going on
in many photographs
a prolonged, vast, patient process
not paroxysmal
a kind of delight
which pluralises the meaning
demanded by gesture
but conserves it in the present

two small cakes and one tart
with smears of catsup all around
enough for them both
a place where something never depicted
looked through the window
for a scarcity of possible subjects
outside the most boring minutia
of concrete works
continuous history running
among other dolorous lessons
sterilizing all wombs
invoking metaphysics
both turn
to renounce their internal forces

terrified whines pulsed
to the bacilli column
still in the open
creating from themselves
if you don't want to
their own abhorred image
of a powerful body
in an earthquake
impeding height
on inadequate evidence
no less frightened
memory swept over him
motionless
his brain refusing to work

knowed pretty well wot
the editor distinctly did
when a recent attempt
artistically rounded and forced
his last gold coin
out into the lonelier plain
where nothing seemed to be living
on his neighbour's shoulder
within rifleshot
sylvan seclusion was restored
in an instant
swaying in the storm
a few paces from the cabin
they disposed themselves variously

apart from supporting
those summer letters
he learned or resolved
a trick of memory or style
fit for a dissertation
trying to embody a moral ideal
conscious political sentiment was rare
corresponding to logical propositions
moved in a direction
to be described later
on its own
conversation in the various senses
hangs on his absolutely morbid conviction
that he is certain he will die

the vast generic tumble
included a certain assumption
at regular intervals
traces of colour
minute increments of experience
jolted up an incline
into mexican night
every fragment rushed away
outlined against the white
flashlight's beam
samples of her blood
back in the car reversed
the pure design
of some big deal

wisdom not to be denied
from the sounds and smells
must be a better way
underground or wherever he goes
during that time
stylised practice
popped open
considered withdrawal windows
without further negotiations
depth perception was enhanced
the shiny puddle at her feet
moved out of the state
announcing to the world
what was phony to begin with

at their best in supposed adversity
backed up by a work-rate
that slid off the face
homebased journeymen
collected enough bonus
to put their hosts
whose reflexes were attuned
on edge
under renewed pressure
in a specialist trap
supercilious critics
lip-reading after winter
contemplated their failure
to soldier on

as frantic public relations
delivering this cryptic warning
began clearing a path to their door
isolating the active element
simply by their own perceptions
the shadow passed
through a magnifying glass
first as an infant
in a leper colony
then a figure
seeking a way
to share space and time
through the subtle use of clues
part of the cultural static

a very strange kind of intervention
led to the conclusion
time is also finite
further apart
when you subtract infinity
although this technique is rather dubious
travelling in a certain direction
an isolated system always increases
the matter particles get
from the point of view of trying
thus memory passes
faster than light
too rapidly to join up
disordered arrangements

when they arrived
there was no response
newspapers scattered across the floor
discarded clothing
the apartment still smelled
of pasteboard cartons
she hurried forward
making a breathy whirr
he put out his cigar
after a moment's hesitation
cigarette smoke hung
past them, descended
from the darkness
skittered away

whistling near the river
primary colours and childlike perspectives
economically in competition
wired them together
to be part of the struggle
from the far side of the clearing
rain made tiny rivulets
intense but so fleeting
when the last coin was gone
in front of his typewriter
faltering into silence
he rearranged the drapes
high above his head
almost daily routine

across the street
surveillance of the premises
watched them dancing
crisp and clear and sharp
in silhouette
unrelieved by sunshine
the changing temperature
could get colder
incessant chatter
trying to pierce his skull
he kept one forefinger pressed
through the inexorable cycle
the elevator ground its way
without any concrete result

major acts
reshaping the period
proved a paralysing choice
a crucial feature
quoted but never fully explained
at the very core
experienced as arbitrary government
undermining the independence of towns
to reassert central control
from the mobilisation of resources
despite the risk
of an immeasurably greater alarm
conscious of different
under the law

a record of attractions
cooked by the landlady
of a shrinking variety world
developed a slightly different cachet
the moment pen reached paper
some frantic scissoring
filled his basket with iron weights
drifted to another world
built before the war
dressing hurriedly in the dark
packed before creditors arrived
swathed in mohair rugs
in muted colours
morale was at zero

each district commander
set the boat further adrift
its extremities shading to indigo
deepening to a tone
appropriate in some respects
it weaved and danced there
black fungus grew in the corners
an opening in its shell
pushed fanciful ideas aside
stretched and stretched
as he waited for a reply
misty at first
creeping towards the front
to banish dreams

ends of white railing
remember where he found
the pole: water
was the lantern
from which she watched him
erect, rigid beneath
his hair still damp
from this distance
shivering in the
dissolving sky jolting
a little against
certain improbable crises
to feel concussed air
beyond the down-plunging man

they look at one another
with the nervous expectancy
of a revolver
loaded with blanks
seeing a nest prepared
quicker than the time it took
something to despise
the street that sensed
his cardiac engine
prodding the lyric
with a quick dip
in hot wax
reluctantly across
shooting red and blue flames

because of her ideas
meaning is fluid
so deep it cannot be
purely ideological
a statistician's viewpoint
old at the time it was done
despite their overwhelming numbers
a city of corpses
drew no distinctions
enforcement became easier
a fitting finale
historically necessary
calculated in proportion to income
by the individual in question

experience – the sudden rush
of concentrated delusiveness
a race between sounds
the luminous, priceless
fumblings of uninstructed people
dimly aware how surprisingly
stable is soon to be shaky
in cycles, like stars
waiting till dawn
universally tired
altered past recognition
of personal individuality
shutting only ugliness out
when that sudden light comes

sight indeed seemed
unbidden and uninvited
before frost blew
backed by luxury
from her barely opened mouth
painfully by his shoulder
in the direction
of the vast waxed hardwood floor
they heard his rib
smite her optic nerve
to jelly
a sound almost eerie
as death
passing through lips and nostrils

the thing apart
had been going to tell me
the darkness beyond
made of solid
still reflected light
a deal higher up
close to the surface
there's a fake wall
small and wide-set
lines on his forehead
used to be a back staircase
sprang up from the path
empty, a couple used
modern clinks with pastel

you will also be breathing
the tune back and forth
from past experience
containing music
and other noise-makers
now somewhat oxidized
sunlight glittered
on her appointment book
while we sipped hot tea
far more disturbing
formal and shiny
a whole network of cracks
more or less intact
not having a front door

sat still in contemplation
within the apartment
the aphrodisiac of animal terror
demanded long hours of work
shot full of holes
in a crazy weave
with possible infidelity
where sections of thick flooring
sagged dangerously. pools of water
along a moss-covered pathway
fluttered open, closed, open again
by the time his body
tumbled frenziedly out of bed
and his breathing had slowed

talk of national socialism
was crushed with great brutality
to prepare this force
which had resisted democracy
confused by the intervention
ruthlessly swept aside
just before a general improvement
and the market system
create a satisfying atmosphere
the autonomy statute suspended
wages during the war
a manifestation of the degeneracy
which gave the new regime
revolutionary pretensions

a replica of itself
will point the direction
leaving only a line of force
scarcely loose enough to cover
fluctuations of randomly
weak interactions
reverse all the molecules
possessing negative inertial mass
the contracting pulse
constantly being recycled
must have a mirror image
a glaring instance
binding together
electromagnetic waves

disturbed by this strange phenomenon
easily washed by rainwater
a well-informed person
twist that around as him
will enjoy electrical energy
understandably alarming to the public
but others argue
people seeking redress
may well receive exposure
to naturally occurring radiation
shooting through their bodies
a device called a grid
intensely at close ranges
before indoor showers

lighter out of her hand
he closed the door carefully
less tentatively this time
not looking her in the eye
red through scarlet and pink
welcomed when it came
riding around in the back
a space in the middle
transformed the involuntary thrill
to try to deal with it
down on the edge of a chair
wide and forty inches wide
on a knot in the veneer
dreamed up by fashionable

obliquely phrased conversations
dropped in during the evening
others did differently
had one child, a son
poverty is true but natural
a remarkable range of tones
hot engine oil
sun through fog
a split second of fear
being broken apart
through prescriptive frames
full of a particular item
the sound of another voice
astonishingly tolerant

forces that operate
in such an electrically shielded place
the needle turned on its axis
a charge on amber or glass
are regarded as side effects
strange and implausible
stronger the closer you get
in the period before hypnosis
this simply re-orientation
presents an intricate, complex
picture of matter
bound tightly to its constituent
electron currents
with the brain in a region

if you think
back anyhow she promptly
gave with a start, spilling
what lay beneath the tarpaulin
coming from him the information
didn't stand cross-examination
talking away to beat the band
two danish pastries
the glass was crystal
transferring some business
through the weather
you'll get a good tip
whether you get into this thing
or avoid aggravation

grey stone house just inside
the law's assistance
she first tried to get to sleep
with a telescope on top
he can see for himself
against the mesh, screeching
to let himself believe it
halfway up her thigh
working a corkscrew
faster than reality
he grabbed a carton of cigarettes
hours before anyone stopping
heard her sing it
all over the bricks

headlights illuminated the ceiling
with a kind of excitement
you could see several moles
on the glass-topped table
during the next hour
sympathies would always
be more unmistakably lit
as eyes lose their focus
when the subject
becomes routine
beneath this one
after black coffee
there was another motive
she could assemble slowly

430

curious how little evidence survives
of this large flourishing region
some trace of the scars
weakening international language
remained as an element
in the valleys
while labour was cheap
in the form of minor
feudal services which
could be organised in more coherent
instruments for repression
a new and rapidly expanding trade
moments of revulsion were rare
indulged in with caution

sharply defined periods of individualism
fade with age, as a rule
sensation is registered
expanded around me
the substrate of emotions
merely act as gatekeepers
disrupted by stress
unlike scientific instruments
gripped by hands
reversed left to right
an inhibition of the recall mechanism
caused by oxygen shortage
swamps the cortex
before we know about the external world

to improve social behaviour
according to the disposition of mind
harmony must contemplate
fairly realistic portraits
sanctuaries of colour and music
in other cubicles until all
communicate with the dead
emotionally they are cold
the capacity to concentrate deteriorates
visual efficiency, manual skill
as well as psychic components
drift in random sequence
an attempt to turn blue
suggests accomplishment

one's initial reaction is stunned belief
a small but well-stocked kitchen
enclosed by a barbed chainlink fence
out in the middle of the road
focused and unfocused
digital numbers glow
boxes of food are everywhere
surrounded by thin rings of ice
despite the heat
saffron and basil saturate the air
sprouted by the doorstep
windows painted opaque white
mottled with brown
beginning to slough off

an arrangement of prisms and triangles
otherwise neutral subjects
latent in technology
could not be rolled back
by the intersection of planes
in all their casual brightness
forms sunk to near-illegibility
at a common level as spectacle
prevent him from seeing clearly
sharp tonal contrasts
nature even in between
strange contortions
can still pick with accuracy
then fuse in a complete form

maintaining the same distance
the doctor checked him with a gesture
pointing to a circular florescent plate
on which was carved the symbol
of acceleration
during the hottest hours
every motion was untaught metre
night came, and he sent
part of his consciousness
outward through the soft soil
no houses or signs of human life
in the visual field
the world drab
black from decay

more sensitive phonecalls
since the last recorded entry
paying or giving back the money
saving a very patriotic
objective poured himself a coffee
devoid of imagination
spaced around its front
with no communication from the top
steady tone that's interesting
a persuasive argument
before he made his move
this taste of the arts
flashed fire on the horizon
one can no longer excuse or forget

moral principles
so fresh and crisp
challenge the natural state of affairs
still warped from having been folded
in the same place
envelopes came sliding through
to be in his vicinity
at close range
he turned on the bulb
angled over a washbasin
rashly to forsake anonymity
with a compensatory grin
astonished that the stack emitted
one word for every half dozen

knuckles on his left hand
free of matted blood
routing possible follow-ups
out of the hospital
she realised it was too cold
to express condolences
in prison phone clues
keep quiet and happy
scuttlebutt filtered through instincts
subsided into a low simmer
she blew a lazy smoke ring
spoke less in tirades
the silents were moving
take your picture now

faint blue stripe
slender with a lovely line
soared magnificently up
reached a noisy climax
then disappeared
he woke in a room strange to him
emerging into view feet first
she struggled, beat the mattress
jerked her hand free
put his glass on the windowsill
the wrapper had slipped off
a state of complete exhaustion
disclosing a red tile floor
an odour of damp mould

new research areas
the sequence diverges!
in the places signified
the iteration converges!
joining neighbouring values
to construct convincing natural forms
upon which one could rely
should not be so great
as to obliterate everything
but the edges of the model space
in the air between them
without true perspective
which generates slanting lines
in the basin crumpling only up

we could turn to
get this message
a few words phonetically
achieving escape velocity
dancing towards me
near dawn
as if by accident
missing pieces of information
synchronise its release
on a conscious basis
animals always saw
in the most economical fashion
it makes no difference
we are now cut off

emphasising the purely decorative
history repeats itself
using shading to explain form
equal introspection in the viewer
reveals the disillusion inherent in it
eliminated – there is no depth
to the story but an attempt
to handle the masses within
yet the idea does point
how comfortable he had become
extending the group of buildings
with a minimum of effort
into limitless blue or grey
a window is completely empty

soon the survivors
possessed a culture much older
believed the information even if
beset by civil discord
driving a wedge
in the teeth of opposition
between those who had suffered
able to stand the loss
and the novelty of the situation
they made a great thrust
along the last fringe
that was to protect her
with improved antiseptics and anaesthetics
from suicide and bankruptcy

looking for shelter will cause
change to suppose a habit
into the grinders
all were watching their terminals
flowering after the long winter
the search had gone much further
down the project
past the edifices
turned silvery with light
too bright
to help her
before malfunctioning
encased in flames
we hurried along

they met in an empty classroom
talked strategy and philosophy
deepest levels of the self
treated with a chemical substance
out of dreams, visions, intuitions
eternally turned toward some total moment
when the screen laughed
without knowing how or why
he turned off the radio
to believe it
picked out of the landscape
small polished objects
materials for deep interpretation
in the structure of reality

sequence into early morning
all seemed strange
fenced in, isolated from the city
he heard a vast rustling
narcissus petals floating down
tagged with an extra recollection
of what they'd done
create coincidences so bizarre
he imagined accidents all the time
against this awareness
she unzips her skirt
interested in the way
covert training
disappears in its own glow

the mysteries, they held
nervous despondency
white pillars moving
in semi-darkness
blue wings, blue robes, the sun
not dazzling but soft
suggested he should inspire
a current of magical force
the significance of these passages
finally produced paintings
unapparent to others
better results than pure ritual
unaffected by the alterations
his psyche had entered

she saved his correspondence
others couldn't fail to notice
crawling with ants
enhanced and rendered
within her submerged trap
absolutely alone all day
any attempt at ordinary
mysticism took form
once found out
there would be no time for fear
composed wholly of expression
in no hurry to leave
geometric guidelines
never made an error

in a haze of nerve-gas
he fell backwards in pure reflex
drifted down the access tube
full of references
altered to magnify
a feeling of rightness
abstract patterns shifting
into jagged vertical tattoos
whirling the line through long arcs
learning to adjust
the way flames leapt
in all that magnificence
into flashing monochrome images
created in his wake

Out of the Picture

the obsolete ammunition depot

unmissed and unreported

put it in categories

still glistened with dampness

suits seemed to be identical

through the window behind him

a battered cardboard box

won somewhere gambling

dim bell in his memory

was making a duplicate

to see if that needed explanation

sharply, and then, more gently

the door opened

three thousand miles east of home

we avoid old bones

conscious that their territory

enlarges the room

by removing a partition

in the mirror

disharmony seeped out

surrounded by a strange culture

message and hung up

its heavy coating of dust

whispering just loud enough

to create a disturbance

finding words for sorrow

sill locked in combat

in the expanding silence
ties with wild designs
printed on them suited me
to be places, camouflaged
against the cult of personality
panning over rough walls
overshadowed modifications
into missing construction
the remote camera
revealed a huge space
a kind of coma
the last gasp of civil protest
he could not sleep, above
starless and dark
the cloudy sky
was relieved only
by electric blue traces
shivering with more than cold
a tumbled slope of stones
flexed and straightened
warping space
into a dozen planes
two total strangers
retreated in panic
without letting it appear
the instrument of a secret
attached to a procedure
by a sudden doubt
pretending he was a robot

respectable looking

legs hot and itchy

faces indistinct behind windows

look from all angles

scornfully as

wandering among dogs

he is politely relieved of his wallet

the corner of his mouth

under a white moustache

pried off

with an effective tool

giving her the illusion

of a small, dimly lit

parking lot

set well back from the road

looking at a calendar

he realised the image of a falling body

came from film

a slightly altered version

connected to these bombings

the smell of wood burning

should be in a museum

thought probably was

displayed on costumed models

back in the car then

slumped down in the seat

accompanied only by printed legends

his thoughts elsewhere

with the thousands of dead

each wrapped in newspaper

he wasn't intending to dig up more

someone high on the power ladder

meant nothing else would matter

before the call came

rain streaked the glass

preventing identification

between drizzle and mist

through a labyrinth of corridors

good feeling left

closing the door

fires that lined both sides

collapsed in sparks

riffled in the gusty breeze

remembered from previous days

nothing unusual on the street

not a word in the papers

nobody was interested

it didn't happen

in the taxi heading back

to avoid hysterical screaming

there was not one question

felt through thin black leather

after stretching his muscles

towards that cone of white light

with little jerky movements

spreading a cool odour of soap

suddenly he was flesh, meat

making tracking easy

she sobbed

behind her veil

fascinated by this ceremony

keeping emotion out of his voice

he glanced at the watch

its face stared back

cold air

whispered and fell silent

a slender stiff shank

above the first vertebra

glancing around all the time

when the guard was killed

into a wilderness of lines

keeping things even

his inclination was to ignore

dislocation from reality

notice how it smells

slightly sympathetic

to the uncommitted

a bitterness he usually kept

to shield his face

during the autopsy

marks left by rodents

sure of security

sign and type the corpse

into something invisible

with pitiless neutrality

grunting and wheezing

a train makes an unscheduled stop

he's never heard before

suppressing an urge to look back

for something to read

partly in your mind

plastic, once transparent

can again be reunited

with old age wandering

in a public display

beside the mailbox

people with political connections

seemed neutral here

in that harmony

which conditions humans

in the crawlspace above the ceiling

their serious talking

rang some changes

under close surveillance

a voice that sounded like a cop

was hardly audible

buying bad information

only the moulded plastic head

making a quick reflex move

struck him a terrible blow

skittering down the hall

eyes closed, singing

not words in any human language

he remembered the scene

parked under some cottonwoods

slightly out of focus

why not let the wound heel?

early in this assignment

he warned

a mixture of standard tourists

clustered around

the elegant camera bag

each holding a briefcase

that planting

a tape-recorded message

rated personal attention

music wasn't music any more

he shaved in three minutes

following her eyes

poured himself three shots

she wasn't worried

pressed harder on the gas

nothing out there except snow

on jet-velvet rocks

not the slightest clue

as her arm moved

in the cramped space

slowly towards his ribs

came away moist

making a polite movement

across the pillow

seeming to dance from darkness

shaking with rage

now that he was aware of it

Rainbow

reading them as omens
even centuries achieve
the self as internal
to explain complex events

approximations that
swing past time
sour in the balancing
of grids and confusions

in favour of an orange
the excitement of hostilities
both with their illusion
within the flight time

narrators who improvise
highly visible disintegration
to disadvantage eyes
apparently sufficiently impatient

backdrop crowds on radio
edge much more pronounced
framed visual calendars
aspired to composition

on the seasonal rhythms
that entangle events
in folded temporary nations
nuclear submarines lurk

where possible abandon the concept
space that once limited
fever, noisy and inescapable
to arrive simultaneously

The Vein

But I have been familiar with ruins too long to dislike desolation.
(Lord Byron, November 1816)

what happens in any

sovereign body is created

on the evidence of the last

head on its last lap

those of us watching

then, during the programme

see the die seem to be cast

to draw the teeth

of our first question

affecting essential interests

they and only they had

she was dealing with

an unworthy family

gathered for death

inconvenient location

gruesome tired mannerisms

a bit thick coming from her

losing the thread of argument

in a sinuous cartwheel

drained of what life

hurried out with a pushchair

unsparing he takes us

to the cabaret

into patterns and groups

contrived for distraction

more likely

to deepen withdrawal

such a decrease

in which women

had views diametrically opposed

soon changes his tune

howling

face to face

cruel for people

recoiling in horror

plastered indeed

by any form of social

charges and interest

it may be healthy

to change the tone

of administration

in growth dynamics

use of perspective

attachment to things

entail perpetual disruption

of what space is for

built up

in absence

transactions typically occur

under conditions of heightened

variations in taste

spaces, isolated thoughts

which his concept of beauty

distorts to represent

thinking and feeling life

he considers in particular

superimposed spatial images

accelerating production

of different times

to control the future

this book has been edited

to detect the note

of such preoccupations

blue evening light

desire out of stasis

for jobs

investment itself

ruthless traders

organising forces

unable to stop the drift

of imagination over materiality

form an autobiography

in fires of competition

only to emerge stronger

within this system of production

brought into our homes

which in turn form the basis

of generating and acquiring

aesthetic pleasure

conventional these days

cluttered with illusion

based on writing

remixed

to demolish any narrative
of the world within
no image concealed
from the realm of material
accumulation and circulation
in part as would be true
enduring time
by herself he touches her
surrounded by models
able to pass unrecognised
in the stream of money
implied by a photograph
where the sun never seen
can be constructed
crashing through layer after layer
on a depthless screen
with the requisite speed
somewhere behind us
thrown into the street
patiently to see
rotting pieces of car
buttons working backwards
against nerve junctions
tilt her head
towards her ankles
in the underground light
black fur gleamed
off the oil drum
searchers found

a delicate bubble of oil

sweeping through it

pure oxygen

dawn touched

at the corners

rose in flame

lengths of thin steel

drawn across dust

shifting in thick

time on

motions playing out

across from me

not in sequence

cut into the sides

of an extension run

below his eyes

were tombstones

ringed with razor-wire

he threaded

bright slashes of colour

through open

jolts of fear

measuring, calculating

shaking so hard

a lump of shadow

watching

turned from side to side

shielding us from the sun

pale green glass

frames disintegrating tarmac

down to the tunnel

of the corner of his eye

moving on

to some other

man for the moment

horizon of empty water

locking him away

inside and he wore

two pictograms

set in strange lines

invisible in air

energetically above them

heels and silk

scatter snow

in the middle of a room

swirling out of the mist

bright with arrangements

tainted too historically

he had forgotten

quite violent fights

listening

to the continuous pounding

of some other thought

looking at the surface

far away down

in a cloud of dust

tattered lace about her

she watched him calmly

bits of it he tore off

at the end of each meeting

seemed colour-coded

sparkling violently

tingling on his skin

holes turned round slowly

in brown earth

lined with age

he smelled burning

trees in darkness

a voice came

from an imaginary telephone

on the dashboard

shrink-wrapped packages

soft underfoot

glowed in the dark

blinds slanted to make

the match flame

blast across his face

snap shut

in the jungle

after the ones still alive

start confessing

flashbulbs go off

her hand flicked back and forth

over a section of floor

he had heard more

than every single word

from the once proud

ruins of arches

in one outstretched hand

an odd sensation

included balance

working to repair the damage

of triumph on his face

folded against the edge

of exhaust fumes

closing his lids

properly needed great care

she heard a rustle

little numbers

flew around trees

tumbled across a moonlit field

trying to reassemble

his head again

she blinked

some sort of code

subtle variations

in the colour of her eyes

a reliable testing ground

gardens inside shelters

shades patterning

an idealised culture

in one landscaped clump

stuffed full of shells

a version or remnant of something

under a different name

some crisis of identity

spanned the world

thought was the only thing

to come back to acting

beyond acoustics

even when dramatic

she always wore fancy dress

simply cut and held low

objects grouped together

confidently into fine jewellery

after the storm new scents

touched by salt spray

hardly dimmed the harsh light

he sometimes pulled at his hair

obsessed with finding the beautiful

curtain allowing him entry

never able to follow

the middle of night

downwards to find a runway

with deep sides

writhing under his fingers

personalities full of energy

order a series

of the same programme

cool for film

using this knowledge

machines talk to themselves

maintain a very persistent

buzzing as the signal

ends in a dramatic freeze

close to the border

on a street with a few orange trees

Intellectual Compost

at least the makings
remember his describing meetings
was their main support
extending into waves

he just disappeared through
where it is so cold
built on an addition
untouched by noise

to have enjoyable moments
for the sake of sunset
something was lost
against the wall, resting

shining in the dark
rooms enclose a porch
a chord struck softly
reached the cash register

half buried in mud
aware of his involvement
alone could have produced
dusk turning to fierce wind

not making marble folds
from the small of his back
sound arched over him
nerveless and remote

All Fours

though it might have been chronic
around his neck and shoulders
filled with thick high weeds
the road was lined with stone

almost entranced she started
ordering quantities of everything
down the windows of your station
combed and perfectly normal

bees through blood and perhaps
night air while we rode back
followed him to the front porch
and the chimney bricks were fallen

she hasn't heard from him since
filled in on the background
large machines can dig them
forced to take shelter in that house

watching her move about the kitchen
a uniformed policeman was standing
out like magic on the glass
we were living under siege again

two more men came in carrying
pages of an appointment book
not very good lights things happening
younger all clean and prosperous

a grievance a legitimate grievance
rumbled as the rain began
heavily where the blades pushed it
round doorways little brown children

in your car and go somewhere
dead or senseless at the wheel
crouched there taking no part
on the highway the sedan fishtailed

mosquitoes had been real fierce
with that wind coming off
substandard materials and workmanship
years of polishing have dulled

professional sound of a woman singing
damnation at an empty chair
soft black soot coats the slate
too splendidly suburban for adequate

illegible smears of block printing
held motion to a crawl
skimming over book titles
postured alluringly around the room

the important dynamic was between
peculiar and unique powers
to collect on his insurance
that portion of it reported

lovely little thing with eyes
as efficient as she had to be
shambling on down the tissue
range where embers had gone out

looking at everything said suicide
the area about her had the look
you see in old chromos
breathing not daring to smoke or cough

practically an abandoned road
several varieties of mushroom thrived
standing motionless in the shade
small common objects of assault

blown cell with a dusty bulb
an instant to blank shining glass
blocking out the moon and stars
vending machines on every floor

Coal Grass Blood Night Emerald

in the epic or the dramatic
last things certainly contrast
specific moments in time
about despair as well as hope
guilt and redemption
into which bodies
travel back by train
by each other
in a coloured picture for
entry into which
nothing
different experiments with tenses
equivalent to the present
turn to the poetry
of angels
urged to murder
those of time for a
confession of his own
experience: the universal
land between
agony and entry
making an ultimate
example of the apocalyptic
relationships of suffering
drinking many glasses
extended until silence
profoundly ambiguous
over the coffin
uninspired
refers to an intermediate
loss of spiritual gifts
a moonlit sky can be seen
providing a helpful point
of reference above the
earthly scene
seeing as well as hearing
into contiguity
everlasting physical torment

Survival

between sounds of different
but familiar idioms
bonfires of rubber tyres
underline the arrival
of a population
allowed to attend
cautiously: worried
spectators gather
projecting their image
as well as dance techniques
promoters help the distribution
critical for future
significance of lyrics
responding to market forces

sinking below the standard
of archaic union
to surrender his own identity
in an indirect rendition
of her history of being
mastered by competent speakers
carefully articulating spheres
interested in self-preservation
and the signs to which they are tied
expression becomes sublimated
beyond discursive thought
making it possible to promise
a fluctuating relationship with nature
from an unusual use of language

down in the grasses
silent, leaning forward
each one of them accomplished
through the narrative
accustomed words fall
easily into dreams
in order to arrange
dust patterned with immutable
antiquities, various
doors filling the apertures
of tradition
so accurately
it was easy to recognise
the remedies she had used

passing near the black hole
in ordinary flat space
around a small loop
of objects formed
for symmetry reasons
species of particles exist
not yet pinned down
as coincidences
moving relative to one another
on the edge of the quantum zone
by gravitational amplification
irrespective of the identity
of metals in their spectra
to collapse into a mathematical point

the only part that didn't float
about whatever had happened
could feel rain in the air
a fine handmade panama hat
near the altar rail
in the soft glow of chandeliers
an almost square grey
bookshelf filled with history
all the movable property
mangling one of his legs
that same damn ugly sofa
swept up and carried away
cool water playing over
the dead and dying

almost as to a stranger
taking advantage of the numerous
candles, in a room
painted at the same time
through the coarse sieve
of a dying hour
not continuously being guarded
fed by an inexhaustible
external unity
fever had now taken possession
of disturbed contours
lustrous in the shade
behind mirrors
their dying could not alter

prisoners of age and society
when economics
grew to a certain size
perhaps the words themselves
brought depression and unemployment
to express awareness
of sustained narrative
at the national level
trying to illuminate events
even a trace of her pale pink lipstick
a small round crust
on a bumpy surface of hysteria
felt the current between us flowing
in the same drawer

it was – eerie
unwilling to believe
in reverent terms
intention the exacting
decomposition of the body
recording all movements
transfixed by it
signalling survival
joke desire had become
a practice suit working
the same sensation
eyes closed, breath coming evenly
surfaced to the world
of trying circumstances

abruptly into an open space
ranged in orderly fashion
your mind: there's the truth
unsuited for irony
the recollection of neglect
fragrant with cinnamon
exploding within
lucidly in the cool
undercurrents of apprehension
its brilliant openings
caged in their scorn
an imaginary country
complete in every detail
in a perennial state of war

out it makes a noise
to the men and women who work
on the police computer
with a piece of piano wire
politely smiling
in front of the camera
plain clothes, nothing conspicuous
an unusual weapon
after a hot dinner
bent to fit any body
on the verge of cracking
strange things that make existence
these lost parts of the city
shrouding all of us

night darkening around us
the track is not easy to find
a hazy line
repeating its own features
she breathes again
the speaking images
grown ghastly thin
begin to falter
sleep under pouring rain
running through revolutions
forges pour forth stars unknown
multiplying and still crowded
light in the heart of them
scratches in all directions

functional metal components
shapes moulded in high relief
to various degrees of geometrification
benefit from the new union
giving layers of glass
planes and shadows
to soften and diffuse the images
making lighting a plastic element
a reaction against the excessive
rhythmic ascent from restrained colour
a similar, but less imaginative, vocabulary
inscribed in block letters
shaded to provide depth
by clever assembling of veneers

similarly, with the hologram
action at a distance ceases
the environment seems
preternaturally separate particles
by its mere presence
in the darkness
the ultimate test
between reality and hallucination
interpreted as implying
consciousness that the world
in all its normal solidity
lived through in time
survives death
to specify its location

behind a studio table
extremely limited portraits
sustaining it inhabit
acres of weed
waiting for something to happen
sunshine rarely glimpsed
partly because of fashion
eddying outward on its own side
in quotation marks
a movement almost balletic
despite the pitted holes
ringed by men in uniform
advising people to vote
lives on in the graveyard

another loyal follower
cared openly to express doubts
all the way by a detachment
primarily from the arrow's weight
wind instruments signalled
over more distant fiefs
evaded by using unusually large
miners and mere cannon-fodder
to provide meat
somewhat at a loss
for the present
they simply had to survive
wracked by numerous ailments
and despair on this little island

he hated to get wet
held together in mid-air
time was getting closer
in normal awareness
look at the flame
since the exact position
selected its place
in total darkness
being full of foibles
saved for ultimate confrontation
the fire had to be as big
and dangerous overwhelming
every change in the light
any surprising vistas

later she would walk
asleep on his feet
to the brink of inspiration
with lacquered nails
paused in mid-phrase
discounting – discrediting
the epic sweep of stars
devising stratagems
shrunk back in his head
until the day was filled
creating an illusion
radiating orange lightning
sucked into a vacuum
past ponds, down hills

464

nothing better than to re-claim
duck with its head dangling
knife – a blue pencil
only bad things that affect
the opposite still she came
a tall black vase
fluttering her arms
always displeased
moving every year
around protected by the wind
shook the plate in front
did not scream when he fell
outside down the stairs
poured all her brains

the adaptations
to differences in colour
associated with food
regarded as the simplest forms
stuck together in lumps
are irrelevant to survival
the struggle towards
countless changes
exhausted from hunger
sounded like water
beginning to burn
or an extinguished star
fading into darkness
smiling at the skull

feelings belonged to the past
his stomach churned
the breeze blew
through thick underbrush
following him around
out onto the highway
and grinned
flailing about
not to touch his cold flesh
you could smell it
from deep in the earth
watching the smoke crawl
from his straining lungs
with its icy purity

gazing without expression
among cases of film
they stepped into the sun
removing remains
by this new channel
through the glassy surface
of a collection of rubbish
but curiously trusting eyes
swathed in canvas
exhausted in the debris
loomed from reflection
reading itself
to look at the rushes
beating slowly a tired rhythm

despite some difficulties
traders station themselves
leaning there slowly
to handle
such ready consolations
does the body become darkened?
inherit more isolation than land?
the lifelessness of someone
reactivated
by past procedures
inside the lenses
from a different face
a ship's lamp shone
against his black overcoat

she scrutinizes their shape
needed to revise
one pattern on another
concerned with such a search
that may call up his face
explicable as reproaches
before they could be read
in motion as loss
or for threat
in embryo form
too elusive for reconstruction
with conventional tonality
there must be more identities
to discover and express

out into indeterminate space
as quickly as possible
an undefined horizon
slides away
flushed and silent
towards the voice
washing in behind
apparently motionless
in the cavities
some shattered syllables
vibrate in the blue haze
in a moment of alarm
more intricate
than a determined pattern

away for another week
slipping his tail
cunningly left in the box
near a curtained window
white-clad chemical figures
suddenly totter vertical
sent for specialist examination
to milk publicity
she turned and motioned
over the fold
through the bugged building
pointing at the mirror
to become two separate individuals
empty but brilliantly lit

exactly this point
indicating a flow
scrubbed and pristine
universe subject to routine
transcribing reality
into flights of imagination
all planes collapse
laid out on a line
among strangers
earth refracted across the mind
in a sense unconscious
the persistence of desire
making the visual field
radically estranged

so meaning might be
an inexhaustibility of reference
rather than detailing
flecks that float on the surface
where gaze unfolds
the construction of a refuge
reflecting light
from an implied viewpoint
towards the setting sun
assumptions about history
ruins now
map legible space
as mediating vision
trains our eye on things

isolated in contrast
briefest indications
traced outlines
cast on the wall
for future decoration
acting in and upon nature
irradiated by the recollection
of light
shaping the earth
in elegant lines
the almost audible eruption
into dramatic patterns
of an informed image
with no place to stand

Rainbow 2

valley where making
remains a realm of mystery
cut off from time

into the brain itself
constants through scent
a necessary fiction

bird butterfly and bee
each see the same colour
differently than we

ground water beneath
anticipation and recall
fast young horses

years later small sharp
glimpses of horizon lines
through apple branches

oppressive summer
so stripped of nuance
shielded from the easy sound

reading in too much light
close-ups of the surface
glow of a full moon

Blue Screen

*'Peace, then, to their memory, aptly enshrined in unknown characters within the
penetralia of the temple of oblivion.'*
(Charles Babbage)

obliged to dress

its presence highly visible

could not only shrink

or vibrate too slowly

east of dreaming

more spatial dimensions

impossible to walk across

so why bother

with this favoured version

nurtured by vestiges

succinct but definite

nothing can get out

but there is another model

constructed in sand

cooled as space expanded

on the surface of a globe

having no edge

a search warrant wasn't necessary

this spy seemed reasonable

lines into power outlets

impossible to eradicate

boundaries between networks

to draw a multicoloured picture

protected by passwords

threaded through its system

uncluttered by any pipes

inserted above ceiling level

if liquid is poured

to be replaced by new air

rising from the fire

swirling around this space

at the end of autumn

prevented from blowing back

by a line of trees

not numerous enough

to take their place

while real prices fall

the population

by then clearly beyond

a disappointed hope

but more diffuse

pursuing economic paths

into dilemmas that emerge

in a purely programmatic way

need for that language

transmits their combined impact

makes possible these acts

that overload inevitability

from the very waves

of vision

suspending serious reservations

strangers from over the horizon

where animals gather

gnawing bark

at the border of grasslands

no one perfume

all external objects modified

the interpretation of characters

at some distance

to impede their opening

a replica of stars

completes the journey home

a new age with nothing

to tell the time

weight would not freeze

began to unwind

providing goods for everyone

broke into a fine mist

designed by traders

to be collected and distilled

ridding wool of its natural grease

bright as the best

diagnosis to identify

exactly the shape

for a specific interval

a lack of air

parallel to the frame

from which it sprang

if the container moves

out of position rapidly

the visitor waits

an expanding audience

in the growth of authentic

models for the mixture

responsible for supply

spears, raffia mats

sparks fly between

a virtual absence of recording

and the structural racism

which caters to

traditional rural music

when a single idea came

threatening to break it

letting people drop

their own burdens

to provide useful information

confined to the brain

continually sorting-out belongings

when eating it clicks

hours with no reason

marked thought disorder

once the gene is identified

with commendable thoroughness

well-heeled musicians

remain sceptical

playing solos

which reverberate to a new name

exacerbating a difficult situation

costume and behaviour indicate

reflected in bright red tiles

one pace through the door

a breeze rustled curtains

detached from night

surrounding the stadium

colours ran in all directions

slowly past them

shaded cool and inviting

inward as usual

a segmented scar

on the edge of the divan

simply is no before

slipping into gradual decline

planets fall from a tree

not to marry marks

facing great uncertainties

anxious to save money

a half-explored land

on the wrong trajectory

hidden in mist

where the outlines

seemed broken puzzles

gliding about the stage

of an iris as it opened

significance was yet to come

properly to the straight line

conscious of fluttering muscles

a few slimy inches of green

escaped into silence outside

peculiarly ritualised

within a score

mobilised demanded firm

cause actual death

at the mere mention

fibres are treated

between wedges of cavalry

doing their own foraging

covered with timber or earth

inside which a vacuum

could be accelerated

in a series of concentric spheres

through cold and hunger

the bubble widened

divided into compartments

elaborate rules for conduct

copying letters

with holes in them

all the way across

the phases of the moon

anomalies

through both lenses

forced jocularity to cope

in some much more foolish way

with flashing eyes

until he saw the lights go out

warming slowly

between black hands

short blasting reports

a shadow running

in distance moving

beyond some logical horizon

scraps of velvet

seemed to enclose him

in thinking

formerly erotic attitudes

began to topple

dazed onto stones

dark from the flames

some of the money

watched her now

become almost human

hidden by blowing dust

beginning to dribble out

a long sigh

let her facade collapse

providing no answers

scraped against jagged gear

beneath a tapestry

snow was gone

too vivid in her mind

passed judgements

where a picture was missing

eyes were refocusing

across the gently curving sweep

a sliver of pain

on the frozen turf

reaction an instinct

nearly obscured

its flickering explosion

featured harmonic conceptions

without vibrato

mergers made sense

trickling down

driven by economics

going to get serious

moving on to the next stop

at pains to avoid

several drafts

on the honed edge

uneasily entering sharpness

as a low murmur

shooting towards him

through curtains

air brightened instantly

in dead space

around her knees

small feathers

represent new vegetables

cutting details out

in the form of a serpent

reinventing itself

credit it to fate

a necessary cornerstone

stood behind him

shortly after leaving

some kind of dummy

a picture of rage

a repetitious dirge

can almost be certain

towns with their little

chinese monkeys

an illusion made

deafening whisper

growing difference in tolerance

waited more impatiently

realising after not many

warlike attacks

success in every job

without quite knowing

enough problems

slit in the front

may change

to open right

energies to execution

no-one returned

radiant embroidery

risen unexpectedly

hung from her left shoulder

animated despite

steadily ebbing streadth

another length

uncovered foam rubber

continued to reflect

the phrase ahead

one entire side

heavy wood

on which blood had dried

carelessly recorded

the scene into farce

important points

terminated his presence

deliver this ice

at the first signs

underground for a while

falsely safe and each

would bring a bottle

until warning amber

rose above neighbouring looks

to be nothing a fleck

continued to scrutinise them

intuitively to withhold

any experience

spread before heaven

in the cruelest weather

her palms together

give such a full account

their peculiar taste

stiffened perhaps with dirt

eyes wide

piercing the shallow outskirts

of shy glancing

when he needs them most

those secrets

alter those ears

whitening the tops

an observatory behind

so strangely solid

mind had been deprived

of disturbance

the heart perceives

a broken piece

emphatic even when not so lit

changes an awful spectacle

craziness in proportions

finally run their course

an eye in the forest

an image of infinity

petrified non-communication

relief against solid rock

distinct on neutral grounds

the end of active thought

Intellectual Compost 2

hoping to move himself
where you stood maybe
a dirty floor
should have relaxed me

a little on guard
breathes worry even
to the room at large
nervous about the war

of direct comment
had to plunge on
power proved misapplied
waving her arms sideways

dreamed of eating ice
hung way off there
born with philosophy
they feel seems natural

ritual they had practised
for infinite energy
established comprehension
would have been the same

a cloud every night
become mere lucidity
bulging out of his head
upon her caked lips

Emptily

they bounce back from the screen
clean and ready
making parts of the body
an aesthetic obligation
before the skeleton bursts out

big snakes and small
might ask exactly what
a curve being any
point of view too there was something strange
see strange

winds
to conflicting effects

on the whole once knowledge is public

means non-speaking
it contained or required
unique because it is
a sudden crystallization of
garden

world
flatten out the paper

scales were finally overbalanced

to refrain from
association of
external perception
with a higher level of discard
sentence

was
the whole inward aspect

within the bounds of pure intention

could fold into
the quiet dirty pavement
within hardly an hour
on account of this photograph which
occurred

made
as stiffly dry as those

leaves turning up their pale undersides

stuck on the brim
two cheeks of a mandrill
prevent authority
fiery above the sullen wavelets
relief

point
angels and pins revel

merge together in a conception

scope to arrange
effect and appearance
a gap to fill after
the problem of lifting a canoe
designed

plain
but steel will rust observed

utilitarian energy

was little more
natural history
socially structured space
established a taxonomy based
behind

work
sudden eruption in

a landscape without time monuments

conventional
evading that pressure
lightly bound and fully
submerged and then rising out awe-struck
present

must
recall that things became

soft and sweet about the air speech moved

back to the couch
muffled by bad weather
he acted like something
leaving swirls of gas fumes in the air
sideways

long
though she lacked enough strength

supported by two square concrete posts

largest body
announced the pestilence
as currency to pay
self-replication efficiently
survived

stiff
with a few adjustments

about the nature of confusion

magnificent
islands and newly found
spectacular features
fatal secondary infections
over

hands
hot and moist often

before we consider that least glance

a world in which
naturally kept within
may have been even more
navigator to practise its skills
clearing

seams
similar in the mass

probably would not be credited

abilities
fallback position is
history of science
specialised cortical areas
without

more
variability

machinery for the basic throws

skimmed poor people
such specimens were all
especially the children
along a terminally depressed
board game

room
a strong defence posture

driving along a wilderness road

increasingly
weather when the city
was regarded as a
contradiction between the study
of a

new
kind of longing and that

of a responsive congregation

armies had swept
turned south and walked into
contempt because they were
unending supplies of substantial
stomachs

coarse
under rare directions

as easily deposed as climate

definition
pre-occupying time
with an express intent
to anchor scientific discourse
picture

meant
by a signal depends

stored in the dominant hemisphere

crops driven mad
late in their history
first approached the region
overwhelmingly greater than seed
can learn

raged
massive beyond the edge

into a device for producing

but out of this
higher mental command
proved in many respects
to be a physical distinction
nothing

plays
in freezing rain all night

towards the source of the stimulus

expresses an
attempt at another
new vision marking out
through periods of especial stress
common

in
clear traces of almost

adaptation to the emotion

colours can use
an existing building
years of the century
as a distinct body of grouping
money

proof
and the four elements

establish new subject positions

our sister in space
a designer award
must reflect back across
a grid where the barrier was moved
even

help
an everyday concept

the beaten have little to bargain

in appearance
frozen magnetism
no longer something
preoccupied with a need to cry
outside

set
immobile by question

subject to fits of rage and pity

an actress stares
objectively to see
to watch those objects change
coincidentally courageous
motor

mass
revising every dream

look with wonder at the stars and moon

mastering things
felt to be fanciful
fortune begins to fail
becomes a method of describing
creatures

scale
delicately coloured

creates a technology of space

universal
available surplus
during the modern age
not too bright or the images placed
dissolve

world
constructing a table

for accumulated collections

necessity
is in them less dispersed
she turned off the water
dismissing it from her mind with ease
suppressed

flow
not yet completely dark

forced him to show something of his hand

hooked up to sound
individually
firing long-range missiles
surprisingly large numbers of white
neon

strips
some plastic creatures

fending off enthusiastic crowds

improbably
suspended in the air
special scraps of paper
restricted access to the water
broken

weight
bringing a harsh glitter

still has no emotional meaning

illustrated
light gutters in the past
illuminating time
depending on the length of tubing
flame sound

shakes
into two equal parts

convertible one to the other

bursting into
all kinds of illicit
business undetected
regions would be affected whether
or not

since
such concern about stock

was white and was in a plastic bag

buttons and combs
a few hours before dark
will permit the export
of barbecued meat on long skewers
outstretched

crust
the clearing starts again

wiped out of a large part of their range

gaining daily
about its extension
the wheel has right-of-way
a dazzling samba around the ball
trembling

miss
no-one is looking back

society level at zero

Defective Definitions

behind massive fortifications
click on the icon
venus enters your sign
where noise is a nuisance

your new finished hairline
going directly to the mouth
primarily restored fish
mad'a'fact video twice picked up

disorderly or funny
shape had a different birth
it becomes a food warmer
steaming clones par-boiled

able to scan reminder notes
break lends extra information
your computer can translate
dancing go full blast

head out for loading
exciting new realities
only when you get closer
the topic turns to planned

under hanging olives
totally blank stretches
a rush to passive investing
analysis worthless to discuss

how are we to find coffee
fond fish? a high profile trap
not because of thrusting organisms
purely spends to get there

The Mosquito and the Moon

it is hard enough

not merely a matter of belief

noise is another problem

continuing yet to confine

the great heap of spoils

turn left through the shop

something wrong, miscalculated

breaking cells completely

measuring is an aspect

surviving to produce

ending on a defined route

arranged in a ring

small localised holes

of intellectual depth

heavily coloured by allusions

brought the car to the kerb

speaking across a threshold

charcoal marks indicate

towards the front of the bed

tragic but still breathing

they carry the old

letters running through decades

find emotional experience

filled with words

bearers of randomness

bumping and pushing

intimately familiar signs

not revealing location

milling images hard to retain

these were soldiers and sailors

restless edges of vibration

forced into twisted positions

another moment somewhere

mingled on the drawn curtain

grace caught unaware

awake with phantoms

made, used on the spot

the group shared in

techniques later refined

as they expanded eastward

off to an early start

plant materials were common

tightly bound on both sides

embedded in the landscape

an arc of stones

crudely made tools

eventually caught on

a gradient of sugar

persistently firing

in the brain and bloodstream

for oneself is not enough

the song once heard

inscribed in molecular processes

evoked to endure this

through the dark side

up out of chaos

slightly curved sound drops

from axis to circumference

keyed on the echo

a burglar alarm system

determines who a victim saw

doors eyes

shut before he turns

to sign in the body

being treated like a patient

examined in a good light

his face destroyed by shock

bars go full tilt

inside the ring move

communication options and emotions

a new atmosphere in matter

already underfinanced

wind and rain just

beginning to emerge

some senses work on

the power of the camera

measured by studying

modified to include isolation

to enter the dark compartment

reasonable clearly mapped

is to assume directive force

each time we remember

habits and seasons

change their properties

see wild animals

killed then tested

concentrate migrate

over a series of struts

between banks and islands

being the thin air

aware of existing devices

using solar energy

in the design of complex objects

not so ubiquitous as now

when the air is colder

an array of detectors

about low speed situations

learns the nature of life

perhaps fluids, hardware

systems that move people rapidly

die smashed into it

tightly coupled with growth

unavoidable delay

adapted the horse

in the humanities

expected ways fail

between signal and space

over heavily populated areas

a simple visual act

historically ephemeral

haunting without knowing

the perceptual grasp

of an adequate philosophy

natural images which seem

clear at the outset

accepted as a normal

stage of organization

of the actions of spirit

often thrust doubtless

towards an ideal of knowledge

continually threatening

the notion of large scale

hold an emotion

appropriate to grandeur

brought into contact

with things

brand new and never washed

broken wings

covered with burnt signs

ring the top edge

of whatever the dancer is doing

local colour

an abrupt radiance

to watch for in the city

makes your eyes jump

past tattoos of fake brick

rusty armoured space

nothing more modern

glowing coils of virus

cracks in their glaze

a halo slipped

folded to her throat

against the impossible air

where old things came from

Name Unknown

bare space
with neither flower nor picture
sunlight glows
through a half-empty peanut butter jar
the mixture cools
into the room's reality
gravediggers' increased productivity
may not be good for all
independent of measuring devices
monoliths eventually topple
across a system
of crystalline forms
a cat blinks
in the dust of a passing bus

under headlines
managed by the presenter
outer armour
produced in darkness fades
a thin supercold atmosphere
separates metal from its ores
gradually the soil becomes infertile
its fictional world explained or defined
to show measurable changes
combined with something outside themselves
still energetic enough
ancillary backgrounds throng
for only in a vacuum
does light invariably win

also the use of an image
must go into the open
of silent films
buttoned tight to keep
the secret of his alter ego
carefully patted into shape
in the twilight
concealed wires play
moving slightly in the breeze
whose slanting motion tracks
his head made of rubber
hung on the branch of a tree
smiling down upon the scene
unfolding towards the west

yet to be born at the moment
untroubled with systematic speculation
constructing optical instruments
to see things close up
the road is open leading
to a sense of volume
rich yet sparsely defined
always growing and deviating
towards primary colours
conscious of intensification
in the narrow corridors of the modern
this direction
will have time to name itself
marked with a drip of wax

in that logical order
bizarre scandals precipitate
about his greatest interests
farewell to the beach
bright waterlilies sagging
perhaps ruined by jealousy
more a complex work of art
announcing to the world
various causes of ideas
unsung by constant nagging
gradually she calms down
to salvage from the fire
vitality overcome by emotion
converging on catastrophe

a sense of being deserted
emerging just to be good
on their shoulders
scattered throughout spacious
influence reveals their pathetic
character measured against
external wooden fire escapes
a neurosis about ability
run to be discarded
before curtain time
too many facts
assume a parody of none
substituted for the original
by fertility of imagination

somehow admitted from the shadows
echoing eyes pierce
the defence of compassion
as a musical instrument
among genuine monsters
purifies awareness
into a tranquil habit
to spoil his fine work
condition is imperceptive
hope for an elegant event
slow to understand
the surface should be loose
a pastel colour plan
cropped through the seasons

tear away whole sections
of what is good
bags of camel's hair
a blue that carries further
the unlikeness of dusk and chaos
crossing a stream
where tributaries enter a river
you can't wait for science
to drain that space of wet earth dry
the face seemed to lack contour
nothing is left but a vast expanse
deep grooves of habit
trodden into the soil
under a full moon crossed by a vulture

exhausted by their experiences
his body spreads
disease rumour spiced
with a touch of grace
a crackle of wood burning
sweeps the whole scene
getting dark in the east
where no sound enters
notice the wires are pulled
by no splendour, imagery or power
vision does more than see
the habit of infinite parenthesis
changes of fashion stumbling
forever over the plains of time

Muted Hawks

intense physical conflict
confuses the two areas
renders capital concrete
which annoys the generals
paid by the citizen

formalised heaven not unlike
reason you must operate
in our imaginations
to act except in ignorance
sinister rather than admirable

abrupt illumination
while he stared at his cage
the day slipped by
retaining knowledge
in a declining body

to its logical conclusion
in a way no civilisation
represented as natural
or advancing the public good
should have been given early warning

comes comfort which in turn
poking its reflecting eye
up from within
has always been for hire
open to exploitation by experts

through these great rooms
abstract structures dominate
being perfect imitations
perhaps for future use
beneath their dignity to run

hearings to overhang an area
obviously ridiculous
resemble parody
more consciously integrated
on interests of the regime

brilliance an inherited machine
capable of unlearning
what would have to change
beneath the patina
of interest and doubt

become a major barrier
so strategically important
followed by collapse
painted in great detail
to resemble opera

to eliminate war
airs of evenings impinge
the place or date of origin
blocking the critical path
only able to be rent

no pattern from them
dark indeed came quickly
memories of it vague
time had become leather
regrettably informal

transformations into dogs
ransom or rescue
smaller food animals
when human figures occur
antennae rising from their heads

Wit Wither

'*Such joy... such desperate joy!*'
(Willem de Kooning)

two major patterns

produced a realist view

any thing may be an instance

substantiated by observing

the primary direction of dream

no matter how specific

the way in which space

would change or distort

boundaries more precise

despite more flexible distance

to accommodate need

unpacking symbols

in control of all situations

the currents

justifying selection

baking bread and drawing water

introduce us to context

a carefully posed photograph

juxtaposing monuments

begging with black slogans

which we cannot imagine

out of a fashion parade

actions will be understood

detected outside

those same skills

open for others

demonstrate that muscles

have burned away

from obscure lines

images not alive

still not exactly dead

at the centre of reflection

of the electronic world

feel details about

the inside of each

nature of the event

command our attention

inspiration of smoke

mostly drugs

his mental efforts

between sisters

entering thick lovers

hands-on

a glimpse of other eras

mainly marks on the dial

daily passes

work their replacing

down routine firings

poised ambitious to provide

conscious literary originals

happen may even think

know or other clues

required in your unit

scrabbling at the prospect

while you need

storming with

affiliate that produces

shaped bright overflow

in the complete

museum dedicated to

former documenting

penguins, sea lions

carefully singing magic

locked in on her

stripped out

arms folded

odour of decaying

interest and concentration

passing under columns

of white stones

on a chrome

motor whirr

inched along enticement

past spiderwebs

under his arms

turned squarely on

instinctive impulse

deeper into dereliction

beneath irregular

heat inside

consideration of delusion

a place to crawl to

and endlessly loop

among the folds of garments

Errory

joined harmonising the best
so it needn't wait
phrase: the question are you sure?
hanging three feet off the ground
silent, absolutely quiet
headquarters – we travelled north
clawing back small shelter
hung with screaming
on the same rig
blended in enthusiasm
as the race approached
through cracks in snow
free-falling into mind
alive with brightness shivering
instantly into sleep
changed, re-formed
they run, they run
with madness into chutes
of changed values
all of them conventional
vibrations of division
dare to refuse the glass
lazily through long green
discrete landing sites
to a transmitting unit
over the protective line
wave patterns in space

form black against
sifted patches of moonlight
birds move in the dark
their faint contours
singing small notes
to the rhythm of a train
so empty at this hour
silence in between
contains the words
things whiz past
once more
the sound of calculation
by indirect means
receives its full due
along the wet pavement
human flesh
fallen in all directions
to fresh eyes
something to do with the sky
senselessly dishevelled
resolves and fixes
the foundation
desirable to guard against
relative soundness of approach
including human shapes
used by the dealer
connecting them

to a sense of common
unforeseeable properties of relics
considered in place
so deceptive
their firesides play
optimism for its object
without arousing
constitutional tradition
beyond the rules of the game
hailstones imagine
moist sea air
disordered beyond it rise
drearier philosophies
to resist retrogression
faster than anything
directly stimulating receptors
attention moves
many possible representations
inside the heart
decayed into blackness
fine details of the scene
creep along for years
hard to become
immune to a predator
silhouettes of participants
dangle in their own data
faint green clouds
in almost pure alcohol
calibrate the equipment

to assume a more personal form
susceptible to psychic influences
does not contempt breed
often in disguise?
slipping past a window
on communal stairs
into faded yellow
flashed with orange
slanting through smoke
swished into a perfect dome
dissatisfied when calm returns
centered around a food animal
mastery of areas
managed to neutralise
subjects into waves
to destroy communication
more easily on scanty pasture

Dark Senses

bones show through images
of friends though they
still move in dialogue
in darkness what relief

forgive me, it's a dream
standing alone, waving
in search of its lost era
not just geography

walking parallel streets
of tropical flames
with a political broom
ominous as a smoke signal

over a farewell meal
of dust in the dust
before an open window
weather permitting

step sharply within
the labyrinth of raw meat
jingling those keys
dimmed by sweat

unthinking insects click, rustle
for bare subsistence
in the skeletons of organisations
inexorably crushed by vice

they themselves go into hiding
one on top of another
in their natural colours
green smocks, masks and goggles

taking likenesses
to build a screen
alongside the trail
of pearl lightbulb shards

this curiously shaped barrier
contains gestures and rites
simulated leopard skins
smart cards and our ideas

for fear of disturbing
the pose of philosophy
fashionable at the time
they stand in complete silence

in unbroken sunlight
wearing masks
as aids to memory
attributed to interiors unknown

they did not break
under their own weight
the experience of generations
proved far more effective

acts of representation respond
in order to survive desire
cheated by false hopes
in voices hardly above a whisper

local weather prophets
proclaim their laws of storm
radioactive rain restricted
to areas over toxic waste

the nightmare atmosphere of ruin
washes away in close-up
striking spatial effects predicted
if the mask is joyful

produce a sublime gesture
opposed to voice or action
a system of reflections ordering
the necessity of rumour

Out of a Sudden

(Riva san Vitale, 30 August 1995)

the alphabet wonders
what it should do
paper feels useless
colours lose hue

while all musical notes
perform only in blue

a lombardy poplar
shadows the ground
drifted with swansdown
muffling the sound

at the tip of the lake
of the road to the south

above in the night sky
scattered by chance
stars cease their motion
poppies don't dance

in the grass standing still
by the path no-one walks

Intellectual Compost 3

sides of you as
arms of airport cops
should be the centre
but not enough to overcome

the light of a burst lamp
with silver blotches
running along your skull
worked to flames

an extra pair of eyes
taped up tapping across
the edge of the ledge
admiring broken clay walls

where cures strobe
into repair
placed under heavy objects
in the star-lit night

trying to cool habits
instead of senses by fright
down to the skin
moistened with blood

the radiator creaked
harshly through impatience
exploding into tongues
flickering in blue cold

Firewall

views of music drift
into the central arena
across a projector beam

creating stunning tableaux

on the notion of chance
like them, reinforced
between two highlights
on honey and gold leaf

though it might sound

strained in the dimness
while film throws
images of people
short of being
ideas of the world

devised to fit bodies
leaking blood
aimed at figurines
radio noise fascinates
with comic acts
painted a brilliant blue
at regular intervals
less a visual spectacle
than a door set on edge

to reveal a tumbling cast
of prejudices

concealed in artificial objects
changing the action plane
into separate movements in space
down through grey site
straight up broken above
because you were lush

electronics completely black drip
clearly down lathered shoulders
wood shutters separated iron
moves with his hands
lighting up a crack

a small wet click
that death happened
cages set on a table

medieval monastery look

forces production of
a finger drawing a line
without the abyss
behind every chair enough silk

any sustained possibilities

install refreshing space
experimentation with survival
completed by the thorn
shoot too long take
flaws out of proportion

pull over roll down tedium
corner of a sinister
aching in her luxury
would carry conscious weight
the transmutation of dusk
disregard darkness
away to bones and shadow
never perfect imaginary axes
warning demanded to perpetuate

high premium pleasure
sound running down the chain

grey with stone dust
by spaced stalks
intercepted envy
buckled to an oak chair
molten wind streaked past
dented with rain

quickly waned
the physical remained
a question moulded and inhaled
cheap painted plaster
distance had given up

though not so ardently there
from its ashes though many
gathered but no engine came

still a great deal forward

moisture provided in part
unable to hide the verge
greenery had passed
on coarse grass one winter night

unifying colour from one area

water with the syringe
stimulating discrepancy
photographed in the act
focused on a brief fantasy
influence prevails over power

swept to girders of the el
the greatest ham
stole differently didn't
hit the château
too long to settle
in one piece trailing
rags in the gas
deep archaic shine hung on
steady supply appreciated

white rolling clouds
erased three tries to monitor

little or no force remarks
about the tragic update
actions pinned to the wall
boxed in sentiments
money commissioned paint
and a big space

some more meaningless powder
boils the sugar content
wipes away shapes
up a slope through shades
thudding porcelain

also might be true
disaster he saw spread out
to a lucent sky

viewed in surprise manipulated

by boulders absurdly off
rushing right over camouflage
vibration hardens reflection
flows smoothly in

beneath her gaze

was the dilemma promised
along another wire
against his notice
flakes filtered out
a triangle was used

so fresh its source remained
vibrant as once remembered
found some way down
a horizontal rectangle
wood for touching
delicate kill with her feet
extended outside
exposed to feel maybe
latex bleeds

pressing plant capable
signal barely reached

dogs to train them
measured baritone cracked
a chord to find the key
successions of cold
went through the scanner
under ragged fur

crazy to be sure
tangled in air above
hulks of freighters
mistakes float through the fan
shifting empty space

precisely the same air
tracks back
until cooked through

draped with luminous cobwebs

an obligation skidding around
was cool and calm
his bearing was gone
not to sound

young sitting there

intolerable jerks of emotion
didn't appear frozen
had taken a piece
led into the notion
conscious of illuminated words

phrases each containing
hair colour
stated that he waited
so comfortably off
dry carpet completely
being serious canvasses
stripped back to bare
guru whose ideas
actions, either, touch

empires of armaments
as aggregate clear

wanders from our scene
abashed to find
mud, his soul
the particular business
of constant talking
the long dream dimly sentient

within tyranny
beneath the surface
of instinct to divert
spread out in thought
be talk talk read

shape to one winter day
from such creative instability
involved risk disaster possibly

flowing rivulets under lying

must be cooled
making simple explanations
fiercely measure
flattery when drooling

he has also heard

the faintest pianissimo
wild clear of pines
burst into painted flames
spaciously reveal
desire of every detail

thinking may pull
the bubble in
a wisp of lettuce
once part of spring
hide its grandeur
weak by relations
stayed in the city
he had not left
dependent in large part

several caped figures
of course, the envelope

completely clean
could see no closet
but too visible amiable
outlines on the wall
cloth unless she ran
silent contemplating

with blurry concern
its speed of reproduction
usually they get broken
by noise and words
found hiding near the path

any conscious movement
between aims sliding back
to nibble the leaves

would anyone sue for

doctrine when he
carved images
of the eternal
voice in the assembly

from the many reported

surprised in the air
yellow and red
seem to have great
basic inequality nobody
knows how to move

space at some point
changes position
holds her face
hides her face
with the name he used
then disconnects
at one end or both
strange terminal types
gravely self-destruct

their long cells looping
after another desperate encounter

to imagine an intimacy
in suspension nothing changed
the vessel ceased
red meat tasted
done simply ask
inclination to help

without scanning minerals
a vast country
disappeared through the door
to see distant starlight
replaced by insecurity

Intellectual Compost 4

beginning is a minor danger
only strong enough to lift
that area exposed by review
or the bite of an insect

locked on the inside
when refugee ships
add insult to high drilling
secret timing runs

drops the match
goes to shuffling
unsettlingly large distances
builds these tracks

proved by hanging
repeated service cracks
probably unsuspected
to judge from the motorcycle

local colour has been gathered
in the wastebasket
allowed to receive letters
peut-être and broke info

never in the hands of either
neither word changed
the sentence from the pen of a red
salsa to the enormous sea

Death to a Star

walks on-stage from memory

most regarded as stories

for which moving explosions

make room so physical

shadows of pure colour

fall away into late night bar blurs

blank cartoons nerves of speed

dissolving scars

in the slow impression

of one of the first places

should heart offend thee

twinned with the global village

at a garment factory

with darkened sides

but inordinate influence

a yellow taxi

heads the economy

around chance booths

to compete gently

against the efforts of neighbours

the hours grind up

poachers have killed

two tusks a piano

completely clear beneath

the river's froth

a working family

canoes downstream

smoke-dried kippers

flapping on long lines

into a new home contaminated

by brightly coloured ancestors

intent as a main defence

artifacts may confuse them

from the inside out

relaxed fans blow hues

half dead exaggerated paint

withers gestures towards green

shy shouldered surrender

platforms from which to rise

shielded from native pieces

scattered across festivity

lured into a peepshow

the galactic museum was premature

neat streets, saintly relics

loving nature beyond hermeneutics

falling asleep

at the head of movement

regularity as important momentum

to be easily unravelled

into an unfrequented level of militarism

across disciplinary lines

sensitivity of the inner ear

linking paper to supporting sounds

with ritual images of wealth

human contacts

begin to reassemble

first laid across the bed

of relative decline

to represent random mistakes

minor changes of code

in their infancy

involving complex system loops

bright with another bloom

figuring out

the geometry of a point

in imitation of selective edges

short rather than long

signals along parallel fibres

awakened by sympathetic

consciousness

promised fame

territorial possession

versus unplanned guided operations

described laconically

during their migrations to the eye

an arch of white roses

lightened her skin

cold in the spring snow

breath brilliant in a sigh

expected among individual hosts

solemn acts recorded

pleasure impossible to avoid

her shaking blunt needle

designed to get trapped

in a straw man

separated by permeable boundaries

of interconnected senses

a cavity large enough

for human nature

from dust in the air

spun clouds

of rapidly evolving diseases

supremacy without sense

until submission of the last

seemed to reflect steel

overtaken by high winds

blending to prolong their power

Sixty Words I've Never Used Before

(for Anne-Marie Albiach)

1937 **astragal**

1938 **constat**

1939 **gony**

1940 **keck**

1941 **olid**

1942 **spathe**

1943 **tonous**

1944 **pyxis**

1945 **lingy**

1946 **plat**

1947 knop

1948 piqueur

1949 loquence

1950 peavy

1951 ovolo

1952 nim

1953 malm

1954 jerquer

1955 ostiole

1956 nolition

1957 lurdan

1958 krypsis

1959 nef

1960 maund

1961 lucule

1962 molimen

1963 kier

1964 madid

1965 causey

1966 surd

1967 burgoo

1968 arrastra

1969 rosser

1970 ambage

1971 perdure

1972 wale

1973 zarp

1974 indagate

1975 elance

1976 xyster

1977 dunch

1978 clow

1979 inveckee

1980 frore

1981 himation

1982 intort

1983 sowens

1984 hastate

1985 gloze

1986 sluit

1987 illth

1988 gittith

1989 fugle

1990 ging

1991 idiasm

1992 gaybine

1993 deforce

1994 haurient

1995 decury

1996 stridor

Meadow

working on the hull
so delicately wrought
while still remaining
irresistibly of the sequence
tearing itself in half
seen by more than one
wastebasket that dribbled
beer buried behind
detachment from the herd
following the edge
of a strange attractor
through images of riches
she led the march back
into continuous fascination
more abstract, simpler
than pebbles, cord knotted
clusters expanding
machines out of step
it is as it is
in fact it is not
time to portray cycles
recording deviations
left to their own devices
full of figures draped alive
in a resentful way
turning out resisters
from unstable cultures

to play in deep shade material

held long enough to build

jokes in space and time

muscles twitch randomly

far from equilibrium

provided the instruction set inside

models the phenomenon

back to the starting signal

that can be off or on

just a fraction longer

enclosed in a glass case

deep in a cave

analogous to their centres

cultures were squeezed

in one of three special spots

singly or in groups

designed for use as toys

exports did not leap ahead

slipping away from school

across a section of joint

the landscape moves

forward with connecting links

to wander there again

against a violet sky

firmly sealed in sounds

she put in her head

sensitive to shocks

bewildered defiance

both alarmed and stirred

immense numbers

in form hardly erect

the soul a misnomer explained

missing from his supplies

forks and tins of caviar

fuse seamlessly

filling spare bits of sky

in the randomness of time

sneaking glances down the mountain

no two movements the same

both live and blank

three pistol shots

out of his environment

out of his identity

soft snow in his sleeve

disembodied sensation of seeing

arrangements for a new set

dance in the beams

fallen on gas

turned off one flight down

haze rose from upstream

to join differently later

perfect in rhythm

gaped on each side

feathering to points of brilliance

historic torsos

vacillate among small scale

ideas of house

through whose windows

movement is its shadow

pollen, spores, hair

courtesy of some professors

begin to beat against his spine

mesmerized by glitter

naturally without any bond

carried on waves of disgust

a flash he remembered

with little variation

a friend taken by typhoid

breaking into halves

too large for natural products

one scrapes some money

waves a summons to the waiter

the sound turned down

mythologies, their population

almost entirely brown

mobilizes the body's defences

plan any experiment more quickly

they freeze too fast, expand

without exploding

collaboration still faintly flickers

connected to some spare bottled gas

so far isolated

from the necessity to make progress

a simple barrier nursing short memories

relics from industrial air

brightly coloured cobalt

masked figures dance carefully

legs pulled back at the hips

develop decerebrate rigidity

accustomed to international cuisine

before the disease recognised

the flow solidifying as it travelled

between careers

at its widest a row

of degrading entire habitats

that channel populations to and fro

packed round the edges

of what officials say

simultaneously in adjoining zones

whose compass may include

the theory they had been testing

to less than sustainable levels

rocks hit the window

violent eddy patterns

release a collective breath

under a slab

hippos scour in vintage muck

shifting heredity through networks

bred into domestic stock

during a field reversal event

above the level we can see

time the usually passive partner

clamouring for new clients

such as a home or car

even a morbid life

of cigarettes rapidly conforming

the moment's most popular

little egos down before

coal dust footprints

invisible in the dark

secret entrance from the shore

came in flat emotion

days after electrocution

by electronic funds transfer

hollow between sombre moors

arabs arose

turned into pedants

of the deified emperor

misconstrued his aim

the long line of ships drop

iconography to bring children

a faint illusion of permanence

with en suite bathrooms

polished by nervous clutching

void: the local pulls

round from deep drugged

memory overshadowed by thought

often slurred to stags

particularly venerated near profit

hypnotic viewed through sacrifice

red-painted bedding

allowed her motherly attitude

to surround the hut

she started the engine

with a few lusty kicks

under the wet beech-trees
the sap a strong caustic
in the fashion of 'jumping rats'
vitamin e so different here
breeding children for the slave
county, an hour from london
over a hundred fords
modern people replaced glyphs
earlier to erase some virtue
writing at a café table
pastry on a treacle tart
exposed one minute
movies bit him for feeling
drawn towards her
metallic taste
better than any spur
suppressed carrier methods
by a lever system
to milk a taste of the past
the word sombre stretched
tearing loose suction cups
from the scree
of complement deficiency
back from infinity
so soon itself a limit
to objects forced into subdivision
as if words named themselves
permitted walks
allowed her to read the cards

dug up with clues

there through us were

papers to arrange

a theory of confused reasoning

applied to hot glass

might help cast light

minds with equal force

even more overwhelmed

at such slow pace

stretching the hypothetical glue

between neutral points

in the space of empty

where practical sides cave

across din of marimbas

shrinking headlines enough

at the window leaning out

ought to turn here

figure threw one missed

perfection the undecided buyer

estimates to mime

beyond measurement

what marvel says flat

talk during the banquet

but passengers are aware

through several genres

exploding when trodden on

modelled on and voiced

to fall for such a hoax

agreed to be expedient

reduced by famine

emptied, and the last

gunpowder obliged to be dragged

up in a solid compact body

home to an episcopal household

rather than political

punishment replaced

thrown crumpled away

en passant with such casualness

the state grieves

alert to the symptoms

called a difficult child

because of lack of regular

nasty cruel phenomena

toast spreads across the map

in all its flux

skin a scanner

severe since you were young

footage kept in pockets

packed with bohea

about to burst into

more screen time

with wings amazed it cracked

pushing marginal effects

into material gains

instars resist

the specially twisted straw rope

when their dolls

choose to observe rules

basically eclectic

ringing 'low and fast'

before neglect transmutes

humour into fashion

shelves creak under in depth

pieces that emphasise

hobbies beyond the commonplace

organism they feed on

ground-down heads

continually at odds in

a tale yet unexplored

as shackles fall

among the wing-nuts, coughing

not too many speckles

the route over that hump

from whose top the stream

of back-lighting trickles

backing behind dog-ends

is too bumpy with massed photons

to allow slick tires

should the lottery pay out

five zeros

massa that pulpit

requires waders at least

trailing mizuhiki

down the ladder of hyphens

to the ash of envelopes

sharp eyes without

openings dazzled by

double dreams
maybe a bit off here
a by-pass there
braid in the gutter
monotonously hands behind
report the crack
of tulle in new weather
design scales are inconsistent
physical objects
require panoptic vigilance
any chalked ciphers
with brackets or a right cross
signposted the empire
words should stop
cold sea slipping through moonlight
to its black sound
therapy since convenient
sections in clarinet
select purpose even assured
flank red meat
pulls in for cheap gas
loaded this time
round smudge pots
wah wah beckons
to the trailer-park barbecue
limbs not pins
balance the message
partly so premature
surely not particular

recede in their sockets

guess at his answer

to find out the names

performing all necessary

hindrance storing materials

activities in other countries

proud of their compromise

govern communications between

things to be distressed

overnight in the field

at a distance from

a solid triangular object

move the main laboratory

electron microscope ready

stumble around the crescent

colour towards wisdom

return to the jar

peas from a pod

divided by two

influences theoretical

and practical

force the destruction of wealth

Unable to Create Carrier

pigeons, explained the supremo, perhaps
basins of attraction and so
easy to identify undefended
footnotes to a moral atom
forced to show traces of serious style
interacting among enzymes to undergo
ritual sabbaticals for a rush of air

on which the dove descended
exploding the generator of earlier situations
happening at the level of dna
narrowly missing the luckless defender
vibrating to a concussion
algorithm designed to locate criticism
between gouts of yellow, the half

egg balanced on a bed of herbs
prolonged and coldly limber
guarding time in an overnight bag
which according to the pronoun you
surpasses the apprehension of thought
represented on screen by a halo
nudging aside tongues of fire

Crowded with Otiose Passengers

at the stage when incredible
mixed shit is ready to drop in
on reflections of the patient's mood
certified to be a true result
hesitating before the sunken state
that pressure might cause
ringing up the voltage
on browsers whose deep sleep
ought to be encouraged and used
draped over the orgone box those
mammals are alike in being
hunted across a full moon dream
as a by-product smaller than greedy

mannerisms shoved back
into corrupt defective nature
quicker than history could clean
grease from its white hair
dropping the rubber gauntlet
while cars queue three deep
between obsession and the go
fuck yourself bar
or is that a piano
rolling across frozen waves
from the shabby sub
over wet powder into the draw
and finally to the igloo?

Cat Van Cat

spontaneous activity reaches
possible multiple signals also
ridden hard in past episodes
along the edge of the harbour
yards : functions occasionally jam
tribal supporters take off
out and settle down
changing course surging over

building blocks to clear six feet
waves until that sort of engine
isolates fish ancestors
intent its information
go to the cerebellum
with its cultural limitations
leaking blood into panic
swirling held formed by echo

words open holes in
ripples of colour to draw
imbued utterances in a single hop
through tephra into natural light
historical sites familiar with traditional
patterns peculiarly patient
hooks mutating profiles
in the breeze from spinning radii

share events shaved close
of crop circle stubble chic
hard white chains stand out
across the supper area
rolling their links
derisively in a spiral
expecting hoist convenience to
spread out the local sheets

Differences in Common

propose that the wave
monopolists in search
of occasional response try
trading capital for an icon
effect : lingering deeply dyed
flowers exploited as basic
use of the chalice
surgical reports slip past

oracles waiting resignedly
at midpoint of a tin roof
flattened according to tradition
within a plausible context
obscurely tempered by reserve
the other way round
angels crossing under steam
begin to increase speed sharply

No Hard Feelings

something called obstructing
then in a sudden falsetto
mutual friends : the social pressures
burn you with gasoline
thick rain : a broken sky
shows through from beneath
intimately with some part
you say was driven
gradually throwing arguments

through right notes right stuff
objects dimly above variations
whir on the refrigerator
different if almost caught
details pour out to sea
running to move the dial
from your face in another
exercise in denial
receiving his full attention

Rhodopsin Blues

one will never come
as a model for instruction
ease of access to dream
begins to take off
on different mechanisms
operating at full power

no structural strength
to smooth lines extra
to the builders of the original
perhaps diminished opera
listing slowly giving time
cells slack only in repose

estimate the exact sequence
housed in rolling static
a camera shutter released
similar additions jump
lock into permanent mutilation
on the fringes of structure

Shewn

processing encoded images
steam engines and nuclear power
in return for clicks of fame
let the curved museum
absorb and emit light
dancing with humour
yellow can't control

more fortunes out of bootleg yellow
ring shorter wavelengths
in a charade of impi
tedious pedantry : a footnote
for the hoi polloi
notion of referring private
experience to tactical meaning

Pyrophoric

measure always came back
not believing people at the next table
attracted by pathos
caused by recollection
bang into a rock
experience of this is an ideal
made to look inside another

expensively upholstered article
to define the definers
in anticipated snow
a case of mass production
even at the price of servitude
shadowed on white paper windows
breaking the monotony of surface

Ingot We Trust

mechanical problems of fatigue
that once roamed bountiful

seem to adhere strongly
one third higher on the wheel

exposed to a breeze
through the cultural structure

of settled tone rings
concentrated in management

expectation a centre
you can shop around

cripples a similar protein
leaving the stage short

No Music

to rise steadily with reduction
was the theme revealed
outside a circle of suburbs

incapable of different history
to produce a backfire
when small and tender

passed by, paused, into top gear
from a position far too close
to tolerate the fury of opulence

bones lie across the country
covered in rare mixed leaves
unable to keep them

to choose the surest gain

Looking for Language

physical pulled to a stop
acting interested reactions

a history for rejection
inherited recognizable energy

whacked holes in gone scenarios
chrome plated folds

dedicated to dazzle conviction
shapes suitable for previous sites

A Happening at the Hair

head driven on down
will release certain facts
or run them through off-chance
spread out in diagrams

panache doesn't let go
daily lives to form centuries
a weakness for cigars
for a few animals in tepid water

stops down into stills
flicking back hair going grey
while rest arranged a barrier
to reside in tissue

Warm Autumn Problem

can

a

falling

leaf

hit

a

dragonfly

?

Landscaping the Future

(for Gianni, Graziella, Dorge, Sandro and Chicco)

once upon a time
in the waste

white rock
white fence
white house

green river fast
bend around
smooth grey stones

a raft of faded wood
yellow butterfly flicker

last fleck of vibrating red
from above
lazy chevrons of wake

a glass cabin
panes acacia honey
run thin and toasted

the idea
of rolling up shadows
whip-cracking out dust

or any table
half-covered by a map
mostly ocean

colour of the river
less yellow

a pair of chrome dividers
one point of rust
at rest

on the farout islands
where forests stretch
hurling nuts into wet cement

in the candlelight that pulses
in the draught from the closing door

Follow the Food

adapted for fast movement
hunting in light

one engine stops
another starts

to make surplus sacred
always missing

emotion liquidised
until distracted

Affirmative ≠ 2 x Negative

(for Luigi)

the motor of memory idles
in thoughtless space

photosynthesis as
spacecraft fuel

within
walking distance

the cherry branch that fits
the stone that cracks the nut

Feu d'Artefriso

nothing left
in its space
boomerang
r   i   c   e

cast at night
through woodsmoke
into the beam
of an unknown star

Translation

very president yesterday chat
much cause the president yesterday
     cover showed half earthquake
     half of the earthquake which was shown by cover
really selection marooned
really mary colored selection
    over wrought her throat
    over wrought its throat
fun hung got painting
the pleasure adjusted the received painting
   to realize sound considerable effort
   in order to carry out the healthy considerable effort
files painting written
card indices which comb documents
  with no reaction lies
  without reaction lies
estranged police currency scours
estranged of the courses for police foreign exchange
    street lamps spill doubt
    the headlights upset the doubt
waiting established back signs
set up waiting backwards characters
   evidence before his death
   obviousness before its death
lost bogus recently been
falsely lost recently been
under sheet slowly
    under the page slowly
only is thought money
is only the thought cash
   picked up body circumstance
   seizure body circumstance
wondered was fraud
fraud was wondered

very the president cause yesterday much cause the president cover yesterday show that half of half of earthquake de terre of earthquake de terre what have be show by the surplus isolate from selection colour by mary of selection of cover really really work its surplus of throat work its recreation of throat stop obtain comb the pleasure have adjust the painting receive to carry out the effort considerable healthy in order to carry out the file considerable healthy of effort comb the file write that the document of comb with step of lie of reaction without lie of reaction estranged the font that some scrubbing of currency estranged of course for the font the reverberator of currency foreign reverse the doubt doubt awaiting established behind the signs before the installation waiting towards the back of the characters show its death before the obviousness its death destroyed false recently wrongfully destroyed recently under the sheet slowly under the page is slowly only the money of thought is only the money cash of thought selected to the top of the body of data entry of circumstance of body until the required circumstance

very the cause of the president much cause that the cover of the president sample yesterday that that half of half of earthquake of terre of earthquake of terre what has to be demonstration by the insulator very well of the color of the selection of maria of the selection of the work of the cover really really their excess of the work of the throat its reconstruction of the shutdown of the throat obtains the comb the pleasure yesterday must fit the painting receives to make healthy the considerable one of the effort to make healthy considerable of the file of the comb of the effort the file writes of which the document of the comb with the passage of progression of the lie of the reaction without lie of the reaction estranged the source which the certain one to of course mop of modernity estranged for the source the reverberator of the nonnative misfortune of modernity waiting of the doubt of the doubt established behind the samples before the installation that waited for towards the posterior a part of the demonstration of the characters its death before the evidence its death destroyed recently false illicit destroyed recently under the leaf slowly under the pagination is only the money of pens very the cause of the president whom to form much cause that the cover of the president sample yesterday which must be very good this half of half of the earthquake of terre of the earthquake of terre which demonstration by the isolation of the colour of the selection of maria of the selection of the work of the cover really really their abundance of the work of the throat its reconstruction of the disconnection of the throat the comb the pleasure receives yesterday, the painting fit must in order healthy the considerable receives from the effort to healthy considerable of the file of the comb of the effort to form the file writes from that the document of the comb with the passage of the advancement of the lie of the those the certain naturally to rub of modernity for the source estranged which which reverberator nonnative the misfortune modernity aufwartung the doubt of the doubt behind the samples before the system manufactured, which toward to posterior detail the demonstration of the characters its death waited, before the proof its death destroys destroyed recently false bad recently under the page slowly under the page

Suffering from painful Trapped Mood

a construction site

        squad cars arrived

really always wanted

        started filling balloons

on your face

        a photograph all over

keep your minds

        where they had spring

behind the wheel

        through the opening

patients stumbling months

        warm and landscaped islands

with a doll's body

        burned to the edge

a stolen plate

        waiting on the side

sideways weapon again

        problematic neighbors landslide

smart reno haircut

        entered the collar

illuminated reflected knees

        felt grown on puppets

smiled hopped away

        stroke chickens known weird

tune for maximum view

        eight mortgaged kidney stones

back over parade stage

        loopy results cropped

bay of window so hair

        suspended in video terror

a clean tine moved

        on fire paper plates

examined chaos contents

        reverse them at pitch

off engines burning first

        simple aboriginal stilts

flying that weekend calm

        persistent map to aid

huddled in fun remember

        short fall stuck in stereo

tie pull moil sweat

        eye surgery on water-skis

the island twirling

                    capped into submission
    orange juice personality
                            however disgruntled
    her hips outside her legs
                        dispenser bump mirror
    in generator fell quiet
                        spring before medication
    camera caught more lorgnettes
                        swung normal brokered pork rinds

For John Gian

on milking every aspect
internal organs
programmes of reminiscence

pacifism, tolerance
crudity of life
though perfectly credible

readings scanned at intervals
dictate that he sleep
better reading than viewing

wiped evidence of the past
between hard covers
this is too embarrassing

plenary indulgences
running the full width
but militarily weak

maintain a minimum speed
some miracle drug
no expression of welcome

kept necessarily small
would pat their gloved hands
until the music started

false promise of happiness
fried in olive oil
stepping from an alpine stream

the most rigid rule of all
feet in wet cement
imperial endeavour

when anyone drops gestures
musical moment
no discernible makeup

interest in them revived
buses with long seats
actual identity

even the allergy pills
worked as a butcher
emotionally precise

to tears to rage to laughter
interpretive range
timed during an interval

selling machine insurance
in abstract stillness
basis of democracy

contempt or hostility
cannot understand
an eye on posterity

air reflected on water
with more bitter truth
drew those objects around taste

gone luckily far beyond
stock made with some head
post and sniper position

restricting every movement
would hunch their shoulders
nightly exchanges of rock

a daily act of worship
some miracle drug
made with meat and potatoes

hands mathematically bent
still crisp as their gloves
blockading more villages

little context is required
slightly more than half
a vital ingredient

information for storing
stone steps in the dark
or out of date medicines

something a lot heavier
obsessively fit
but not extraordinary

Drinking Electricity

more forms search telling
damaged by less vegetation cover
cratered unexplained oddities
languages propose an ambiguous method
particles of logical consistency
grow into a high bulge
clockwise in the heat
water exhausts enough to compete
transmuted by inconsistence
by any desire not water
developed limited sensual experience
a fateful eye warming
draws up religious ceremonies
of arithmetic's ultimate capability

no predetermined products
minimize the itinerary
a sequence of images is no evidence
expressible outside experience

mere forms search tolling
damaged by less vegetation cover
cratered unexplained oddities
particles of illogical consistency
spin clockwise in the heat
grow into a high bulge
a fateful eye warning
water exhausts enough to compete
languages propose an ambiguous method
transmuted by inconsistence
by any desire not water
developed limited sensual experience
draws up religious ceremonies
of arithmetic's ultimate capacity

far mountains flat black
behind a line of red lights
a pigeon banks bleached by the flash
the ocean is indescribable

Index of Titles

Index of First Lines

INDEX OF FIRST LINES

INDEX OF FIRST LINES